Willow Creek Church is a remarkable evangelical phenomenon by anyone's standards. This humble, honest story of the principles and pains, visions and victories of this ministry makes for endearing and enriching reading.

Stuart Briscoe
Elmbrook Church

Bill Hybels is a great leader, and Willow Creek Community Church is a reflection of that leadership. Bill and his congregation have influenced thousands of pastors and churches in this generation. Both have influenced me.

John C. Maxwell
Speaker, author, founder of INJOY

This book is about what it takes to build a good and faithful church. The bigness of Willow Creek Church is only incidental to what makes this church special. Those who take cheap shots at super churches must read this book.

Tony Campolo

If you're like me, you have asked a thousand times: "How does Willow Creek do it?" Now, instead of asking one more time, you can read Lynne and Bill Hybels' new book, *Rediscovering CHURCH*. What an exciting acc͟o͟u͟n͟t͟ ͟o͟f͟ ͟r͟e͟a͟ching the lost for Christ and seeing record-breaking church growth!

C. Peter Wagner
Fuller Theological Seminary

Willow Creek is about spectacle and about supp͟o͟r͟t͟i͟n͟g͟ ͟e͟x͟c͟e͟l͟lence. It's no less about tenderness and touching. Thank God that Bill Hybels were not content to stop with a church where the footlights and spotlights create a behavior setting for the beautiful people with stellar performing gifts. They pushed beyond entertainment until they had created a ministry structure of small groups and serving teams, where Willow's people are not afraid to show they care. When I see here how the struggling people are helped, I am deeply moved. It reads like *rediscovering family*.

Carl George
Parish Analyst, Consulting for Growth

Bill Hybels is one of the most innovative Christian leaders of this century. People in many countries are wanting to learn from his Willow Creek Church. Don't miss this book!

The Reverend Dr. Michael Green

Forged in the crucible of sacrifice and pain, Willow Creek was launched and grew to maturity under the leadership of Bill Hybels. *Rediscovering CHURCH* documents its conception and growth. A book for everyone who takes growth seriously! A threatening book for those who bypass godliness and look to gimmicks to light the flame.

Joe Aldrich
President, Multnomah Bible College and Biblical Seminary

Lynne and Bill Hybels tell the amazing story of Willow Creek Community Church as only they can do it—honestly, humbly, helpfully. Theirs is a story of vision that leads to missions that leads to community that leads to more vision, more mission, more community. Not size of congregation but quality of love—that's the secret of Christ's Church of which Willow Creek is but one remarkable example.

David A. Hubbard
President Emeritus
Fuller Theological Seminary

Here is the fascinating "untold" story of how, by God's grace, the Willow Creek Community Church came into existence. It reads like Acts 2! This is a recitation of how God moved in the heart and mind of young Bill Hybels, its dynamic Founding Pastor, to bring into being a new paradigm in rediscovering CHURCH. It's a remarkable and moving testimony to God's powerful working to bring His life-changing message to today's seeking generation.

Ted W. Engstrom
President Emeritus
World Vision

Real People, Real Church, Real Gospel ... Lynne and Bill Hybels tell the Willow Creek story from a gripping, new, inside-out perspective that is inspirational, informational, and motivational.

Russell Chandler
Former religion writer, *Los Angeles Times*, speaker, writer,
and author of *Racing Toward 2001*

Rediscovering CHURCH is an exposé. It shares the joys, pain, struggles, and victories of the most amazing church-growth story in this generation! Hybels' openness and honesty sets the standard for an evaluation of contemporary ministries.

Kenneth M. Meyer
President, Trinity International University
Deerfield, Illinois

Lynne & Bill Hybels

REDISCOVERING

·chûrch·

n **1. A building for public, esp. Christian, worship. 2. People who demonstrate their love for God by loving and serving others.**

THE STORY AND VISION OF
Willow Creek Community Church

ZondervanPublishingHouse
Grand Rapids, Michigan

A Division of HarperCollinsPublishers

Rediscovering Church
Copyright © 1995 by Bill Hybels

Requests for information should be addressed to:

🏭 ZondervanPublishingHouse
Grand Rapids, Michigan 49530   -

Library of Congress Cataloging-in-Publication Data

Hybels, Lynne.
  Rediscovering church : the story and vision of Willow Creek Community Church /
Lynne and Bill Hybels.
      p.   cm.
  Includes bibliographical references.
  ISBN: 0-310-59320-4
  1. Willow Creek Community Church (South Barrington, Ill.) 2. South Barrington
(Ill.)—Church history. 3. Hybels, Bill. 4. Church growth—Case studies. 5. Big
churches—Case studies. I. Hybels, Bill. II. Title.
BX9999.S65H83   1995
280–dc 00   95–18577
                                                                                              CIP

International Trade Paper Edition 0-310-20408–9

This edition printed on acid-free paper and meets the American National Standards
Institute Z39.48 standard.

Edited by John Sloan and Robin Schmitt
Interior design by Sue Koppenol

Printed in the United States of America

---

95 96 97 98 99 00 01 02 / ❖ DH/ 10 9 8 7 6 5 4 3 2 1

CONTENTS

ACKNOWLEDGMENTS

We never intended to write a detailed history of Willow Creek. Our goal, rather, was to tell enough of the story to convey certain values we have held and lessons we have learned during our years in ministry. Even given that limited scope, however, the history of Willow Creek that follows is incomplete. Missing are the names and stories of the many people who have lived out those values and learned those lessons with us. We began this project intending to include these personal stories of heroic devotion to God, to the church, and to hard work. But once we began "dropping names," we didn't know where to stop. Daily we faced a growing list of people who "just had to be included." There were …

- High school students in Park Ridge, Illinois, whose abandonment to the untamed winds of the Spirit gave birth to a miracle.
- Students and leaders in Palatine, Illinois, whose vision and extraordinary sacrifice gave birth to a church.
- Unpaid staff and lay leaders who started everything from a children's ministry to a bookstore simply because they saw a need and felt compelled to meet it.
- Early module directors who were driven by love to draw people together and translate church into something warm and personal.
- Board members—bona fide adults!—who had no logical reason to sign on with a bunch of kids, but did it anyway, and with grace in their hearts have stood by us all the way.
- Elders who came on the scene amid crisis and who throughout the years have exhibited wisdom and have faithfully carried more than their share of the "heavy" side of ministry.
- Management team members whose blend of professional competence and spiritual depth has enabled them to provide God-honoring staff leadership on a daily basis.
- Staff members whose contributions to Willow Creek have prompted us to say time and time again, "I can't believe God led that person to us. We are so blessed."
- Invaluable volunteers who do everything from directing traffic to serving food to cleaning bathrooms.

- Financial donors who invest significant percentages of their income in what seems at times like a high-risk Kingdom venture.
- Musicians, actors, and production people who spend more time in late-night rehearsals than most people would imagine and add so much "heart" to our programs.
- Small-group leaders who are, both in theory and in practice, the backbone of Willow Creek.

Despite our original intention, as this book goes to press, few of these people have been mentioned by name. Some names have been provided to avoid confusion. Certain people have been named because of their unique contributions at critical points in the church's development. A few additional names have been included in order to pull the story out of the abstract and tether it to the concrete reality of individual persons. But for the most part, the heroes of Willow Creek have remained unnamed simply because there have been so many of them; their stories could have filled many books! We have not forgotten them, however, and it is to them that we dedicate this book, with deep and lingering gratitude and respect.

We offer special thanks to our friend Lee Strobel, who did major manuscript work on the second half of this book, and to John Sloan at Zondervan for being the perfect editor for us—again.

PREFACE: THIS IS CHURCH

"He's gone." The paramedic speaks slowly and softly as if to ease the truth into Karen's mind. But the truth strikes like a missile and explodes in shock and loneliness. She feels jerked from reality, thrust into a twilight zone of pain. Then the gentle touch of Ann's hand draws her back. Jeff's firm embrace surrounds her with strength. Jenny's whispered word reminds her she is not alone. The tears that fall from David's eyes help her find her own.

For over two years Tim and Karen had poured time, energy, and love into each member of the small group they led. Now the love circles back and soothes the raw edges of grief.

This is church.

Twenty-nine years old and worth a million. Headed straight toward the top. Then the rich young ruler meets Jesus. "Lay it on the line," the Savior says. "Put your money where your mouth is."

It's December. Building-fund time. The rich young ruler stares at the stage in the overcrowded, rundown theater that the young congregation calls home. He shifts in the dirty seat and smashes another kernel of popcorn under his heel.

"Lay it on the line," the Savior says. The rich young ruler tucks his hand into the pocket of his corduroy coat and gently fingers the tiny paper that defines his success. When the offering plate is passed, he carefully slides a check that shatters his net worth beneath the mound of crumpled bills.

This is church.

Angie pulls into the parking lot as she does every Monday night, but on this night she drives past her usual parking area and parks her car by the maintenance building at the rear of the church property. Walking back toward the church building, she silently thanks God—again—for the mechanics who volunteer their time on Monday nights. While Angie attends the ministry for single mothers and her daughter attends a class for children of divorce, a grease-smeared hero with his back on a concrete floor replaces the U-joints on her car.

This is church.

"This isn't about sports. This is about one man's journey to faith." With the agenda clarified, the discussion begins. The thousands of people who come to multiple services that weekend hear Mike Singletary, former linebacker for the Chicago Bears, speak openly about family, faith, and forgiveness.

It is a mixed crowd. Many are first-time visitors to the church, most of whom have been brought by a friend or relative who regularly attends. Some of them have been invited repeatedly before, but only the likes of Mike could break through their resistance.

Afterward, a young girl sends this note to the church office: "I've been trying to get my father to church for years, but he would never come—until I told him Mike Singletary was going to speak. He really listened to what Mike said about Christianity. We had a good talk afterward, and he said he might come back. I can't believe it. Thank you!"

This is church.

Peanut butter. Spaghetti. Baked beans. Powdered milk. Coffee. Cereal. Soup. Canned stew. Diapers. Shampoo. Toothpaste. Sue continues down the list, buying three of each item requested. The checkout clerk comments on her triplicate buying, but Sue only chuckles.

On Sunday, Sue wraps the bags of groceries in black garbage bags and leaves them on the pavement behind her car while she attends church. During the service, volunteers load thousands of the black garbage bags into pickup trucks and transport them to the Food Pantry, which feeds hundreds of needy people each month.

This is church.

The young man weeps as he reveals a story of childhood abuse so cruel that its victim, his wife, buried the memories in her subconscious mind for fifteen years. But now the surfaced memories haunt her, shatter the tranquillity of their home, and threaten the security of their marriage. Both husband and wife are leaders in the church, with visible, responsible roles, but now they feel helpless and exhausted and scared.

The husband sits alone in the middle of a circle of his peers. When he finishes his story, one man reaches out and rests his hand on the young man's shoulder. Another grips his arm. A woman holds his hands in hers. Soon he is wrapped in a corporate embrace. Quietly his friends begin to pray, and for nearly an hour their words go to heaven on his behalf.

This is church.

"But I tell you that anyone who is angry with his brother will be subject to judgment.... Anyone who says, 'You fool!' will be in danger of the fire of hell. Therefore, if you are offering your gift at the altar and there remember that your brother has something against you, leave your gift there in front of the altar. First go and be reconciled to your brother; then come and offer your gift."

"You know what these words mean," the pastor says, "but are you willing to act on them? Please don't come to the communion table with unfinished business." As he speaks the rustle of movement begins to filter through the auditorium. Within minutes, hundreds of people have left their seats. Some line up at pay phones. Others meet in empty classrooms. Some go home. The work of reconciliation has begun.

This is church.

"I baptize you in the name of the Father, the Son, and the Holy Spirit." Dale and Ellen are well into the "later years" of life, yet as they rise up out of the icy water of the pond, they seem like kids. And in a sense they are. In terms of faith, they are in fact mere babes, toddlers at most.

But what happy toddlers they are. And what a sensation they cause. On the grassy hill, there is applause and cheering, an out-and-out carnival of joy. Their small-group leader laughs so hard he cries. Their daughter runs to greet them with bear hugs and warm towels. Their unchurched neighbors are a bit confused but delighted to see their longtime friends so happy. It is a celebration fit for heaven.

This is church.

"They devoted themselves to the apostles' teaching and to the fellowship, to the breaking of bread and to prayer. Everyone was filled with awe, and many wonders and miraculous signs were done by the apostles. All the believers were together and had everything in common. Selling their possessions and goods, they gave to anyone as he had need. Every day they continued to meet together in the temple courts. They broke bread in their homes and ate together with glad and sincere hearts, praising God and enjoying the favor of all the people. And the Lord added to their number daily those who were being saved" (Acts 2:42–47).

This is church.

INTRODUCTION BY BILL HYBELS

A few years ago I called the Willow Creek management team together for a daylong strategic planning session, complete with a meticulously detailed agenda and outside consultants. Our goal for the day was ambitious, but we could meet it; we meant business. Then, shortly into the meeting, I received one of those inexplicable "audibles" from the Holy Spirit: *Forget the agenda. Look around this table. Focus on the people.* I sent the consultants out of the room and said, "Let's slow down for a minute here. We can attack the agenda later. What's going on in your lives?"

What followed was a pleasant update on personal and family life—until one of the team members revealed a personal tragedy in the making. It hadn't been obvious to others, but beneath his cool image were the smoldering ashes of pain and fear and loneliness. The story came out slowly, with jerks and starts and sighs and tears, and then finally it was over, his energy drained, his words spent.

We all knew the time had come to move on; the day was slipping away. But we just sat there. Finally one man said, "I'm sorry, but I'm not done with this yet. I feel as if I'm trying to shift without the clutch, and I just can't do it. I'd like to pray about what's happening right now." So with highly paid consultants pacing the hall beyond the locked door, we prayed around the circle, begging God to strengthen and sustain this brother in need.

Later that night I thought, *We knocked heads all day trying to figure out how to lead this church, but the most important thing that happened was that for two hours and fifteen minutes, we* were *the church.* We were the church—to each other.

That's what this book is about: being the church. It's about people coming together to be Christ to each other in community. Interdependent. Vulnerable. Giving of themselves.

I don't know how many people believe me when I say this, but I never set out to build a big church. I don't say that carelessly or naively. I know that every motive I have is to some extent mixed. I know that I am not immune to sins of pride and self-promotion. I have an unconscious drive to succeed, to prove myself, that I have only begun to understand in recent years.

Still, I can honestly say that building a big church was never the conscious desire of my heart. I never set out to see how innovative I could be with drama or music, or how many cultural codes I could crack. Those were simply a few means to an incredibly valuable end. What motivated me twenty years ago, and what motivates me today, is the priceless goal of seeing redeemed people become the church. To one another. I am reenergized every time I see people who were formerly lost in darkness now giving and receiving love, walking through valleys with one another, rescuing each other, and helping each other with their physical and spiritual needs.

If ever there was a time in history when the ministry of the true church was sorely needed, it is now. Though church attendance dropped drastically in the decades following 1960, the rising surge of spiritual interest currently moving across our country suggests that many people are anguishing over spiritual emptiness.

Pollsters attribute much of this rising interest to growing disenchantment with the modern, materialistic lifestyle. In the secret places of their hearts, many people are concluding that there has to be more.

Another reason for the spiritual search is the increasing breakdown of relationships. Marriages are failing, families are fragmenting, and friendships are falling apart. As interpersonal trust levels sink to an all-time low, some people are beginning to look up. *Can God be trusted?* they wonder. *And can He somehow help me put my marriage, family, and friendships back together?*

Spiritual interest is also prompted by the growing awareness that social engineers, government programs, and increased funding for education are not going to eradicate the evils facing our society. Alcohol and drug abuse, pornographic exploitation, domestic violence, and general crime rates continue to rise. Temptations facing young people are greater than ever; casual sex, alcohol, and drugs are accepted aspects of high school life. Many baby boomers who are now parents watch their children live out the sixties morality they themselves once celebrated and wish they could rewrite the past. With the entertainment media pumping out a constant antimorality message, parents must look elsewhere for a healthier perspective.

The complexity and stress of modern life also prompt spiritual interest. Technological advances designed to ease the demands of life have actually forced us onto a faster track. "Psychologists and counselors contend that many people are 'overwhelmed and anxiety ridden' because fast isn't fast enough anymore in a modern world paced by timesaving products and services."[1] Technology, particularly in the medical field, has also complicated our lives by raising ethical issues unimagined in past years. How should we respond to issues like genetic engineering, fetal tissue research, and euthanasia? Is there spiritual truth to guide us?

Fear of environmental doom adds to our stress. Oil spills and hazardous waste violations anger us. The breakdown of the earth's atmosphere, the depletion of the earth's resources, and the contamination of the earth's water supply put our future in jeopardy. Many feel trapped in a fragile world and wonder about the world beyond.

The fear of another kind of doom has recently taken center stage, spotlighted by the Oklahoma City bombing on April 19, 1995. Terrorism has brought the subject of evil and the search for its cure into the daily dialogue throughout our country and the world. "Why do these things happen?" people ask. "How can we stop them?"

In an increasingly dysfunctional society, individuals are becoming increasingly aware of their emotional wounds, their loneliness, and their need for help. Victims of childhood abuse need a safe place to heal. Those recovering from divorce need understanding and guidance. Single parents need emotional support and tangible help. Though many of these people reject the distant-God image and the impersonal church environment of their childhood, they long for what they call a "higher power" to reparent them and for a loving "family" to take them in. Can they turn—as I believe they must—to the God of the Bible? Can they find what they long for in His church?

Granted, many of these spiritual searchers have chosen *not* to take their spiritual questions to church. "Today we are living in a spiritual renaissance that perhaps is like no other in history. One of the things that makes it unique is that the search for spiritual values is not associated with any institution and does not depend on traditional religious terms or symbols. Rather we see these spiritual concerns guided by the heart."[2]

Why, I wonder, are contemporary Americans convinced that true spiritual answers are only to be found outside the church? Is it because they seek answers that are self-centered rather than God-centered? Or is it because they have become sincerely disillusioned with a church that for too many years was more concerned with its identity and traditions than with the concerns of the human heart?

Years before I read the statistics about increased spiritual interest, I knew it was there. As a young adult, I rubbed shoulders with people who had spiritual questions: What is the purpose of life? What is beyond the grave? Is Jesus more than a myth? How do I make moral decisions? Is there absolute truth? Does prayer really work? Is there meaning in suffering? Some thought Christianity was a "good idea" but didn't know much about it. Others knew that their lives were falling apart and wondered if the Bible might offer wisdom and help. They had lots of questions but few answers.

In 1975 a group of friends and I began to call these people "seekers," and we decided to start a church that could reach them—a church that would answer their questions, address their needs, introduce them to Jesus Christ, and give them a taste of His kingdom on earth. We wanted to "be the church" for people who thought church was irrelevant but who needed it so desperately.

What was true in 1975 is every bit as true today. People need the church—not the lifeless institution that has often passed as the church but the true church, the Acts 2 church. Nothing else is going to change the course of individual lives and the direction of this country. We need authentic heart-change that will transform the way we operate in relationships, the way we respond to social injustice, the way we use the earth, and the way we treat the weak, the poor, and the unborn.

In some corners, Willow Creek has become known primarily for the avant-garde, laser-age style of its preevangelistic events, in which we release the considerable creativity of our music and drama teams. The truth is, I struggle with what it takes to put on these events. I wrestle with the amount of money and time it requires. I regret the personal toll it takes on the programming staff and the volunteers and myself. I dread the letters of criticism I receive for "putting on programs" when I should just be "preaching sermons."

So why do we do them? Because some lost man or woman, who matters more to God than we can possibly understand, might come on the arm of one of our believers and get a first glimpse of what Christianity is like. And that glimpse might set the dominoes falling, so that someday that person will come to understand who Christ is, then build a relationship with Him, and eventually sit in a small circle of believers in which he or she can experience the church.

That's what this book is about. It's not about how to build big churches. It's not about how to create high-tech programs. Nor is it about might and power and strength. In fact, I am slowly coming to believe that being the church to one another is nearly antithetical to might and power and strength. You see, I'm not sure you can taste biblical community apart from personal weakness. I didn't believe that when I was younger, sitting tall in the saddle of a powerful stallion, charging ahead, fiercely running down obstacles for the kingdom. I was mighty and powerful and strong back then, but I didn't know much about giving and receiving love. I didn't start learning that gentle art until my stallion began to stagger a bit and the obstacles became almost overwhelming.

I might as well level with you. I was the man described at the beginning of this chapter—the man with the broken heart at the strategic planning meeting. I was the man who needed to draw strength from others, the man who sat in that circle and received through human conduits what felt like a direct infusion of divine love. If I could rewrite the script of my life, I'd write in more scenes like that and fewer big-screen scenes with charging stallions.

So if your goal is to build a big church or to learn how to create the latest in laser-age programs, don't read this book. And if you're into might and power and strength, don't read this book.

But if you long to be part of a church striving to truly *be the church*, then I invite you to turn the pages of this book. You won't find all the answers you need. But you'll find the story—written down by my wife, Lynne, who has had a front-row seat the whole way—of some people who have experienced enough of the true church to fall madly in love with it. Then, in the second half of this book, you'll discover the vision, values, and strategies that have made my heart beat fast in ministry for over two decades.

In case these introductory pages have left any doubt in your mind, let me state it clearly: I love the church. I am convinced it is the hope of the world. I think I understand why Christ called it His bride. And I humbly thank God every day for letting me be part of it.

NOTES

1. Russell Chandler, *Racing Toward 2001* (Grand Rapids: Zondervan, 1992), 84.

2. Hal Zina Bennett, Ph. D., and Susan J. Sparrow, *Follow Your Bliss* (New York: Avon, 1990), 7.

REDISCOVERING
·chûrch·

part one

chapter one

SON CITY

1972–75

We were living a miracle. We don't just say that in retrospect. At the time, in the midst of it, we knew it was a miracle. We knew something very powerful was happening, something far beyond our own abilities. The questions we had to ask were: How do we respond to what God is trying to do? How do we maximize this? How do we experience this to the hilt?

DAVE HOLMBO,
SON CITY COFOUNDER

Unlike Bill, who turned to Christ as a teenager at a Christian camp, I became a Christian as a child through the ministry of a local church. And throughout my grade-school and teenage years, I faithfully attended two services each Sunday, one each Wednesday night, and nearly every event that was sponsored by the youth group. Yet at twenty-one, on the brink of graduating from a Christian liberal arts college, I was thoroughly disillusioned with church. I read of the early church and it seemed so alive and life changing; I looked at the twentieth-century church and it seemed so dead and unproductive. Did the Bible overstate the life of the early church? Or was that really the ideal for which the contemporary church was to aim? If so, the church seemed to have fallen far short.

The frustration in my spiritual life paralleled an equal frustration in my relational life. I had planned to marry Bill Hybels in April 1972, during my junior year of college. But I broke the engagement in January of that year. I returned to college and to a series of casual dating relationships, determined to forget him. At the same time, he took off for South America, determined to forget me. Rereading the letters he wrote to me during that time and remembering the passion with which

I had first read them, I can see now that neither of us forgot the other, no matter how hard we tried. Still, for the next year and a half we continued to go our own separate ways. Bill's "way" turned out to be a dramatic departure from what I—and he—had expected.

WORK HARD, PLAY HARD

Half a year before I broke our engagement, in the summer of 1971, Bill had decided to put his business major to practical use after two years of college. He had returned to his hometown of Kalamazoo, Michigan, to take his expected place in the family-owned wholesale produce company. Since childhood that had been his plan. He had a natural aptitude for business, and his father had prepared him to excel in the marketplace by teaching him the value of hard work and by instilling in him an entrepreneur's love for challenge and risk taking.

From kindergarten on, Bill had spent Saturday mornings at the produce company with his father, first sorting produce and cleaning refrigeration bins, later loading and unloading trucks, then delivering produce to area restaurants and grocery stores, and eventually driving eighteen-wheel tractor-trailer rigs to Chicago to buy produce at the Water Street Market. During high school it was not unusual for Bill to drive a semi nonstop to Florida to pick up a load of produce, arriving home just in time to go straight to his morning classes.

During summers, Bill had worked on family-owned farms. While his friends were at the beach Bill spent hot, humid, dusty August days heading up crews of migrant workers and planting and harvesting fields of potatoes and onions. Often he came straight from the farm to my house for a date and would arrive looking more like a field hand than a high school heartthrob. Our first stop would be his parents' home, where he would shower himself into dating condition.

The clearest illustration of the work ethic passed from father to son was the day Bill had to empty a truckload of rotten potatoes. After hours of unloading bag after bag of slimy, smelly potatoes, he complained to his father about the number of bags still remaining. "Don't worry, Billy," his father said, "you only have to unload them one bag at a time." Though in later years I was often frustrated by Bill's propensity to pour too much time and energy into work, at seventeen I fell in love with that hardworking, disciplined part of him. Over the years his ability to face any challenge "one bag at a time" has served him well.

Still, life wasn't all work and no play for Bill. There were the ski boats and the summer cottage. There was *Ann Gail*, the forty-five-foot sailboat his father sailed across the Atlantic; Bill and a friend sailed it alone on Lake Michigan when they were in seventh grade. There was the Harley-Davidson motorcycle and the glistening black Pontiac GTO (I had to make sure I didn't scratch the paint with my fingernails when I opened the passenger door!). There was the airplane Bill had soloed in at sixteen. There were the credit cards.

And then there were the trips—the trips designed to expand Bill's worldview and to "grow him up." In grade school Bill's dad gave him skis and put him on a train bound for Aspen. Bill took the train to the end of the line, asked the conductor how to get to the Aspen Inn, and was gruffly informed that Aspen was twenty-five miles away and the train didn't go that far. Bill learned quickly how to ask questions and come up with alternatives. When he was fifteen, his dad gave him a stack of airline tickets and a travel itinerary that led him on a solitary eight-week journey through Africa and Europe. In Nigeria Bill ran out of cash and slept on the dirt floor of a one-room hut with a Nigerian family of six until his father wired him money.

It was a life of challenge, opportunity, and promise. Bill felt sure he was on the fast track to success.

TOUGH QUESTIONS

"What are you doing with your life, Bill?"

"I do a little work. I do a little play. I have a little sweetheart. I raise a little Cain on Fridays and Saturdays. Then I go to church on Sundays." Barely out of his teens, Bill thought his answer clever and appropriate. His interrogator didn't.

"Get serious, Bill. What are you doing with your life that matters? What are you doing *that will last forever?*"

"Not much, I guess." A more honest answer, Bill now says, would have been, "Nothing." And the most honest answer would have been, "I'm bowing in front of a full-length mirror. I'm serving myself. I'm bowing down to . . . me. And I don't give a rip about other people or their problems or their eternity." That man's simple question made Bill face the truth about himself, and the truth hurt.

Shortly thereafter Bill took the South American trip I mentioned earlier, and we temporarily parted ways. On that trip, he visited various missionary friends of his father. He was becoming increasingly restless at the produce company, sensing that God was calling him out of business and into some form of ministry, perhaps as a missionary. One night toward the end of the trip, he had dinner on the top floor of a restaurant that overlooked the Copacabana Beach in Rio de Janeiro, which was then considered the jet-setting capital of the world. While he sat pondering the yearnings of his soul and the direction of his life, he overheard the conversation of a sixtyish couple sitting near him. "Well, it's all been worth it," they said to one another. "All the years of working and saving have finally become worth it now that we are on this vacation and enjoying this evening."

Bill was overwhelmed by the absurdity of it all. Years and years of hard labor so that one day they could eat a meal in a restaurant overlooking the Copacabana Beach? He returned to his room, fell on his knees, and said, "God, there has got to be more to my life than this." He was twenty years old.

ROCKIN' ON THE EDGE

After spending the rest of that winter and the following spring working at his father's company, Bill made his annual trek to Fredonia, Wisconsin, to work as a summer counselor, lifeguard, Bible study leader, and coach at a Christian camp run by a Chicago church. Camp Awana was where at age sixteen Bill had become a Christian. One night as he had walked the path to his cabin a verse he had memorized as a child made sense to him suddenly: "Not by works of righteousness which we have done, but according to his mercy he saved us" (Titus 3:5 KJV). The awareness that salvation was a free gift of love stopped him dead in his tracks. "I thought my heart was going to explode," he says. "I couldn't imagine that kind of love. I remember just standing there saying, 'You've got to be kidding. This is too good to be true. If this is real, this is the greatest thing on the face of the earth.'"

So there he was in July 1972, back at the scene of the most important decision of his life, facing his second most important decision: what should he do with his future? He loved the marketplace but no longer felt satisfied there. He felt called to ministry but didn't know where to go or how to start. He was a college dropout at a kids camp in the middle of Wisconsin.

In the midst of that summer of confusion, a visitor arrived at camp. Dave Holmbo was a few years older than Bill, but they had been friends for years, each spending part of their summers up at Camp Awana. Dave wasn't working at camp that summer because he had just taken a job as the assistant music director at South Park Church in Park Ridge, Illinois, a Chicago suburb just twenty minutes from the downtown "Loop." During his visit, he told Bill about the high school music group he had started at South Park. Dave was nothing short of a musical genius, but the style of music he loved was a far cry from what was typically heard in churches in the early seventies. In fact, Dave had left the church he grew up in because he felt stifled musically. Church leaders didn't appreciate his ability to play any Beach Boys tune after one hearing, and they couldn't understand his constant need to "contemporize" the music of the Christian faith.

South Park, an independent church, was squarely evangelical and mainstream in its theology, but it was marked by an unusual degree of openness and spiritual authenticity. Prior to Dave's arrival there, South Park's pastor, Leroy "Pat" Patterson, had started a contemporary service that met after the traditional Sunday morning service and featured modern Christian choruses and an informal "share time." That was a fairly radical move in the early seventies. By the time Dave started the high school singing group, Pastor Patterson had left and South Park was between senior pastors. With the absence of strong adult leadership, Dave found even greater freedom to "do his thing." Having stored a lifetime of musical energy in his soul and having suppressed his creativity for what seemed like an eternity, Dave was a musical volcano just waiting to explode.

The explosion resulted in a Christian rock and roll group called Son Company, complete with singers, guitars, saxophones, trumpets, French horns, flutes, an oboe, and, of course, drums. Dave had an amazing ability to take the mediocre talents of inexperienced kids and fit them together in such a way that the end product was extraordinary. Within months Son Company was traveling throughout the Chicago suburbs, putting on concerts in churches and community centers. Eventually the group was traveling regularly to Wisconsin and Indiana, and ultimately put on two concerts in the famed Orchestra Hall, the elegant home of the Chicago Symphony.

Dave wrote much of the music himself and was inspired by the cutting-edge music of Californians Michael Omartian, Larry Norman, and Chuck Girard, leaders in the contemporary Christian music revolution that flowed out of the Jesus People movement of the sixties. Their songs echoed the longings and beliefs of the kids' hearts but set the lyrics to the music they loved, the music of the seventies. Kids like my own, who have grown up with Christian contemporary music, can't appreciate what this meant to a generation of Christian kids who had grown up without a music to call their own. It was exciting. It was emotional. And Son Company was on the leading edge of the contemporary Christian music scene in the Chicagoland area.

A STRATEGIC MOVE

By the end of the summer camp season, Bill had decided to move to Illinois to accept a job at the national headquarters of the Awana Youth Association, then located in Rolling Meadows. After settling in he visited South Park Church, where the Son Company was singing at a Sunday evening service. At that point the group had only been together for a few months, and Dave was preparing the kids for their first full-concert performance. He needed another guitarist and some help with vocals, so he asked Bill to join the group. According to Dave, Bill was a "hack guitarist," but again, Dave specialized in the transformation of mediocre talents. When it came to music, Bill fit perfectly into Dave's specialty.

When he left the family company, Bill had to turn in his credit cards and the keys to the boats and airplanes. Sliding them across his father's desk was sobering. "That's when I realized I was making a serious choice," Bill recalls. But he was undeterred—and grateful that his father let him keep the GTO and the Harley-Davidson. When he arrived in Illinois, he had little money in his pocket and his household possessions fit into a plastic laundry basket, but he earnestly believed he was heading out on a path prepared by God.

The kids at South Park knew nothing about Bill except that he was Dave's friend from some place called Kalamazoo and that he had interesting wheels. But when Dave asked Bill to lead a little Bible study for the kids after their weekly music rehearsal, the kids were willing to give him a listen. In fact, they had been praying for a teacher ever since they lost their previous youth director. They were hoping for a permanent replacement; in the meantime they would listen to the guy from Kalamazoo.

A SIMPLE FORMULA

Bill had no teaching background nor aspiration, but he had led a Bible discussion group during college, so he continued that format. He asked the kids to come prepared with verses on a particular subject—confidence, prayer, confession of sin, friendship, or obedience—and helped them apply the verses to their everyday lives. It was a simple formula: read a verse and apply it. But it began to awaken the kids' spiritual sensitivities. Many of them had previously experienced a dichotomy between their Christian lives and their "real" lives. They knew Jesus as Savior, but they didn't know what it meant to walk with Him Monday through Saturday. They didn't know how to live out their Christian lives at school or how to share their faith with their friends. As one former student says, "We were moral kids. We were Christian kids. But we didn't live and die for Christ on a daily basis. Then all of a sudden the principles of Scripture began to 'live' for us. We made a transition from Christ as Savior to Christ as Lord."

During that winter, some of the kids began inviting friends to the Bible study. By the early spring of 1973, there were nearly eighty kids coming each Wednesday night. This created an awkward situation in that the kids had to sit through the singing practice before they could attend the Bible study. For some this was great, but others had neither ability nor interest in music. Even the inspirational genius of Dave Holmbo was no match for a choir of monotones. So the decision was made to move the music rehearsal to Sunday afternoon and keep the Bible study on Wednesday nights.

Shortly after that, in May 1973, I graduated from college. Since breaking my engagement with Bill seventeen months earlier, I had received numerous letters from him chronicling his move from Michigan and the produce company to Illinois and the youth ministry. For over a year I had left the letters unanswered, but eventually my curiosity about the changes in Bill's life prompted me to write him. Immediately he called and asked if he could visit me at school. I agreed. By the time I graduated, we were toying with the idea of patching our broken romance, so I decided to visit him in Illinois.

I arrived on a Friday night, just in time to experience for myself the emotion of a Son Company concert. I stayed for nearly a week, attending another concert and also the Wednesday night Bible study. The youth group had not yet reached the size that would later bring it notice within the larger Christian community, but to me it seemed like a page straight from the book of Acts. God was doing something real in that little group of high schoolers. Kids who had yawned through fifteen years of church were suddenly charged with the kind of spiritual electricity I had read about in the Bible but never seen. And together they formed a community of love that would eventually prove irresistible to hundreds of local unchurched students—and to me. I moved to Illinois shortly after that first visit and began to play my flute in the Son Company band. I felt as if I had fallen into a miracle.

WHAT IF...

The Wednesday evening Bible study continued to grow, with a few students becoming Christians along the way—almost as if by accident. Bill and Dave began to wonder what would happen if they actually planned an event specifically to present the Gospel to unchurched kids. Bill decided to teach a five-week series on evangelism to the core kids, then challenge them to bring their unchurched friends to a special outreach event that he and Dave would develop. By the time the plan became a reality, Bill and Dave had decided to organize a weekly outreach event in order to provide more opportunities for Christian kids to bring their unchurched friends. The two of them would continue meeting separately with the core kids on another night of the week.

When they presented this idea to the core kids, the kids were revved up but also a little wary. One guy raised his hand and said, "Hey, you know, Bill, I like you and everything. But I would be a little embarrassed inviting the halfback of my football team to this group. I mean, we're sitting down in the basement on these carpet squares. I've had a carpet square since fourth grade, so it's OK for me, but my friend isn't going to know what to think about carpet squares. He's going to think it looks a little strange down here."

Bill said, "That's a very sensitive observation. I'll talk to the deacons about moving this meeting upstairs into the activity room. Anything else?"

Another kid raised his hand and said, "I'm not sure the guard on my basketball team is going to enjoy singing 'Kumbaya' and 'It Only Takes a Spark.' And about that twelve-string guitar that only has nine strings. It's got to go."

So Dave said, "No problem. We'll use the Son Company band. We'll use biblical lyrics—but we'll make them rock!"

Then a girl raised her hand, adjusted her chewing gum, and said, "Well, did you ever think about using drama?" The blank expression on Bill's face told her that in Kalamazoo, Michigan, people didn't talk much about drama. She explained, "It's where you put on a little skit. If you were talking about love, I could get some kids together to put on a little skit about the opposite of love so it would get kids thinking. Then the meeting wouldn't just be talk, talk, talk. There would be some acting going on, and kids like that stuff. You know, TV generation and all that."

"You know how to do that?"

"Sure, we do it at school all the time."

"Then it's all yours."

Another kid raised his hand and said, "Why don't we do media?" Again Bill had to admit his country boy ignorance. "You put together some slides," the guy explained, "and then put a computerized soundtrack behind it. It's very powerful."

"You know how to do that?"

"Sure."

"Then you're in charge of that."

Then one kid said, "And about your teaching, Bill." *Here it comes,* Bill thought. And it did. "You see, Bill, one of the reasons we listen to you is that we like you, but my friends don't like you yet. So instead of these long walks through the sticky pages of the Bible, where you hit six or seven topics at one time, why don't you just narrow it down? Make a point that is biblical but relevant to kids' lives, tell some good stories to illustrate it, and keep it down to about twenty-five minutes. I'm not asking you to compromise the Bible—but just give it to us in manageable doses."

"All right," Bill whispered. It was like taking an elbow in the stomach, but Bill knew the guy was right.

FLASHBACKS

After the kids left, Bill sat in that empty room in the basement of South Park Church and remembered a conversation he had with his dad when he was in junior high school.

"Hey, Billy, remember Bud Johnson? He just found out his wife has cancer, and he's really scared. He's not a Christian, but I think he needs spiritual help. He's going to be in town this weekend. I think I'll invite him to church."

Bill remembered thinking at the time, *I can't believe it. Dad's an intelligent, world-traveling guy. How can he even consider bringing an unchurched businessman to our church? It's Sunday afternoon. Has he already forgotten what we experienced just two hours ago?*

"Dad, whatever you do, don't do that. If this guy does have a spiritual spark flickering, you take him to church and it'll get extinguished in a matter of minutes! Spare him!"

In his brief conversation with his dad, Bill had no intention of discrediting their church. To this day Bill appreciates the values and doctrinal teaching he received while growing up. However, it was clear to him at age eleven that the church he grew up in was strictly for the already convinced. If you had grown up in the church and were accustomed to the routine, you were fine. But it was no place for the unchurched.

Bill remembered another time, in senior high school.

The wildest kid in the school was the right fielder on the baseball team Bill pitched for. He was, by any account, a character. He routinely abused alcohol, but beyond that—this was the late sixties—he was the first guy in school to experiment with marijuana. He also spent weekends with a college girl, and he was a great storyteller. On Monday mornings kids gathered around his locker to hear every sordid detail of his weekend sagas.

Bill didn't share most of this guy's leisure-time activities, but they were friends. He said to Bill, "Look, you live on the religious side and I live on the wild side, but let's just play baseball and have a good time." So they did.

One day all the other guys left after a game, but Bill's friend hung around, obviously wanting to talk. He sat down on the dugout bench and said, "Bill, my life is a wreck. My girlfriend dumped me. I'm drinking way too much. And the funny cigarettes are messing up my mind. I need help. I know you're pretty religious. I wonder if I can come to church with you and get squared away."

Before Bill could catch himself, he said, "Well, sure."

On Sunday morning Bill picked him up, drove out to his little white church in the country, and experienced the longest sixty minutes of his life. It was the first time Bill had attended a traditional church service with a genuine, downcast, openhearted unbeliever on his elbow, and it was an unmitigated disaster. Everything that happened was wrong for an unchurched kid. During the prelude, the kid looked as if he were going into shock. The "already convinced," who had grown up on this liturgical diet, were accustomed to hearing ancient hymns "interpreted" by ten-year-old flautists or less-than-proficient pianists; they appreciated the "heart behind it." But it was unlike anything Bill's friend had ever heard in a public setting. "Why aren't people throwing things?" he asked in a bewildered whisper.

From there it went south. They did a stand-up-sit-down thing several times, and the kid never did catch on. He listened, mystified, as a vocalist sang of seraphim and cherubim. Then there was the Creed. This was a hit, since the veterans had it memorized and Bill's friend had to stand there conspicuously mute. The Law was a hit too, because he'd broken nearly all of it, which made him think he was probably not too welcome there. Then came the sermon. *No, please no, not the minor prophets,* Bill pleaded silently. But sure enough . . . Amos . . . locusts . . .

It went on and on and finally ended. On the way home they talked baseball, girls, school, anything but church. They didn't see one another for three days. Finally Bill tracked the kid down.

"Hey, what gives? You avoiding me?"

"Look, Bill, I'm going to shoot it to you straight. I live on the wild side and you live on the religious side. But in spite of that I've always appreciated the fact that you are normal. You dress normal. You drive normal. You pitch normal. You talk normal. But what you took me to on Sunday was not normal. I've just been wondering why a normal guy like you goes to a place like that."

The face of his lost high school friend lingered in Bill's mind as his thoughts returned to 1973. *This is what the kids were trying to tell me here tonight. And it's what I understood at age eleven and relearned at eighteen. The typical traditional church is no place for the unchurched. To anybody but the already convinced, the average church service seems grossly abnormal. It makes no sense to those who haven't grown up in it, to those who don't know the drill. The music we sing, the titles we choose, the way we dress, the language we use, the subjects we discuss, the poor quality of what we do—all of these lead the average unchurched person to say, "This is definitely not for me."*

SPIRITUAL GIFTS AT WORK

As I settled into a new job as a receptionist (so much for the career in social work I had anticipated) and a new home (actually a tiny room I rented from a single woman with a young son) I focused my after-work hours on getting to know Son Company students and reestablishing my relationship with Bill. Though Bill and I enjoyed—thoroughly—the personal time we spent together, finding that time proved to be a challenge, because he and Dave were so busy charting a new course for the ministry. Taking the kids' suggestions, they planned a series of weekly outreach events that would be creative and energetic, contemporary and practical, but absolutely biblical. They would provide a safe place for unchurched kids to hear the dangerous, life-changing message of Jesus Christ.

There were about 125 kids that first night. John Ankerberg, a respected teacher-evangelist, spoke for the first three weeks. By the fourth week, when Bill took over the teaching, there were 150 students. Then 175. Within six months there were 300. Each week, Bill offered a biblical perspective on a subject relevant to students' daily lives and also talked about how to build a relationship with God. Some of the kids were becoming Christians and funneling into the believers group that met on Sunday night. We called the Wednesday night outreach service Son City, and the believers meeting Son Village. At Son City Bill explored what the Bible said on important topics. At Son Village he taught in more of a verse-by-verse fashion, and he and Dave led worship.

When Bill first started teaching weekly at Son City, he was so intimidated by the teaching responsibility that he asked a respected Christian leader for advice. "Teach through Berghof's *Manual of Christian Doctrine*," the man said. Bill took his advice. The first week, he started talking about theophanies, or the special appearances of God. Five minutes into the message, he realized the kids were lost. He put his notes away, apologized to the kids, and said, "If you'll come back next week, I promise I'll talk about something that is relevant to your life." From then on he always asked himself, "How does this passage, this biblical truth, this doctrine, relate to daily life?"

It soon became evident that Bill had the gift of teaching, though no one was more surprised by that than he. After one message on repentance and confession of sin, he said to me, "I don't know what was going on tonight. I suggested that kids repent before God and one another, and they did. Genuinely!" It was true. As Bill spoke kids had gotten out of their seats, walked over to other kids, and said, "I've wronged you. I've carried a grudge against you. I'm sorry. I want to confess my sin before God and you." Bill was mystified by the impact of his teaching, but those of us who listened weren't. His teaching was practical and relevant, yet thoroughly biblical and challenging and—in an almost uncanny way—empowered.

Part of the reason I fell in love with Bill was because I always had the sense he was going somewhere. He had strong convictions, he was decisive and energetic, and he made things happen. I didn't realize I was responding to his natural leadership abilities, but those gifts became even more evident during the Son City years. Bill inspired confidence. Kids wanted to follow him because they felt they could trust the direction in which he was going. Bill took that trust very seriously, and he and Dave together did their best to lead the kids wisely. While Dave developed the musicians and actors, Bill discipled student leaders.

A PERFECT PARTNERSHIP

Nearly every morning, Bill and Dave met at a little coffee shop in Park Ridge—The Tasty Platter—to brainstorm about the next ministry event. Over breakfast they would light a match to each other's ideas. Both were infectious, creative dreamers, "big picture" people, optimists, risk takers, and—to one degree or another—rebels, sharing a common frustration with church as it had always been done. But there were important differences that made their joint leadership of Son City so effective. Dave was the artist, Bill the businessman. Dave provided the programming direction: music, drama, and special events. Bill provided spiritual leadership and the businessman's feel for the nuts and bolts; he had a great sense about what was logistically possible. Dave would filter his really radical ideas through Bill, and together they would shape them into workable forms. When an idea came together, both had engineered and implemented it, but each in his own areas of expertise. After an event that bore the fruit of transformed lives, they would go out together and celebrate.

Many people have wondered how Willow Creek "came up" with the idea of using the arts so intensively in our services. Actually, the idea was the inevitable result of the collision of Dave Holmbo's gifts and the talents of the initial core kids at South Park Church. Why were these kids special? Because many of them attended a high school where the arts were highly honored and enjoyed, where it was as "cool" to be involved in music or theater as it was to play football or basketball. These kids understood and responded to the arts and knew how to use them. I think God was well aware of this and chose that particular time and place to harness the contemporary performing arts for His purposes.

TWO HANDS

Evangelism became a way of life at Son City. Both Bill and Dave were evangelists at heart, so that mind-set constantly filtered through the arts and teaching. Together they were always casting the vision of caring for those on the outside. When the youth group had reached about eighty in number, Bill and Dave split it into four teams, each led by student leaders: a captain, cocaptain, and secretary. When these teams got too large, they were split again. When the kids initially dug in their heels and didn't want to split into teams, Bill challenged their value system. They had to divide in order to embrace new kids. Eventually there were twenty teams, each averaging fifty to sixty students.

There was always the reality of heaven and hell hanging in the balance, which created an incredible sense of urgency. Dave wrote a song called "Crossroads," in which one line asked, "Have we all forgotten there really is a hell?" These kids hadn't forgotten. And because they were young, the concept of eternity had not grown old to them. They hadn't developed sophisticated defense mechanisms to cushion the blow of truth or rationalize away their responsibility. They just said, "Oh my gosh, if this is true, my friends are not going to be in heaven with me. I better do something."

I remember prayer meetings in the church basement in which kids would literally weep for the lost. Perhaps there was a Son Company concert coming up, and their parents or their best friend had agreed to come for the first time. There would be little groups of four or five kids on their knees on a cement floor, pleading that God would draw their loved ones to Himself. The kids carried that same intensity and spirit of prayer onstage with them when they put on concerts or led team meetings or sat through Bill's messages with their unsaved friends beside them.

The kids sang a song called "Two Hands," which could have been the theme song for Son City. It said, "Accept Him with your whole heart / And use your own two hands / With one reach out to Jesus / And with the other bring a friend."[1] That's what these kids were doing. God honored their sincerity with a steady stream of conversions. Baptism services in local park district swimming pools were the highlight of each ministry season.

TOUGH COMPETITION

On Thanksgiving Day, 1973, Bill and I became engaged—again. We had each grown during our long separation, both in our commitment to God and in our understanding of our personal goals and values. We seemed, more than ever before, to share a similar vision, and we were united by our mutual desire to make a difference with our lives. Son City offered us a way to do that—together.

Son City evenings started with team meetings, in which newcomers were welcomed and team events announced. Then all the teams came together for team competition. When weather permitted, there were outdoor competitions at the local park district—volleyball tournaments, obstacle courses, jungle ball. While Bill led competition, I joined in. One night I broke my toe during a chaotic game of line soccer, in which four teams competed at once in an "organized" free-for-all in a giant square on a football field. In the adrenaline-charged excitement of that evening the pain was easy to ignore, but in the coming days I earnestly wished I had played with a little less intensity. Perhaps my participation in such a game was not a very dignified way for a "leader" to behave, but one of the beauties of

Son City was that we made so little distinction between leaders and followers, between teachers and students. There was very little "us" and "them." We were all in this adventure together, learning as we went along and enjoying the moment, whether it was a moment of earnest prayer or raucous fun.

In the winter, we had to move inside, so we staged creative competitions in the church sanctuary, from Frisbee throws down the center aisle to "challenge the champ" spectaculars, which could have provided ideas for the *Guinness Book of World Records*. Sometimes teams had to prepare something ahead of time to present for competition, like a giant cake (one team used sixty-five cakes to create a huge telephone complete with musical push buttons) or huge posters or a complex papier-mâché creation.

These competitions built team unity and helped kids move from a spectator mind-set to a participant mind-set. They also showed unchurched kids that Christians knew how to have fun. And not least of all, they drained off energy. We thought it better to use that youthful energy creatively than to fight it for an hour. After thirty or forty-five minutes of fast-paced competition, kids were ready to settle down for the program.

HIGH IMPACT

The program often opened with a song the kids heard every day on the radio, like "Mighty Clouds of Joy" or "I Believe in Music," perhaps with lyrics slightly altered to reflect a deeper message. Drama provided a transition as unchurched kids learned through true-to-life skits that "these people understand me." Multimedia slide shows illustrated the theme of the upcoming message. Before Bill got up to speak, a high school girl might sing a song about a "Stranger" who "died to set men free." Or a guy's group would earnestly repeat the line of an Imperials song that said, "Christ means more to me than you'll ever know." Or the Son Company might sing, "He'll set you free from sin / And you'll be born again / When the Son comes in."

Though Son City lifted fun and games to new levels of hilarity, there was never any doubt about the ultimate goal—to compellingly present biblical truths to lost high school kids—and the entire evening led up to that. By the time Bill was ready to speak, you could have heard a pin drop. He would give a talk called "Jesus Is God," "The Bible Is True," "The Rich Young Ruler," or "How to Become a Christian," or he would present a three-week series, such as "Jesus the Forgiver," "Jesus the Friend," and "Jesus the Leader of My Life."

After Bill's message, little huddles of high schoolers would gather all over the sanctuary, talking and praying. Night after night we would have to lovingly kick them out of the sanctuary and send them home before they broke their curfews. Weekly, kids were becoming Christians, which created an energy that propelled students and leaders alike to further growth. Core kids were forced to keep growing in order to shepherd the new kids they brought. At Son Village these new-believers-turned-disciplers were challenged with messages like "You Are the Light of the World," "The Courage of David," "The Call of Moses," "Your Dream or God's Dream?" Any students who attended Son Village will remember Bill's challenges to make careful decisions about their master, their mate, and their mission and to yield their resources of time, talents, and treasures wholly to God.

These kids were serious about their Christianity. Sure, they wanted to have fun; they loved the excitement of crazy competitions and the emotional impact of creative programs. But what they seemed to want more than anything else was to be transformed from the inside out. Hundreds of students studied Brother Lawrence's book *Practicing the Presence of God* and earnestly tried to be conscious of God's purposes every moment. The kids' celebrations of communion at Son Village were authentic outpourings of love and gratitude to the Son who had died for them and transformed them.

The natural result of this life transformation was the development of strong community life. Just as Bill taught boldly about our relationship with God, so he taught about our relationships with others. He taught about dealing with anger, resolving conflicts, ministering to the hurting, and being an encourager. He taught about patience, compassion, forgiveness, and gentleness. And the kids put what he said into practice.

Son City turned the social order of the local high schools upside down. If a castaway freshman boy was on Red Team with a senior cheerleader, they were buddies, equals; they went to social events together, competed for their team together, laughed and cried and prayed together. Local high schoolers wanted to be loved the way the Son City kids were loved. Sometimes they came just to find out what was behind all this relational warmth.

Often once they came, they stayed. Hundreds of kids spent nearly every night at church or at a team activity. And they weren't content to merely take the benefits of community life; they wanted to contribute to it. Those who had jobs donated money for team expenses and set up funds for kids who couldn't afford to attend Son City retreats, or they put gas in other kids' cars so they could bring their unchurched friends to church, or they loaned out their own cars. Whoever had money on a given day would pick up the tab for a late-night snack for his or her team members. If for any reason a student ever needed a place to stay, he or she could always find a "home away from home" with a Son City friend.

Another reason kids enjoyed coming to Son City was that everybody had a contribution to make. Kids who liked to paint or draw joined the Art Module and made posters to decorate team rooms. Kids in the Construction Module built sets for the stage. The Production Module was responsible for sound and lights at group events. The Photography Module took slides for media presentations. The Cooking Module provided food for team events. Other kids made phone calls to newcomers or memorized verses for team points or played in the band or helped lead competition or acted in skits. Kids with obvious leadership skills were groomed for team leadership. All of this built a sense of ownership. Every student had a job to do, a contribution that was important to the entire group. Though we had never heard of the term, we were reaping the rewards of "gift-based ministry."

THE TEAM

Throughout the history of Willow Creek Community Church, the assembling of the ministering team has been one of the most obvious signs of God's intervention, and it all began back in Son City. In addition to the openness to the arts, there was also an extraordinary closeness in that original South Park group. Many of the kids had grown up together since infancy, so they knew each other well and had a history of working and playing together. Most of them had grown up in stable families and had strong character and healthy values. They had also benefited from the foundation laid by previous youth workers, particularly Bruce and Loita Dart, a gracious and gifted couple who had taught the original core kids the meaning of "love fleshed out in relationship."

When Bill and Dave came on the scene, these kids were ready for God to do something in their midst. They had been prepared. They were primed to grow and to reach out to their friends and to assume positions of leadership. For many of them the call to ministry that they received when they were fifteen or sixteen years old is still alive. Nancy Moore, the girl who had to adjust her chewing gum to explain to Bill the meaning of drama, became Nancy Beach, Willow Creek's programming director since the early eighties. Laurie McLennan, secretary of Red Team, is now Laurie Pederson and has been an elder at Willow Creek since 1978. Don Cousins, Red Team's captain, was Bill's associate pastor throughout the eighties and early nineties. Purple Team's captain, Bruce Horgan, was active in the Production Module and later became Willow Creek's building trades manager.

Other kids from that group are active members at Willow Creek or key leaders in churches throughout the country. Frequently they attend church leadership conferences at Willow Creek and sit in the front row with a knowing look on their faces, remembering our basement beginnings.

A NIGHT TO REMEMBER

Bill and I were married in Kalamazoo, Michigan, on Saturday, May 18, 1974. Like everything else in our life at that time, our wedding was a Son City event. Team captains served as ushers, Son Company flautists played during the ceremony, vocal groups sang at the reception, and smiling students were stationed everywhere from the guest book to the punch bowl. In addition, nearly one hundred kids made the four-hour drive simply to attend the wedding. Arriving on Friday night, they "crashed" our rehearsal, enjoyed a late-night meal that Bill's father graciously hosted, and kept the local Holiday Inn—and Bill—hopping until dawn.

But our wedding was not the most important Son City event that month. During the 1973–74 school year, Son City had continued to grow steadily, but the Christian kids clearly had not gone all out in inviting their friends. There seemed to be a sense that we had just been practicing this outreach idea. But one night at Son Village, Bill suggested that we choose a Son City evening in May and target it as a major outreach. If the kids would bring their friends, Bill would give the clearest Gospel presentation he could come up with. "Let's make a pact," he said, "to fast and pray and bang on the doors of heaven. Let's ask God to be merciful and to take the blinders off the eyes of our unsaved friends. Let's trust in the power of the Gospel to lead people unto salvation." So we agreed, set the date, and served notice to the Evil One that we intended to do damage for the kingdom.

The kids began inviting their friends.

Bill tried to remain calm as he worked on his message for that night, but the pressure was on. A freckle-faced freshman girl would say, "I have my whole pom-pom team coming that night. Don't blow it." A senior jock would say, "I have the defensive side of the football team coming that night. Counting on you, big buddy." Bill's knees were already shaking. He tried to put a message together made up of all his best illustrations. He wanted the kids to like Jesus, of course, but I think he was also concerned that they like him too, so he wrestled with what to preach on. Then he had what can only be called a leading of the Holy Spirit: *Read the story of the crucifixion of Christ and tell the kids why Jesus died.*

Oh, brother, Bill thought. *That's a barnstormer. How about Plan B?* But the Spirit gave him no way out; he stuck with Plan A out of sheer obedience.

The night came and there were kids hanging out windows. Nearly six hundred charged-up students filled the church auditorium, and everything—from the opening jam (our version of a prelude) to the prayer at the end—was designed just for them. We had great contemporary music, sidesplitting drama, a powerful media presentation, and moving lead-in music. Then Bill walked out in jeans and a T-shirt with an open Bible in his hands. "Let me read you the greatest story in the history of the world," he said. "It's about a God-man named Jesus." Then he read the story of the crucifixion and made some brief comments. At the end of the message, he said, "The reason Jesus did what He did is that He knows that kids like you have rebelled and sinned against Him, even at your relatively young ages. But you still matter to God. So He sent His Son to die in your place. If you'd like to receive Him now, stand to your feet."

So many kids stood up he thought they had misunderstood him, so he had them all sit down. He was so nervous he barely knew what he was saying, but he did his best to explain the story again. Again they stood up—nearly three hundred kids. The meeting ended at half past nine, and from then until almost midnight kids stood in lines twenty deep, waiting to pray with someone to receive Christ. Eventually we dragged the church deacons out of their Wednesday night meeting to help pray with kids. What, we wondered, could they possibly be doing that was more important than this?

The events of that night remind me of Paul's words in 1 Corinthians 2:4–5: "My message and my preaching were not with wise and persuasive words, but with a demonstration of the Spirit's power, so that your faith might not rest on men's wisdom, but on God's power." There was nothing in Bill's words that night which could have touched the hearts and souls of those high school kids—except the simple truth of the Gospel, and the dramatic intervention of the Spirit. It was a night like so many we have experienced since then, a night when God used weak, inadequate human efforts to accomplish his extraordinary purposes.

Bill was the last one to leave the building that night. He walked slowly out the back doors of the church and leaned against the red brick wall. His knees began to give way, and he slid down the wall of the church, collapsing on the sidewalk. Suddenly he was crying like a baby. "I couldn't figure it out," he said later. "I was the quintessential thinker, devoutly antiemotion. I hated tears. And there I was, heaving and sobbing on a concrete slab." Then it all came together for him. The Holy Spirit was giving him a message he would never forget. It was a question, actually, and it went something like this: *Where would those kids who received Christ tonight be if there hadn't been a service designed just for them, a safe place where they could come week after week and hear the dangerous, life-transforming message of Christ?*

That simple question overwhelmed him. That night, he made a commitment that shaped his future: *God, with your strength and for as long as I am in ministry, I will always make sure that our strategy includes a regularly scheduled, high-quality, Spirit-empowered outreach service where irreligious people can come and discover that they matter to You and that Christ died for them.*

A SERVICE FOR SEEKERS

I'll never forget that evening, when the Holy Spirit squeezed tears from the heart and soul of a twenty-two-year-old kid from Michigan who had just witnessed the miraculous outpouring of God's redeeming power. I look back in awe of that moment when Bill committed himself to the concept of what we now call the "seeker service." I thank God for protecting that moment. How easily it could have been missed. A lingering student or a conscientious custodian could have interrupted Bill. Or an internal preoccupation could have distracted him. But on that night, as on so many occasions since then, God grabbed the moment and spoke his message. I'm glad Bill was listening that night. I'm glad he embraced the vision that has shaped our passion for over twenty years.

Later when we started Willow Creek, we formulated our plan around this given: a weekly seeker service that would provide a safe and informative place where unchurched people could come to investigate Christianity further. We've paid a price for that decision, both in terms of the hard work it has taken and in terms of the criticism we have received throughout the years. But those of us who were there on that unforgettable night in May 1974—as many of the current leaders of Willow Creek were—know that God was calling us then in the same way he calls us now: to be aggressive and intentional in providing learning opportunities for the unchurched people in our community. And time and time again we have seen God draw people to Himself through the outreach ministry of a seeker service.

I remember the series Bill taught at Willow Creek called "Faith Has Its Reasons," in which many seekers heard for the first time a clear apologetic for the Christian faith, and hundreds trusted in Christ. I remember the concluding message in the series "Fanning the Flames of Marriage," in which Bill told seekers that even more important than pursuing marital growth was pursuing a relationship with God. Many became Christians after that message. A sober aura hung in the auditorium throughout the series "Your Ever After." Many people turned to Christ as they faced for the first time the eternal realities of heaven and hell. I could mention many such illustrations. Twice each year we have baptism services in which hundreds of people give public witness to their newfound faith in Christ. Many of these new believers have become Christians after attending a seeker service with a believing friend.

I will never forget the weekend Bill gave a message called "Show Me the Way." The service as a whole offered perhaps the clearest and most compelling presentation of what it means to become a Christian that Bill and the Willow Creek programming team had ever come up with. Bill gave our adult core of believers the same challenge he gave the Son City kids almost twenty years earlier: "You

41

bring your friends; we'll make sure they hear the Gospel." The auditorium was filled at each service. As Bill gave his message, a charge of electricity ran through the entire congregation. Believers were vibrating with excitement and anticipation, because on either elbow were people they had been trying to lead to Christ and bring to church for years. If we could have harnessed the energy, we could have lit up Chicago.

There is today at Willow Creek the same pulsating passion to introduce people to Jesus Christ which marked the early Son City years. Introducing people to Jesus is just the starting point, of course; our ultimate goal is that they would become true disciples. Similarly, the seeker service is just one part of the Willow Creek story, just one step in an overall ministry strategy designed to encourage people along a path of ever-increasing devotion to Christ.

On that May night in 1974, we had no idea what the future would bring. As Bill sat with his back pasted against that knobby brick wall he knew only one thing: he had to keep reaching out to unchurched people. He had no grand view of what that commitment might mean. He had no long-term plan. The thought of someday starting a church had never even crossed his mind at that point.

But something had happened inside him. He was gripped by the soul-level awareness that an all-out effort to touch the lives of lost people pleased God and reflected the heart of Christ.

NOTES

1. Tom Coome and Chuck Butler, "Two Hands," 1970, Dunamis Music, *Love Song* album, 1972, Good News Records, North Hollywood, CA. Distributed by Myrrh Records, Word, Inc.

chapter two

TRANSITION ERA—"BE THE CHURCH"

*I remember walking into South Park for the first time, into a church
that looked like the church I had walked away from years earlier. But
the band was playing loud and kids were having a great time. It just
floored me. Then I went to a Son City retreat, and everyone I met
seemed to care about me. They seemed genuine. That weekend I
heard a message about the Gospel and about true discipleship. I was
ready to hear it. I said, "OK, this is it." And I trusted Christ.*

TIM VANDENBOS,
DIRECTOR OF WILLOW CREEK'S WILDERNESS CAMP

Recently on a crisp May morning I sat in the sanctuary of the stately red brick building of South Park Church, which housed Son City over twenty years ago. I sat beneath the white arched ceiling, my eyes trailing the length of the giant white molding that marks the line where the ceiling reaches down to meet the sky blue walls. I counted the tiny panes of frosted glass that fill the ten arched windows (forty-nine panes in each). I walked past the thirty-six white pews and stood before the white wooden pulpit with its three arched panels. To my left was the white grand piano, on my right the white organ with its glistening pipes. I rested my hands on the white communion table where gold letters read, "This do in remembrance of me."

In my mind there is a time warp, and suddenly I am back in Son City. I can't help but smile, delighted and amused. *Why me?* I wonder. *Why was an ordinary girl like me plopped in the midst of something as extraordinary as this?* I am not the only one asking that question. For me and so many others, leaders and students alike, Son City is our family, our friends, our social world, our recreation, our passion, our vocation. It is, in fact, our life—our wonderful, exciting life that day after day bursts with meaning.

Years later we pile word upon word as we try to describe it, but in the end we sink helplessly into a cliché: "You just had to be there." Many of us have described that intense spiritual and relational era as Camelot.

But Camelot had a shadow side. Not many of us had to spend time there, but those of us who did felt caught between two extremes: a breathtaking ministry experience that gave life more meaning than we could ever have hoped for, and a heartbreaking personal disappointment that bordered on despair. Perhaps a glimpse into Bill's calendar from November 1974 will provide a hint about that darker side:

- Sunday morning: "Church Service" (Bill sang or led the "share time.")
- Sunday afternoon: "Music Rehearsal" (Bill sang.)
- Sunday night: "Evening Service" (Bill often participated in these services.)
- Monday night: "Son Village" (Bill taught.)
- Tuesday night: "Awana Club" (Bill directed.)
- Wednesday night: "Son City" (Bill taught.)
- Thursday night: "Son City" (Bill taught.)
- Friday night: "Retreat" (or "Team Event," "Overnight," "Concert," "Discipleship"—Bill was involved in all of these.)
- Saturday afternoon: "Tournament" (Bill led these.)
- Saturday night: "Gym Night" (Bill led these.)

In addition to these activities, Bill spent hours each day in Son City program planning, ministry leadership, and message preparation. He was also a full-time college student. If ever there was an empty crack in his schedule, there was inevitably a needy high school student ready to fill it.

In my mind I am walking again along the quiet, tree-lined streets from the church to the tiny home where we had just begun our married life in May 1974. I am sitting at the round kitchen table with the red tablecloth. Another lonely meal. Another empty evening. An hour earlier I had begged Bill to stay home. He had looked at me in disbelief. "Kids are dying and going to hell, and you want me to stay home and hold your hand?" I am too young and too insecure to know how to respond. The words echo in my mind, and I hear them over and over in different forms: *Don't bother me, Lynne. How can you demand that, Lynne?* Six months into marriage, I am convinced I have made a horrible mistake. I love the man I married. I love Son City. But I hate our marriage. I hate the pain of disappointment. I hate mourning the death of so many dreams. And I hate the loneliness.

As I look back I realize Bill didn't intend to hurt me. He had simply lost perspective. He was caught up in something so powerful, so fruitful, so enticing, so wonderful, so much bigger than he was. It would have taken an incredibly mature man with a long-term view of life to have responded any differently. But how mature can you be at twenty-two? And how can you look to the future when the present is so extraordinary? Bill speaks now of the addictive nature of fruitfulness, but he didn't know about that then. All he knew was that slowing down seemed like disobedience or laziness. If God was pleased to bless his efforts, how could he not do more and more and more? The blessing of youthful energy is that it allows you to keep going and being productive. The drawback is that it allows you to run past insights that exhaustion might have forced you to notice.

Today I can look back at Bill's insane schedule with understanding. Back then I just felt hurt. Too often my hurt turned to anger and erupted in hostility that pushed Bill farther and farther away. Similar dynamics touched the marriages of other leaders and the family lives of many students. But just when one of us would work up the courage to question the pace, there would be a new wave of conversions. We would be astonished anew by God's redeeming power and would feel guilty for even thinking of pulling the plug on the flow of divine electricity. There seemed only one option: to continue on. But could our marriages survive?

A COLLISION COURSE

Unfortunately, our personal struggles mirrored a larger relational struggle. The marriage between Son City and South Park Church was also experiencing strain. And for good reason. Son City was not an easy spouse to live with.

Another memory comes to my mind. I walk back into the elegant sanctuary and see hundreds of kids in muddy shoes come in from outdoor competition and stomp down the carpeted center aisle to the rock and roll music screaming from oversize speakers. Strobe lights flash wild patterns on the pristine walls. The pulpit is nowhere to be seen, and I know that the communion table has been stuffed into a closet somewhere. A team scoreboard is set up on top of the white organ. I see a freshman boy, a little too zealous, forget to remove his shoes before he jumps onto the organ to write in the scores.

I see another evening. A mammoth rope is stretched down the main aisle; nearly a hundred kids dig their heels into the carpet as they wage a giant tug-of-war. I see a whiffle ball football game played down that same center aisle, Frisbees tossed aloft from the balcony, and weight lifting contests held on center stage.

I remember the week we used the entire church facility for a Halloween competition, giving each ministry module a different room to decorate. The Art Module ended up in the baptistery, which was converted into a very creative haunted house. The next morning, one of the church trustees had a lengthy conversation with Art Gay, who had recently become the senior pastor at South Park, about why the winning of souls necessitated the painting of polka dots on the baptistery walls.

Every piece of carpet and every inch of wall in South Park had Son City's mark on it. And people like Art were beginning to take heat for it. Every pew was loose and scarred. On Son City nights the front pews, which would normally have held thirteen or fourteen people, repeatedly had twenty high schoolers—not sitting quietly, mind you. One night the load finally broke the physical laws of lumber and glue and nails. The end of a pew literally fell off.

Today we regret the way we treated that facility, being adult stewards of a church building ourselves, and we regret our impatience with trustees and church members who complained about our behavior. "Don't they realize these are kids' lives?" we used to ask. "Don't they hear the teaching that goes on here? Haven't they seen the genuine life transformation? Who cares about buildings when eternity is at stake? So what if there are repair bills? It's only money." We have since learned that money doesn't grow on trees, that somebody *must* worry about buildings, and that lives can in fact be transformed without the wholesale destruction of facilities.

South Park was remarkably tolerant of the excesses of the youth ministry. In fact, many people in the church were enthusiastic supporters, providing vehicles for distant events, meals and lodging for leaders, financial support, and prayer. Others displayed incredible patience and a forgiving spirit when their kids returned from retreats hours behind schedule or when their sons or daughters missed family events because they "just had to be at Son City" or when the family car was brought home filled with the same mud that decorated the carpet in the sanctuary. We remember these people with deep gratitude and affection.

But eventually there were over twice as many kids in Son City as there were adults in the church. The youth ministry budget had grown from $300 in 1972 to $80,000 in 1975, and while high school kids are great at spending money, they're not very good at bringing it in. We also had events scheduled nearly every night, which changed the maintenance budgets and schedules and crowded out other church activities.

As tension grew between Son City and the adult side of the church, Bill began to wonder what God had in mind. Son City was as exciting as ever; kids' lives were still being transformed, and the leadership was unified. But in some ways the ministry was becoming a monster. It was beginning to create an impossible, destructive situation at a great church. What should we do?

The answer had been in the works for nearly two years.

A MODERN-DAY TRAGEDY

During those two years, Bill had been pursuing a degree in biblical studies at Trinity College in Deerfield, Illinois. During his first semester there, one of his professors asked, "Do any of you students want to do something truly great with your life? Do you want to sign up for the most compelling, far-reaching challenge in this world? Do you want to discover real excitement?" Without apology he added, "Then commit yourself to Jesus' vision of establishing communities of God here on this earth. Devote yourself to the church!"

Bill thought, *He is joking, right? Compelling challenge? Excitement? Does he think I was born yesterday? I know all about church. An hour a week is enough for me.*

But periodically that middle-aged professor would finish the subject matter of the class period early, step in front of his wooden lectern, and with a wistful gaze fixed on something only he could see, employ his intriguing French accent in some unsolicited vision-casting.

"The early church," he would say, "was *alive*. It was Spirit-led, so it was fresh and energetic and creative and dynamic and unpredictable. It wasn't about maintaining the status quo or going through the motions. It was about the Holy Spirit working dramatically and explosively in people's lives."

The professor talked about how the early believers actually let the Word of God rule their daily lives and transform their attitudes, goals, and relationships. He described true Christian fellowship and talked about what it means to take off our masks and be strugglers together, to weep and rejoice together, to be "brotherly and sisterly." He portrayed communion as a deeply moving opportunity to reconnect with amazing grace and to celebrate the ultimate act of love. And he described prayer as a matchless privilege and the conduit of power that brought energy to the early church.

His litany about a church of New Testament strength went on. A consciousness—no, expectation—of miracles and the anticipation of supernatural surprises should mark a Spirit-led church. Redeemed people would see private property as available for the common good—not communism but commonism, with God's material gifts viewed as potential relief for the needy.

The early church found favor because it was filled with loving people who were attentive to one another, responsive to suffering, and committed to social justice. Bill's prof matter-of-factly pointed out that the early church "added to its numbers daily" because that's what happens when the church is really being the church.

The captivating Frenchman passionately lamented that reality in too many twentieth-century churches is a far cry from the biblical picture. Preaching is insipid and unrelated to daily life. Fellowship means little more than superficial conversations in the church lobby after a service. Communion is an autopilot ritual, and prayer a formality. Surprises—in terms of programs or sermons or policies or life transformations—seldom occur, and a sense of the miraculous is an outdated notion. The "haves" give little thought and even less help to the "have-nots." The church operates as an isolated island of subculture, wondering why it is ignored and unappreciated by the community at large. Evangelism is, more often than not, "something we ought to be doing" but aren't.

"This is a modern-day tragedy," he would say.

Dr. Gilbert Bilezikian proved to be a masterful vision-caster. Bill took every class he taught for two years. It didn't matter what the class was; Bill was there for the occasional five or ten minutes when Dr. B. exposed his soul, when he went on a tangent about the church. The picture he painted seemed beyond the realm of reality, but Bill found himself asking, *What if it could be done? What if a true community of God could be established in the twentieth century? It would transform this world and usher people into the next.*

CAUGHT!

To say Bill caught the vision is inaccurate. The real truth is that the vision caught him. It captured him, overwhelmed him, blocked out everything else. Suddenly it was the only vision that made sense, the only vision that seemed worth committing his life to.

"Within a matter of months," says Bill, "every other goal I had considered seemed to pale in comparison to the thought of establishing the kingdom of God here on earth. Bowing down in front of a full-length mirror had lost its appeal. Going for money or toys or pleasure or fame seemed like a trivial pursuit. Climbing some corporate ladder would be child's play. I lived out those visions in my mind, and none of them seemed to warrant the investment of the only life I had. Because of my family background, I had already discovered that the fun-fixes get old. I knew that the travel spots didn't measure up to the brochures and that earning another thousand dollars wasn't going to change the quality of my life."

Finally one day Dr. B. said, "Maybe someday one of you students will try to build a church like this."

Says Bill, "I wanted to jump up and shout, 'Sign me up! I'll do it!' I had no idea what my spiritual gifts were; I certainly didn't think I was destined to be a pastor or a church leader. But whatever contribution I could make, I wanted to get about the business of making it. I felt like a kid who'd been playing T-ball and suddenly discovered he could join the major leagues. To me it was a no-brainer. 'Sign me up!'"

Signing up for the major leagues did not mean starting a ministry for adults. To Bill at that point, "church" still meant Son City. Just prior to his first class with Dr. B., he had launched the first major outreach of Son City. So Dr. B.'s inspirational teaching on the church paralleled the inspirational reality of the transformed lives of the early Son City converts.

ACTS 2

As Dr. B. spoke it became apparent to Bill that the church was the only hope for the world. Only the power of Christ, unleashed through the activity of the local church under the direct influence of the Holy Spirit, could change the downward trajectory of individual lives and cultures. Left unchecked, the systems and organizations of ungodly men and women would lead to the society's downfall. But the church could have tremendous—ultimately strategic—importance in the world.

In private conversations Bill asked Dr. B. how he could apply the lessons he was learning to the high school kids he was leading. "How serious are you?" Dr. B. would ask. "Are you just trying to build another youth group based on slick activities, athletic tournaments, parties, and trips to the beach? Or do you want to infect these kids with the real disease of Christianity?"

"I want to infect 'em."

"Then just do Acts 2!"

It was Dr. B. who challenged Bill to call students to wholehearted discipleship. It was Dr. B. who challenged Bill and the other core leaders to provide the model for true Christian fellowship by building relationships of vulnerability and trust with one another. It was Dr. B. who challenged Bill to create an environment in which prayer and worship and communion were meaningful, and in which kids would share their resources with one another. It was Dr. B. who challenged Bill to teach the kids about spiritual gifts.

In their private discussions, Dr. B. became increasingly impassioned, yet frequently Bill detected a sense of futility, a desperation almost, in his demeanor. He asked him about it once, and Dr. B. said, "I have felt for many years like John the Baptist, a lone voice crying in the wilderness. I understand that God wants me to continue crying out even if nobody listens, but I am getting weary."

Is he crying out for me? Bill wondered. Dr. B. taught at Trinity College for only two years, the exact two years Bill attended there. Was that an accident of fate or a divinely staged collision?

Bill struggled with the radical nature of Dr. B.'s vision. *Forget it,* he found himself thinking. *This is spiritual utopia. Evangelical nirvana. Antiquated Bible history. It could never happen in the sophisticated culture of the twentieth century.* But he was just young and idealistic enough—or perhaps Spirit-led enough—to think, *But what if it could happen? What if I could be part of it? And what if I missed it because I didn't believe or wasn't willing to try?* The thought of missing what just might be possible had begun to haunt him.

With tensions rising at South Park, Bill turned again to Dr. B.'s words and wondered if Acts 2 could come alive with adults as it had with high school kids.

Would adults be flexible enough to try something new? Would they respond to the challenges?

DREAMIN'

Late into the night we would sit with Dave and his wife and other core leaders and talk about what *could be*. We dreamed of a place where the Word of God would be communicated in an irresistibly compelling way. We dreamed of people getting together informally in small groups and meeting in homes and taking meals together and talking about real-life issues. We dreamed of a community in which prayer would unleash the prevailing power of God. We dreamed of a church that would be distinct and countercultural, in which affluent members would say, "Enough is enough," and would funnel their excess resources back into the local fellowship for distribution to the needy. We dreamed about church members displaying so much love and integrity that good rumors would begin to circulate among the lost, and when unchurched people would come to see what was going on, they would find Christ. We dreamed of a place where there would be a sense of the miraculous, where what was happening couldn't be explained in human terms.

We didn't dream about how to be a big church. We dreamed about Acts 2. We dreamed about what it would feel like to be part of a biblically functioning community. We dreamed about how to *be the church*. And we believed that the dream was straight from the heart of Jesus. The church is, after all, His vision. It didn't originate with a scholarly Frenchman in a college classroom. It wasn't dreamed up by a bunch of kids in an all-night coffee shop. The picture was first painted by Jesus, who said, "I will build my church; and the gates of hell shall not prevail against it" (Matthew 16:18 KJV).

But in reality what did that dream mean for us in the winter of 1975? Was it just stimulating food for thought? Or was it a call from God to leave South Park and start a church? Increasingly, it seemed to be the latter, as Bill felt a growing passion to minister to adults. *How,* he thought, *can we really make a difference in the world unless we reach the entire family?*

When Bill ran this idea by his mentor, Dr. B. was wary. "You're biting off more than you can chew," he said. "I think you'd better stick with kids. Just move Son City to a different location and start an independent youth ministry." Dr. B. wasn't convinced that adults would be open to a new paradigm for ministry or that they would respond to music, drama, and media the way kids did. "But," he said, "if you really believe God is calling you to do this, I'm behind you. I'll do whatever I can to help."

A DEFINING MOMENT

In March, Bill and I went to Florida for a much needed vacation and talked more about starting a church based on the principles and strategies developed in Son City. When we returned home, Bill told the team captains that he thought the Holy Spirit was leading him to start a church, and he asked them to pray about it. In April he read Robert Schuller's book *Your Church Has Real Possibilities,* which affirmed Bill's belief that one could reach unchurched people through the local church. In May he presented his resignation to the deacons of South Park Church.

The biggest test of God's call was when Dave Holmbo said, "That's great, Bill. You go start a church, and I'll stay here and keep Son City going." Other core leaders said the same—understandably. Son City was at its peak, with nearly twelve hundred kids coming each week. We all had thought we would be doing Son City for the rest of our lives. The attitude was, "God is doing a mighty thing here. Let's play it out till the end." Now suddenly Bill wanted to give it all up and start something new, with no guarantees, no precedent, and no backing from any church, organization, or significant donor. Bill could understand Dave's decision, but it was unsettling. The entire Son City miracle had happened under the joint leadership of Dave and Bill. How could Bill do ministry without him?

Walking down the sidewalk one evening, Bill asked himself—and God— that question. The only answer he received was, *You can't make a real difference in the world until you reach adults. Now is the time. Get going.* It was a defining moment, a "Though none go with me, still I will follow" conversation with God. After that Bill had perfect peace about the two of us venturing out alone.

Thankfully, however, God was at work in ways we were unaware of. By the time Bill presented his formal resignation to the church body in June, Dave and his wife, Sue, and a handful of other gifted core leaders had decided to go with us. Together we entered a two-month transition period, during which Bill and Dave handed their responsibilities over to others. In August we all performed for the last time with the Son Company and officially left South Park Church. Bill and I were twenty-three.

We decided to start our new church in Palatine, Illinois, a suburb twenty miles west of Park Ridge, because a group of dedicated Son City kids from Palatine—kids who had taken buses into Park Ridge each week for two years—was eager to have a home church in that area. We did not conduct any demographic studies. We knew nothing about Palatine or nearby Barrington. We just knew that one of the leaders of that group—a longhaired drummer named Mike Bourbon, who had an infectious smile and a burning passion for the lost—was convinced that God was "going to do something great in Palatine." What more did we need to know?

So we were ready to start a church for the unchurched. All we lacked was money, a facility, and adults. Bill did the first thing that came to mind: he bought twelve hundred baskets of tomatoes on the Water Street Market in Chicago and recruited the Son City kids to sell them door-to-door in Palatine, hoping to sell them for $4 or $6. What Bill didn't know was that Palatine was a "garden community"; the last thing its residents needed in August was more tomatoes. By the end of the day, baskets were going for $.25. But we earned about $4,800 that day, enough to buy sound and lighting equipment, with a little left over to begin our facility rental fund.

In September we started Son City West with about 250 kids. About 100 were kids from the core committed students who had attended Son Village—and who would eventually form the nucleus of our new church. The rest were new "recruits" from the community.

A NEW ADVENTURE

For Bill and me the decision to leave South Park Church came when our personal situation was improving. Despite the tension in our marriage, our life had finally become a little less chaotic—Bill had graduated from college, the church had begun paying Bill a more generous salary, and we were comfortably settled in a tiny two-bedroom home in Park Ridge. Yet I was excited about starting a church in Palatine. Like Bill, I earnestly believed that God had called and that there was no option but to obey. I had total confidence in God's power to use Bill to bring the dream to reality. I probably should have been worried about finances, but I wasn't. We had already learned to make do with little. Bill had started at South Park as an unpaid volunteer, then gradually moved up to part-time pay. I had earned minimum wage in the office of a Christian organization and later in a Christian bookstore, and I had taught private flute lessons on the side. We had sold possessions and taken in boarders to help pay bills, and Bill had been moonlighting as a produce buyer for his father's company. On more than one occasion we had found an anonymously donated bag of groceries on our front porch just when we needed it most.

We were young, childless, free from encumbrances. We had just survived one extraordinary adventure. Why not try another one?

People said it wouldn't work, but we didn't believe that. The odds were stacked against us, but we didn't know that. We just knew that God was calling, and since He'd proven Himself faithful in the past, we decided to trust Him for the future. It was His church; surely He had a greater vested interest in it than we did. We would pray for guidance and move according to His leadings.

A TANGLED TALE

This idea of God *calling* us to start a church has been at the center of our activities and decision-making processes for over two decades. In recent years Willow Creek has been analyzed, dissected, and systematized—both by sympathetic insiders and critical outsiders—to the point where the Willow Creek "paradigm" seems more like a prepackaged formula, complete with a money-back guarantee, than a church. But what could seem like a patterned formula is actually a twenty-year response to the fluid, daily, unpredictable leading of God. The unimpressive truth is that we made the whole thing up as we went along, trusting the Holy Spirit for each next step, rarely seeing which direction the path ahead would take. It was only by following the voice of God—by listening for his particular call to us—that we could move forward with confidence.

My personal awareness of God's calling frees me to wholeheartedly affirm and support Willow Creek's ministry. Still, I am forced to acknowledge the many ways in which Willow Creek has failed to live up to its calling. I'd love to tell a story of a God-given dream fleshed out in unmarred perfection. But that's not reality. The truth is that the Willow Creek story is a tangled tale of feelings, thoughts, and actions touched both by the strength and beauty of the divine and by the weakness and ugliness of sin.

If you glean anything from this book, I hope it will be that the Willow Creek story is a story of grace. Years ago God accepted our flawed efforts, wrapped them in His love, and poured His blessing out upon them in extraordinary ways. "They're just a bunch of kids," I can almost hear Him say. "And pretty wounded, immature ones at that. But I love them. And I think I can do something with the blend of craziness and devotion that they have offered me. So I'm going to lavish them with grace."

Presumptuous words to put in God's mouth? Read with me these words of the psalmist: "As a father has compassion on his children, so the Lord has compassion on those who fear him; for he knows how we are formed, he remembers that we are dust" (Psalm 103:13–14). A comfort to me for over two decades, this passage says that God knows we are "but dust," creatures of the earth. Does He call us to soar above our dustiness? Surely. But He doesn't expect perfection. He knows that no matter how hard we try, the story of our lives and our ministries on this earth will always be a tangled one.

For years Willow Creek had the reputation of being the black sheep of the Christian community. The "can do," "whatever it takes," "sky is the limit" mentality that seemed to us to be the only appropriate response to an ideal as noble, worthy, and strategic as the church frequently elicited strong and unfair criticism. We often were—and still are—misquoted, misunderstood, and misjudged. We've been called entertainers by those who didn't ask why we chose our methods, and we've been labeled a cult by those who didn't listen to our message. At times fighting the attacks of Satan has seemed easy compared to fighting the attacks of some in the Christian community. We have become weary of unfounded rumors and unfair criticisms.

On the other hand, we have often deserved the criticism. We were young and incredibly mistake-prone when we started Willow Creek. And we still are—mistake-prone, that is. I have seen Willow Creek's weaknesses, its imperfections, its reactionary imbalances, its pendulum swings. I've seen enthusiasm turn to carelessness, zeal become workaholism, and creative expression fall on the side of irreverence. I've seen difficult staff changes that should have been handled better. I've seen people who really needed help slip through the cracks and eventually leave, disillusioned and hurt. I've seen the results of immaturity and inexperience and, yes, sin. As with anything touched by human hands, there is a downside here.

But I've also seen the awesome and overwhelming movement of God at Willow Creek. All along the way, He has guided and challenged and chastised and blessed us. Willow Creek would never have moved beyond the dream stage without that.

In the second half of this book, you will read about the vision, values, and strategies of Willow Creek. They are presented not as an exact pattern around which other Christian leaders should shape their churches but rather as a set of principles we've seen work, principles that can be considered and possibly applied under the guidance of the Holy Spirit. I've seen them make a difference in people's lives and in churches scattered throughout this country and others—England, Spain, Germany, Poland, New Zealand, Australia. I've seen them work, up close and over the long haul.

AN EARNEST EVANGELIST

In addition to believing in the principles presented in this book, I believe in the man whose words and ideas are behind so much of what you will read on these pages. Part of the reason I married Bill Hybels was because I knew he wanted to make a positive difference with his life. I didn't know the specific direction our life together would take, but writing this book has reminded me afresh of how thrilling God's unfolding plan has been. For months I have loaded my mind with the history of Willow Creek. I interviewed Bill during long walks, talked with friends and colleagues at church, and searched through the disorganized files in my own mind. Then I littered my office with pages and pages of transcripts, which I sorted and outlined and rearranged. As I actually began typing the words I found I believe in both the material and the man more than I ever have.

I believe in the material because it is biblical and it works. I believe in the man because of his honest passion. Bill Hybels is truly committed to the church and to the lost. That is not just something he talks about to inspire other church leaders. It's something he lives. Some time ago I took a phone message from one of Bill's unchurched friends who said he was sick and couldn't attend our Saturday evening service as he had planned. Bill's response seems strange when you consider he was preparing to speak to thousands of seekers that weekend, but he said, "I can't believe it. This service is perfect for him. I don't even want to give my message without him there." He did give the message, of course; but without *his* friend, for whom he had prayed and with whom he had shared his faith, it just wasn't the same.

A PERSONAL NOTE

For me personally the past twenty years have been exceedingly difficult. Ministry is always hard. Building a marriage is always hard. Raising kids is always hard. Discovering one's gifts and putting one's talents to work is always hard. For me these challenges have been intensified by internal battles and wounds that I have only recently begun to understand and by the pressure of visibility that has been, I must admit, an unwelcome dimension of our lives.

Still, when I sit through a baptism service, as I did last night, and weep as I watch nearly two hundred adults give a public witness to the saving and transforming work of God in their lives, I know there is nowhere I would rather have been during the past twenty years than at Willow Creek. There is no endeavor I would rather have devoted myself to than the mission of reaching out to unchurched people, introducing them to the truth of the Gospel, and helping them along the path toward full devotion to Jesus Christ.

So where was I? Oh yes. It's August 1975. We have just sold tomatoes door-to-door. Now it's time to start a church.

chapter three

THE WONDER YEARS
1975–78

Bill stopped at our house, asked us a few questions about our church habits, and invited us to come to a Willow Creek service. We hadn't gone to church in a long time, but our oldest son, Brian, had joined Son City, and he convinced us to go. We attended the first Christmas Eve service and thought it was tremendous. We decided to go back, and we've been at Willow ever since. During the first year I experienced a slow conversion. The more I heard, the more I understood that I needed Christ as my Savior. After that first year I started attending New Community, because I wanted to keep growing.

QUIGLEY FLETCHER,
CHARTER MEMBER OF THE WILLOW CREEK BOARD OF DIRECTORS

"Do you regularly attend a local church?"

"No."

"Would you be willing to tell me why you don't?"

Though the church is Jesus' first love, it has certainly not been loved by contemporary Americans. In the years following 1960 there was a steady and dramatic drop in church attendance. Walking door-to-door throughout Palatine in September of 1975, Bill and several other core leaders tried to find out why.

One frequent answer was that church was irrelevant to daily life. A typical response was, "My marriage is in turmoil. My oldest son is out of control. My husband doesn't know how to show love to our kids. I'm losing hope, and I don't know what to do. Sometimes I get to the point where I just want to end it all, but I'm afraid to die. I used to wonder if maybe God could help. But when I went to church, I found no answers. Pastors talked about issues that had nothing to do with my daily life. They never even mentioned the struggles that are tearing me apart. I left feeling more hopeless than I felt before. So I don't consider God or church anymore."

Imagine Bill, an idealistic twenty-three-year-old convinced that the Bible and the church held the answers to *everything*, standing fourteen inches away from a woman who was headed for a Christless eternity and who had deemed the message of the church irrelevant to her life. He vowed then that if he ever had the responsibility of teaching in a church, he would do whatever it took to communicate the practicality and relevance of biblical truths.

Another complaint was that church services were lifeless, boring, and predictable. One man said, "I don't have to go to church anymore. I went to one for fifteen years, and I figured out the whole routine. I haven't been back in five years, but I could tell you who sits where, what the choir will sing on Mother's Day, the order of the service, and what the pastor will probably preach on. If I need a little 'shot' of church, I can just sit at home and conjure the whole thing up in my mind. I can attend vicariously!"

A third complaint was against "pontificating pastors" who preached down at parishioners and made pronouncements and judgments that seemed harsh or even cruel. One divorced woman said, "My husband ran off with a woman from work. He left me with no car, a big mortgage, and three preschoolers. I kept going to church, because I thought I could find some encouragement there, some spiritual strength, a glimmer of hope. Instead I received a steady stream of condemnation for a divorce I didn't even want. I can't take that anymore."

A man said, "I get beat over the head every day at work. I can't take getting beat over the head on Sundays too. I'm not saying I want a pastor who will just tell me what I want to hear, who will never challenge me or call me to task. I'd just like someone who would spend as much time providing solutions as he does pointing out problems."

The fourth complaint was that churches were always asking for money. The reasoning seemed to go like this: *If the messages are irrelevant and the services are lifeless, boring, and predictable, and if every week I leave feeling more beat-up than when I arrived, how can anybody expect me to be excited about supporting the church financially?*

Dr. B. would say, "This is a modern-day tragedy." The hope of the world, conceived in the mind of the all-wise God, comes off as irrelevant to real life. That's unthinkable. Services aimed at revealing truth about the *Creator* are called lifeless, boring, and predictable. That's the ultimate contradiction. People walk away from the church carrying a heavier burden than when they approached. That's a travesty of the Gospel. That's a modern-day tragedy.

"How'd it go today?" I'd ask when Bill came home from a day of surveying the community. Repeatedly I was amazed by the emotional impact his conversations with unchurched people obviously had on him.

"If I ever preach an irrelevant sermon," he would say, "if I ever bore people with the Gospel, if I ever pound the life and hope out of a needy person—drag me out of the ministry! Don't let me do it. It's killing people. It's driving them away from the only thing that can lead them to faith."

A TEMPORARY HOME

The first thing we needed in order to start our church was a facility. Bill chose the Willow Creek Theater, because its proximity to main roads gave it easy accessibility and because it had adequate parking. Also, it seated up to 970, which meant we would be able to stay in it until we could buy land and build our own facility. Unlike most movie theaters, it had a huge stage that was perfect for our programming. It also had a large lobby that could be subdivided and used for Sunday school.

The theater manager told Bill that the owner was stridently anti-Christian; there was no way he would let a church use the theater. But Bill did a little homework, discovered that the theater was never in use except during show times, and calculated the profit that our $250-a-week rental would net the owner over a three-year period. Then he went to the theater owner and presented his offer, assuring the owner that we would leave the building better than we found it. The man asked what kind of church it was. Bill said, "The kind of church that leads people out of spiritual confusion, helps families come together, and guides kids onto a straight path." The man called his manager and said, "Sign them up." We held services in that theater from October 12, 1975, to February 8, 1981, eventually having three services each Sunday morning.

Bill also discovered a warehouse we could lease for three years at $700 a month. There we could build offices for the daily operations of the church. We could also build a conference room that would seat approximately fifty people and give us a place to start our midweek services. The landlord was "a bit" skeptical about our ability to pay our monthly rent: we hadn't yet started the church, and Bill was unemployed. Bill said, "If we can't pay the rent, you can take me to court for the lease amount, and one way or another I'll get you the money. Then you can double-lease the space." Within twenty minutes the man had pulled out a lease document and Bill had signed it. I didn't know until years later that Bill and I were personally responsible for the fulfillment of that lease.

With donated labor and with money from the tomato sale, we put up drywall to make offices. However, we were so low on money that we decided to forgo luxuries—like HVAC ductwork. Two furnaces blew heat and air conditioning up above the acoustic ceiling. For the next six years the only way to circulate that heated or cooled air was to slide the acoustic tiles out of the ceilings. Old-timers still talk about the unique ambiance created by those gaping overhead holes.

In late August 1975 about thirty of us, including former leaders from the original Son City and team leaders from the new Son City West, began meeting together on Sunday mornings. Bill gave a devotional, we sang some songs, then each week Bill cast the vision for a vibrant church to reach the unchurched. He also challenged every person there to give as much as he or she could to the savings account of the church—and he wasn't talking about tithing! He was talking about each of us giving everything above what we needed to live on. And that's exactly what we did—gladly. We were probably the most "cheerful givers" any church has ever known. We had absolute confidence in how the money would be used—for theater and office rental and necessary supplies and equipment—and we believed wholeheartedly in the cause. We were convinced that we were making the wisest and most worthy investment we could possibly make. Bill kept the checkbook in his desk and applied a Dutchman's skill to overseeing the finances. We managed to get by on the contributions of our little core group until our first service in the theater, in October.

COMMITTED TO THE CAUSE

People have often asked how we managed to get Willow Creek off the ground with no paid staff. What they don't realize is that we had a huge unpaid staff. Bill was the point leader and communicator. Dave Holmbo was the programming coordinator and music director. Randy BeMent was our administrator. Dave Swetman and later Don Cousins led Son City. Rory Noland directed Son City music. Joel Jager handled production. Rick Wold directed drama. Rick Meredith and Virginia Meredith produced multimedia. I could go on and on. We probably had an unpaid staff of fifteen to twenty people. Many of them worked forty or fifty hours a week for the church. To make ends meet, they worked part-time jobs or night shifts, or even enlisted friends to help support them.

During that era, I continued working to support us personally. Our boarders, also active members of the church core, continued to contribute what they could to our household expenses. And Bill still made occasional midnight runs to the Water Street Market to boost our meager income. Dave Holmbo was financially supported by his wife, a gifted schoolteacher and an invaluable member of our music team.

This system worked because most of the core people were single. Those few who were married had no children. So we were available; there was nothing holding us back or tying us down. And the fresh memory of the three-year miracle we had just experienced in Son City turned us all into zealots for our cause.

And we knew our cause. Our goal, to which every member of our core was sold, was to reach unchurched adults, lead them to Christ, disciple them, and establish the kind of community of faith we had experienced in Son City. We were excited about the goal and excited about reaching it together. We were a team. We were colleagues, yes, but also friends. We loved being together. Whether we were onstage or behind the scenes, we enjoyed great camaraderie, unity, and bonding. There was nothing we'd rather do than work together.

And I do mean work. We had a remarkable work ethic—an attack mentality that said, "Don't quit until the job is done. Do whatever you do to the best of your ability. Never say, 'That's not my job.' If something needs to be done, then get out there and help do it."

But we didn't just work hard, we worked smart. Our "smarts" didn't come from seminary, since none of us had been there. But we had all acquired tremendous on-the-job training. We had led numerous kids to Christ and discipled them. And we already knew how to use our gifts and talents in a complementary way to bring out the best in one another.

Beyond the staff leadership team, we had a broader circle of about one hundred Son City kids who were willing to contribute whatever they had, whenever they could. They picked up the slack and worked behind the scenes. They didn't care about the spotlight. For them the experience of "being the church" was so incredibly wonderful that they wanted their friends to experience it, too. They practiced relational evangelism. Without them we would have had nothing more than a program, and programs do not reach lost people.

Bill and I had been willing to start a church on our own if no one chose to go with us, and I think God was pleased with our willingness. However, I think God knew it would take a strong, multiperson effort to get Willow Creek going, so he put together a fantastic team. We have become convinced that any seeker-sensitive start-up venture needs a similarly "stacked" team.

AN UNMISTAKABLE CALL

But even a stacked team is an unworthy match for the rigors of starting a church. We would have given up the dream had we not believed, at the center of our being, that we had been called by God to start a church. To choose not to start Willow Creek—or to give up each time it seemed impossible—would have been rebellion, betrayal, and disobedience. In fact, we *had* to start a church for the unchurched if we wanted to sleep at night.

Along with the unmistakable call of God came an unquestioned confidence in God. We had come out of Son City with a faith portfolio that taught us that "with God nothing is impossible," and we had seen firsthand how God could use the illogical, the unexpected, the foolish, and the weak to accomplish His purposes. We knew it didn't make sense to start a church in a movie theater. It didn't make sense to use contemporary music and drama and multimedia. It didn't make sense to try to reach adults when you're twenty-three years old. It didn't make sense to step out on faith, with no outside backing. But did it have to make sense?

At a defining moment in his life, Martin Luther said, "Here I stand, I cannot do otherwise." I am not using poetic license when I say that's exactly how we felt.

HELLO, WORLD!

Everything You Wanted to Know About Sex But Were Afraid to Ask was the movie title featured on the glittering marquee. But the 125 people who filed into the Willow Creek Theater on Sunday morning, October 12, 1975, were convinced they were going to church. Mostly kids from Son City, a few of their parents, and some friends and relatives who came as curious well-wishers, these enthusiastic adventurers were not to be disappointed.

Our truck, an old produce truck donated by Bill's father, had arrived at the theater at 4:00 a.m.—as it did every Sunday morning for the next five and a half years—ready to be unloaded of the newly acquired speakers, microphones, monitors, transformers, sound board, lighting trees, and miles of electric cord, which would be snaked throughout the theater and secured in place with silver duct tape. Joel Jager, Bill's childhood friend from Michigan, was the "king of setup and takedown." That morning he and a handful of other early risers transformed a dark, silent movie theater into the first home of Willow Creek Community Church.

Dave Holmbo's music and drama teams had arrived at 6:00 a.m. for rehearsals and sound checks, and at 9:00 a.m. they opened the service with the very best they had to offer. Then a captivating multimedia slide show filled the giant screen. Finally Dr. B. read Scripture and Bill presented a message called "New Beginnings."

Our seeker services have grown up and mellowed over the years, as we have, but back then all the energy and boldness of youth flowed through everything we did. The music was loud, the drama was raucous (sometimes crossing the line of acceptability), and Bill walked onto the stage with no notes, no pulpit—just a Bible, and an outline engraved in his mind. But those services were electric with the power of God and our earnest desires.

We desperately wanted to provide a place where unchurched people with a spiritual hunger—seekers, we called them—could come and hear the truth that could transform their lives both here and in eternity. We wanted to use contemporary Christian music with lyrics that would communicate real-life spiritual experience. Sometimes we used crossover music, secular songs with a message that addressed the frustrations and longings of lost people, songs like "Desperado," which hauntingly chronicled the spiritual emptiness of the seventies. With our dramas and media presentations, we wanted to show lost people that we understood the challenges and longings and heartaches and joys of their lives. Through Dr. B.'s comments and Bill's messages, we wanted to show unbelievers that God's Word could speak with clarity and power to their situation, whatever it was.

From the very beginning our desire was to lead people to a moment of truth, when they would decide to go God's way, when they would repent of sin and turn to Christ for salvation, when they would become part of the community of believers, the church.

A GROWING CHALLENGE

In the weeks to come, as the curiosity-seekers and well-wishers went back to their previous Sunday morning plans, our attendance plummeted. "This is an interesting thing these kids are doing," said many, "but it's not for me." Many Christians were uncomfortable with our unique philosophy of ministry, and we had not yet established credibility with the unchurched community. We were in a kind of no-man's-land. Sometimes during that first winter, there were more people onstage than in the congregation.

And the early-morning movie theater transformation was beginning to lose the glamour of "newness." Many mornings found Joel desperately trying to start a very temperamental truck. Sometimes those of us who went in early for music rehearsals had to sweep popcorn from the aisles or, worse, wash vomit out of the carpets or clean the bathrooms, which doubled as nursery space for infants. As more families began showing up with young children the maze of burlap dividers that defined our children's classes became increasingly complicated and difficult to set up. Later when we went to multiple services, we had to scramble to get the equipment out in time for the early-afternoon movie matinee. Often members of the production team had to haul equipment out and let it sit in the snow while they methodically loaded the truck, carefully tucking cords and boxes and stands into ridiculously overcrowded corners.

But the seeker service wasn't the only challenge. By January 1976 it had become evident that the core believers, who were working so hard and giving out so much, desperately needed deeper Bible teaching and corporate worship. So we started the New Community, our midweek believers service. Dave and Bill programmed and taught at these services, as they did the weekend services. They both also stayed heavily involved in Son City and Son Village, mentoring the younger leaders. Bill was still involved in the weekend music groups, so he had to show up for nearly every weekly music rehearsal. He also provided pastoral counseling and personal discipleship, and carried nearly the full weight of the financial responsibility for the church.

Forgive me if I repeat myself, but *building a church was proving to be far more difficult than we had anticipated.*

Still, there was more to life than building a church. Less than a year after we started Willow Creek, Bill and I became parents. Our daughter, Shauna, was born on August 17, 1976. I continued playing in the band, situating Shauna in her car seat beside me onstage during our 6:30 a.m. Sunday rehearsals. Bill was there for the rehearsals too, of course, so it was a genuine family affair that continued for several years. Shauna was a charter member of the "Willow Creek nursery," and she and I became pioneers in the young moms ministry. Years later when she reached Son City age, we felt as if we were reliving the past.

IT'S WORKING!

Throughout the early years we were vehemently criticized by traditional churches, often publicly from the pulpit. We were called deceivers and phonies. It was rumored that we were backed by the Moonies. Youth leaders warned their kids to stay away from the Son City *cult.*

But among the unchurched, we were slowly gaining credibility. Our attendance steadily increased. Some of the parents of Son City kids became Christians, then brought their friends. We had baptism services that celebrated God's grace and fed our zeal. These new Christians were fresh and alive, unencumbered by expectations from previous church experiences. They weren't trying to do church the way it had always been done—most of them had no idea how it had always been done.

As in Son City, Bill taught about both the vertical and horizontal dimensions of Christianity, so people were coming to Christ *and* finding deeper human relationships. Soon it was time to divide the church into smaller groups, like the teams of Son City. We called the groups modules. By the church's first anniversary we had six to eight modules and nearly a full house on Sunday.

It was like Son City all over again, yet with the added excitement of seeing adults coming to Christ, marriages strengthened, and families united.

Our giant faith gamble seemed to be paying off. By our second anniversary we were nearly filling two services.

THE DISCIPLESHIP CHALLENGE

Yes, it was Son City all over again. But as I've said before, how much harder it was to work with adults than with high school kids! Adults' lives were so complicated and entangled; they had so little discretionary time. Spiritual growth was slower, and emotional defenses harder to break through. High schoolers craved community and jumped headlong into it; adults needed it but were afraid of it. While the team concept was an automatic hit in Son City, it was extremely difficult to build a sense of community in the adult modules. Module directors put heroic efforts into planning creative events to build unity and camaraderie, but we didn't know how to nurture the deeper relationships that had developed so naturally with the high schoolers.

We had no formal discipling program at the time, but Bill soon realized that new adult converts would not mature spiritually unless they had a one-on-one relationship with a more mature Christian. He also realized that in order for Willow Creek to survive, we needed a cadre of strong adult leaders. Thanks to his close relationship with his father and his background in business, Bill knew how to relate to older men, particularly the entrepreneurial types so prevalent in our community. He also knew how to detect leadership skills and discern the direction of a person's potential. Immediately he began meeting individually with men in the congregation.

Since racquetball was *the* male bonding rite of the mid-seventies, Bill spent hundreds of hours on the racquetball court with men from the church. He planned ski trips to Colorado and invited spiritually sensitive men in whom he saw leadership potential. Nearly every day, he had breakfast and lunch appointments in which his conversational style was direct and gutsy: "Where are you spiritually? Where do you want to be? How can we help you?" On paper napkins, he outlined the "plan of salvation" and sent his new friends back to their workplaces with questions to ponder and challenges to face. Many of these men were quite resistant to spiritual change and probably needed Bill's confrontational style to get them thinking about spiritual issues, but I was constantly in awe as Bill recounted to me his conversations with these new friends. "You said *that*?" I couldn't believe the guys kept coming back for more.

In time, as these men became true and growing believers, the "How can we help you?" questions often turned into "How can you help us?" and "We can't do this church without you." Many of the men today on our board of directors were led to the Lord and discipled this way.

Unfortunately, few of the young adult leaders in our start-up core had the life experience or the relational skills necessary to work with the kind of adult men who were beginning to fill the seats in the Willow Creek Theater. This put a tremendous discipleship challenge on Bill. The impossible weight of that responsibility was a major motivation for the extensive discipleship group program that we developed later.

SPECIAL EVENTS

One of the major hurdles in any church start-up is to get to the point where you have the "critical mass"—in terms of money and labor—to support an ongoing ministry. During the early days when we typically had more people onstage than in the congregation, we realized that our survival as a church depended on drawing new people in quickly. So we planned special events, such as concerts or musicals or special holiday services on Good Friday, Easter, and Christmas Eve, and encouraged church members to bring their unchurched friends. We found that many people who wouldn't visit a church on a normal Sunday were open to a one-time event.

Of course, many such events ended up being a *first* visit rather than a one-and-only. "I came on Easter with a friend, and I liked it. I decided to visit the next Sunday, and I've been coming ever since. I became a Christian two years ago." That is a story we have heard repeatedly throughout the years.

In those early years we also planned beautiful baptism celebrations and discovered that unchurched friends and family members are often willing to come and share this significant experience with a new Christian. Many of them are genuinely moved by the music, the message of grace, and the witness of a transformed life—and they come back to learn more.

We also held women's luncheons and men's breakfasts featuring special speakers who would talk about personal growth from a Christian perspective, tell the story of their personal journey to faith, or offer a biblical perspective on issues of concern to seekers. These events were designed specifically as a place for our believers to bring friends who were not ready to come to an "official" church service. I've heard of other start-up churches sponsoring family picnics, marathons, bike trips, baseball clinics, parenting seminars, gym nights, and kids fairs to provide entry points for seekers.

For us special events proved to be invaluable for drawing people in and introducing them to Christianity and to our ministry, but they demanded a huge investment of time and energy from a small group of people who were already wearing too many ministry hats. Yet each time we heard another story of a onetime visit leading eventually to salvation or witnessed another baptism, we were motivated to start planning the next special event.

FACILITIES AND FINANCES

Before we moved into our permanent facility in 1981, our midweek New Community service was bumped from building to building, and even from evening to evening, on a regular basis. The theater was a stable home for the weekend service, but just barely. If we would inadvertently leave a piece of equipment in the theater or commit some other minor misdemeanor, the rent would be raised and we would be threatened with eviction. Fortunately, one of our early converts was a businessman with an extraordinary gift of diplomacy. More times than we want to remember he had to go to bat for us and renegotiate our lease for another week. Sometimes we didn't know until Friday or Saturday whether we would be permitted to use the theater, and we usually didn't have a Plan B. A year after we moved out, the theater went bankrupt and was converted into a banquet hall. On Willow Creek's fifteenth anniversary we held a banquet there for all our staff and lay leaders who had been part of the church during "the theater days." It was a wonderful event for remembering—and for rejoicing that those days were long behind us.

For us, as for many start-up churches, the facility pressure was second only to the financial pressure. I am not exaggerating when I say we were always just one week away from total financial ruin. Because we knew how sensitive unchurched people were about being asked for money, we didn't take an offering for two years; we simply left a basket on a table in the back of the theater and announced in the printed program that if anyone wanted to make a donation as they left the service, they could. Apparently, few newcomers wanted to, and those who did found the bottleneck of increasingly crowded aisles enough to squelch their motivation to "drop their donation in the basket."

An average offering was $600 a week, out of which $250 went for the theater and $300 went for multimedia presentations. In retrospect it seems ludicrous that we spent half our weekly income on media, but in the mid-seventies this was a fresh form of communication that proved extremely effective in driving a theme, value, or biblical truth through people's defenses and into their hearts. Certainly it wasn't a logical expenditure, but being logical had never been one of our driving forces.

Eventually we started taking an offering at the weekend services, but always with a qualifier, which we still use: "If you are visiting, this part of the service isn't for you. You're our guest. Please feel no obligation to give." When the giving increased enough to provide Bill with a salary of thirty-five dollars per week, we thought the windows of heaven had burst open upon us.

HOW DO YOU DO THIS?

During the latter years of Son City and the early years of Willow Creek, Bill traveled periodically as a consultant to youth groups. One group with whom he had an ongoing relationship was the high school youth group at Garden Grove Community Church in Garden Grove, California (now the Crystal Cathedral). During one consulting visit there Dan Webster, Garden Grove's gifted high school director (who later joined the Willow Creek staff and directed Son City for over a decade), asked Bill to describe in detail to his high school leaders the process Son City had used to bring unbelieving students to a point of sincere devotion to Jesus Christ.

Bill had an hour before he had to make the presentation to Dan's student leaders. Tucked away in an office in a youth ministry building in Southern California, Bill looked back through the Son City years, trying to re-create in his mind a clear picture of the processes that had been at work in students' lives. On a paper napkin, he sketched out what he saw. Moments later he stood before Dan's leaders.

First he described how he had challenged Son City kids to build relationships with unchurched kids. Lost people matter to God, he had told them, so Christians need to get to know them and discover how to love them.

Then he told the student leaders how he had encouraged the Son City kids to give a verbal witness of their faith and be prepared to speak simply and authentically about the reality of Christ in their own lives.

When our students had discovered that their friends were interested in finding out more about Christianity, they had invited their friends to the weekly Son City outreach event. As the kids came week after week they received answers to their questions about the Bible, about Jesus, and about what it means to become a Christian.

Once they became Christians, the new kids were invited to Son Village for worship and deeper Bible study so they could grow spiritually.

After that for the new kids came involvement in more intimate accountability relationships with individuals on their teams, so they could learn what it meant to practice in daily life the lessons they were learning through teaching and Bible study.

As they continued to grow they were challenged to discover their unique gifts and use them to serve God and others. Service was considered an act of obedience to God, but it also offered kids the camaraderie and "belonging" that comes from being part of a ministering team.

Finally the kids were challenged to submit their resources of time, energy, and money to God out of gratitude for what God had done in their lives.

Then Bill described how kids like these who had gone through this gradual process of ever-increasing devotion to Christ had ended up initiating the whole process again as they in turn reached out to their unchurched friends and shared with them the reality of their faith in Jesus Christ.

Willow Creek's seven-step strategy for "turning irreligious people into fully devoted followers of Jesus Christ" came, then, from an outline scratched in red ink on a white paper napkin. It appears in fuller form in Chapter 11.

Actually, the strategy had come to life long before Bill gave it words. It had been born out of common sense and the Spirit's direction. It was a series of steps that had built naturally upon one another. It was a simple, pragmatic approach to loving kids—and later, adults—into the kingdom of God.

DIVINE ENCOUNTER

In the fall of 1976, Bill took another trip to Garden Grove—this time to take the staff, module directors, and other lay leaders of Willow Creek to a pastors conference there. During the conference, our entire entourage somehow ended up in Robert Schuller's office, which at that time was in the upper floors of the Tower of Prayer. Bill told Dr. Schuller about our efforts to establish a church for the unchurched and about our seeker services and about our tentative plans to buy land for a future building. Bill asked Dr. Schuller if he could give us any advice regarding our next step.

Dr. Schuller answered, "If you give God a thimble, perhaps He will choose to fill it. If you give God a five-gallon bucket, perhaps He will choose to fill that. If you give Him a fifty-gallon drum, perhaps He will choose to do something extraordinary and fill even that. If God chooses to do a miracle, you'd better be ready for it. Don't buy a thimbleful of land. Buy a fifty-gallon drum."

Was there any logic in that counsel? By all rights it was ridiculous for a ragtag bunch of kids like us to dream even of a thimble. And here we were, huddled in that sky-high office, committing ourselves to the pursuit of a fifty-gallon drum. Had we been mesmerized by the emotional appeal of a clever communicator? Had we been lured into a dream that was more about self-aggrandizement than obedience to God? Had we been "puffed up" with the affirmation offered us by a man so highly esteemed—the only credible adult who had given us any encouragement? Had we become victims of our own youthful enthusiasm?

As I look back through the years I can't help but think that what happened that day was exactly what we thought it was at the time: a divinely staged encounter. We returned home changed. We had been given a glimpse of the future, an augmented sense of destiny, and it catapulted us forward. We were humbled by the responsibilities and potential challenges, yet we were excited by the possibilities and convinced anew of our unmistakable calling.

We recalled the words of the old hymn "Trust and Obey," and we earnestly believed that no matter how absurd it seemed, we had to move out in faith and prepare for a possible outpouring of God's miraculous power. We had to find a fifty-gallon drum.

GOING FOR THE IMPOSSIBLE

About six months after starting the church, Bill had formed an ad hoc committee of adults to serve as a financial advisory board for the purpose of holding him accountable, helping with decision making, and generally overseeing the financial affairs of the church. As Bill began looking for land these people played a critical role. All astute businessmen, they had the legal, financial, and real estate expertise that Bill lacked. But as growing and zealous new believers, they shared his unwavering belief—"with God nothing is impossible"—and his optimistic commitment to step out in faith. So when Bill discovered that 104 acres just 10 miles from the Willow Creek Theater were selling for $600,000, the board members checked out the land, prayed for direction, then agreed with him to "go for it." The acreage was on a prime corner in the suburb of South Barrington.

On a Saturday night in June 1977, Robert Schuller graciously came and spoke at our fund-raising banquet in the ballroom of the Sheraton Hotel in Des Plaines, Illinois. We had prepared a moving multimedia presentation chronicling our brief history and lifting up our vision for the future. Dave Holmbo had written a song especially for the occasion: "What more could you want / Than to help lives come together? / What more could you want / Than to look into eyes that were blind but now see?"

Over and over we sang the words together and committed ourselves anew to the dream that God had given us, the dream of building a permanent home for a biblically functioning community that would reach out to the unchurched and help them become fully devoted followers of Jesus Christ. Dr. Schuller affirmed the value and potential of the dream to the 1,000 people who attended. Finally Bill presented the need: $600,000 to purchase 104 acres at the corner of Barrington and Algonquin roads.

We knew it seemed like a ridiculous goal for a new church with a handful of kids at its core. But we were convinced that people would give sacrificially. In fact, the leadership core had led the way. Prior to the fund-raising banquet, the advisory board had secured an arrangement with a local bank whereby the bank would offer low-interest loans, in increments of $1,000 and to be paid back within two years, to anyone who wanted to donate to the building fund. Those of us in the core who had already poured our savings into the church were the first to line up for loans. Bill and I each took out $2,000 loans. Other core members gave $1,000 or $3,000. As one core member said later, "The question wasn't, 'Could I or should I?' The question was, 'How much can I?'"

We could only imagine how much "adults with real jobs" would give, especially when they heard about the available loan option. On Friday the church office buzzed with speculations: "I think we'll raise . . ." " No, I think it'll be . . ." We were confident of reaching the goal; we were already looking forward to a victory celebration at the Sunday morning service.

A SWAN DIVE INTO REALITY

After the banquet Bill went to his office and counted the money and pledge cards. The total was $425,000. Bill was crushed, devastated. It was the first major ministry setback he had experienced. What did it mean? Where had he gone wrong? What should he do now? He was confused, but he knew he didn't have the luxury of wallowing in confusion. Somehow he had to come to terms with his own despair so he could lead others through their disappointment. He had to pull himself and others back to the truth that had seemed so apparent in Son City and that he so wanted to believe: God was in control, and He could be trusted.

The next morning Bill announced that we didn't make the goal and "we won't be able to buy the land right now." We would, he said, regroup and decide what to do next. It was hard to make the words come out, and he had to work hard to hold back the tears that threatened to blow his cover of confidence.

The mood was anything but electric that week. Bill wasn't upset with the people. It just appeared that there wasn't as much money out there as he had thought. Sure, there were pleasant surprises. People he didn't think could give anything took out multiple loans. But others he had thought could give $10,000 or $15,000 or $20,000 gave only $5,000—or nothing at all.

Immediately after the Sunday service in which Bill made the announcement, a businessman from the church said to Bill, "This is a good start. Leave the fund open, and we'll get there in a few weeks."

Bill said, "You don't understand. We have all given every last dime we have."

"No," the man said, "I don't think so."

The man was probably right, but at the time we couldn't see that. We couldn't conceive of anyone holding back. It never dawned on us that not everyone would charge out on the limb of faith the way we had. In years to come Bill learned that one-night fund-raisers are unrealistic. It's natural for people to hold back initially, then give more liberally as they have time to catch the vision and assess the need. But Bill was a rookie in 1977.

HUMBLED

The woman selling the land wanted cash. She refused to accept anything but the full amount. What did this mean for the dream? How did God want us to respond? What was He trying to tell us?

We learned soon enough exactly what God was trying to tell us: that He loved us more than we knew and that He wanted our dream—His dream—to succeed. If He had to intervene in ways we didn't understand in order to protect us and the dream, He would—and He had.

Shortly after the real estate deal fell through, we learned that the parcel of land we had wanted had been condemned by the state and set aside for a forest preserve area. Had we purchased the land, we would have eventually gotten our money back, but it probably would have taken years, and we may not have received the full amount. I can't tell this story without experiencing viscerally the jumble of emotions we felt then. We had come face-to-face with an almost scary awareness of divine intervention. We knew we had been lovingly rescued. We felt gratitude. Hope. We were humbled by the affirmation of the calling, which had followed so quickly on the heels of doubt.

Within months we learned that a piece of property adjacent to the original piece was selling for $660,000. The owner wanted partial payment, then a land contract for the rest. At 2:00 p.m. on November 26, 1977, just six weeks after Willow Creek's second anniversary, we closed on 90 acres of rolling hills, meadows, and woodlands at 67 East Algonquin Road in South Barrington, Illinois. We were in awe of the mighty work of God.

The three-year miracle ride of Son City seemed to be continuing.

chapter four

THE TRAIN WRECK
1979

For me the Son City days and the first years of Willow Creek were exhilarating—time and again the hard work of ministry was eclipsed by the deep joy of "doing it together." But in 1980 I left Willow Creek. Though I lived only seven minutes from the new building, I didn't drive on the campus for over three years. I felt as if I had gone through a wrenching divorce. The journey back was long and painful.

NANCY BEACH,
WILLOW CREEK DIRECTOR OF PROGRAMMING

The unpaid staff and lay ministry team that moved from the leadership of Son City to the leadership of Willow Creek enjoyed an extraordinary sense of community. We were drawn together by a great cause that we each owned as our own. We were like soldiers together in the foxhole, battling the forces of evil; we knew the stakes, but we believed that together we could face the challenge.

But our relationships went beyond the cause. We were friends, we were family, and we enjoyed relationships of love and trust and vulnerability. Outside church we spent time together, too, simply because we enjoyed being with one another.

Our shared ownership of the dream, and our authentic friendships, led to a real sense of team. In Son City, Bill and Dave had clearly been known as the leaders of the ministry, but their leadership never had a hierarchical feeling. They were involved in ministry right alongside the kids, and Dr. B.'s teaching on *servant leadership* provided their leadership model. A leader was not to "lord it over" those he led but rather to encourage and support them.

The result of this commitment to friendship, team ministry, and servant leadership was that when we started Willow Creek, we did not appoint a senior pastor.

Bill was called the coordinating pastor. His responsibility, in terms of staff leadership, was—obviously—to coordinate the efforts of other staff members. "Coordinate" was a loosely defined term that did not include the concept of authority. In fact, there was no staff authority structure. There was also no ruling body of elders. So the church was run by a staff team with no formal configuration of responsibility or authority.

That sounds incredibly naive now, but it had worked in Son City. For three years Bill and Dave had headed off in the general direction they each thought God was leading them, and they always seemed to end up going in the same direction. Everyone else followed in step, and it all worked beautifully.

By Willow Creek's second anniversary, however, it had become obvious to Bill that the system had lost its beauty. Because nobody reported to anybody, there was no accountability. Bill could coordinate the efforts of other staff members if they felt like being coordinated; if they didn't, there was nothing he could do. And increasingly, it seemed to him, they didn't feel like it. People seemed to be running off in all directions. A call would come to the office for a particular staff member, and nobody would know where the person was—sometimes for hours, sometimes for days. A staff member would make a church purchase for which there was no money. Another staff member would fail to complete a necessary task or would exhibit signs of spiritual confusion or poor judgment in personal matters. Bill would schedule a staff meeting and prepare an important discussion agenda, only to have people straggle in according to their own internal clock. If Bill tried to confront any of these issues, the response would be, "Who are you? You have no authority. We're supposed to trust each other."

THE PRICE OF SUCCESS

It was not that staff members had lost their commitment to the dream or their enthusiasm for ministry. On the contrary, the excitement was building, fueled by the steady stream of converts and by a weekend attendance that had reached nearly two thousand. We owned ninety acres of prime real estate and could envision the expanded ministry that a permanent facility would allow. The dream was as big and brilliant as ever.

But what the dream demanded was nearly destroying us. Staff members were working harder than they ever had before. The pace of our lives was insane. Since the beginning we had struggled with the tension between personal life and ministry. During this era the tension almost vanished, because ministry was winning every minute of our schedules, hands down. Our personal lives got the leftovers—if there were any. Too often there weren't.

Bill's and my marriage often felt like a marriage on paper only—and sadly, we were doing better than several other couples in the leadership core. Friendships were going the same way as marriages; there was no longer time for shared recreation or shared meals. Bill's early-morning planning sessions with staff members had given way to separate discipleship meetings with men in the church. The joyous celebration of comrades who had worked hard toward a goal and witnessed God's gracious blessing was a luxury we could no longer afford; always the next deadline, the next service, the next program, the next need, loomed larger than the pleasure of the moment. Time with God Himself had almost become an unaffordable luxury. For many, the unending demand of planning public meetings *about* God had squeezed out the possibility of having private meetings *with* Him.

Bill saw the dangerous splintering of the staff. He also felt the increasing weight of concerns he had never had to worry about in Son City: land, buildings, mortgage commitments, million-dollar budgets. Increasingly, he was having to ask lay people to make tremendous contributions of time and money. They wanted to know, "Who's in charge here? Who makes the calls? Where does the buck stop?"

A RADICAL MOVE

In the spring of 1978, Bill rented a conference room in a local Howard Johnson and called the entire part-time and full-time staff together. "We're falling apart," he said. "We're spinning off in too many different directions. We need a staff reporting structure. We can have any structure we all agree on, but there has to be somebody riding point. There has to be a designated leader." He suggested they choose the person according to giftedness. "Who has the strongest leadership gifts?" he asked. Silence. "Well, I think I do."

Then Bill drew up a possible organizational chart. There was some discussion, but no one presented an option that everyone could agree on. Some staff members signed on wholeheartedly with Bill's proposal; others accepted it with a sullen silence. Bill knew there would be fallout, but he was already facing fallout in the church as a whole. In fact, he believed the whole dream would collapse if he didn't do something. Clearly without a mandate, Bill left the Howard Johnson as the senior pastor of Willow Creek Community Church.

Hindsight offers numerous and better ways in which Bill probably could have handled that organizational crisis. But he was twenty-six years old, bearing the weight of the probable destruction of a dream into which hundreds of people had poured their time, their talents, and their treasures. He had never taken a class on negotiating change. He hadn't been taught to think in terms of outside mediators or management consultants. He just knew there was a serious problem and he had to solve it—fast.

At church leadership conferences, when Bill stresses the importance of designating the point leader and clearly defining the staff structure and lines of authority before starting a church, he does so because he has experienced the painful ramifications of failing to do that. Inevitable splintering of staff will eventually require the adoption of a new structure, and this will almost certainly result in a difficult transition, as we learned all too well.

Some staff members viewed the change as a natural and necessary progression and welcomed it. Others never did accept it. They submitted to it but never bought into it. From their perspective, trust had been broken, ownership had been snatched away from them, friendships had been undermined. It was no longer *we*.

But the tension didn't erupt. For months there was just a low, underground rumbling. Bill should have addressed it directly, but there was never time. Life went on. Ministry went on. Programs had to be planned. Decisions had to be made. Messages had to be written. The pace continued, accelerated. *In time the tension will pass,* Bill thought. *Everyone will get on board. This won't be a problem.* His natural optimism calmed his fears. The demands of the church kept him moving forward.

For Bill, moving forward included a not-so-subtle shift in his teaching. Listening to tapes by John MacArthur had convinced him that he needed to engage in deeper Bible teaching at New Community. Previously he had primarily taught using a topical format, but on March 15, 1978, he began an expository study of 1 Corinthians that would continue for the next year.

Moving forward also meant clarifying and formalizing the spiritual oversight of the church. From among the existing module directors and lay leaders, Bill selected three people who seemed to evidence an exceptional degree of spiritual maturity. At a meeting of the module directors, he suggested them as potential elders, and the module directors voted to affirm Gilbert Bilezikian, Dick Swetman, Laurie Pederson and Bill as the first elders of Willow Creek Community Church. Though Bill considered this action prudent, he had no idea how critical the formation of this elder board would be in the year to come. Neither he nor anyone else anticipated the disaster ahead.

YOU CALL THIS PARADISE?

Shortly after we started Willow Creek, Bill's father donated to the church two hundred acres of Michigan woodland on the Tahquamenon River in the Upper Peninsula. Pristine and beautiful, accessible only by boat, cut off from electricity and every other vestige of civilization, it was a perfect spot for a wilderness camp.

Under the direction of one of Bill's childhood friends, Tim VandenBos, and with donated materials and volunteer labor, we built rustic cabins and a dining lodge and borrowed the true-to-life name of the nearest town: Paradise, Michigan.

During the early years of Willow Creek, we held an annual weeklong leadership retreat at Camp Paradise, inviting staff, module directors, other key lay leaders, and their spouses for a time of recreation, Bible study, relationship building, and strategic planning over the week prior to Labor Day. For the noncampers in our midst it was a challenge, but without the distractions of "real life," it always proved to be a refreshing time.

But the Labor Day camp of 1978 broke the charmed spell of our wonderful annual retreats. On Friday night of that week, Bill discovered that a staff member had been involved in a pattern of behavior that threatened the stability of the staff member's personal life and the integrity of the rest of the staff. Months earlier Bill had become concerned about behavioral trends in this person's life and had confronted him but was angrily accused of being overly suspicious, judgmental, and prone to the legalistic excesses that we were all trying to escape. Wanting to believe the best, Bill backed off, but his suspicions had in fact been correct.

I'll never forget Bill's agony as he walked into the darkness of our cabin and described to me what he had just learned. In the shock of the moment, he could see nothing but absolute disaster. "The dream is over," he said.

Immediately upon returning home, Bill called the first meeting of the newly formed elder board and disclosed the tragic truth. Personal feelings of intense sadness were forcibly pushed aside as these inexperienced elders faced an immediate problem: what do we do now?

It was a destructive, ongoing pattern of behavior; it could not be ignored. But the person involved was a beloved friend, a member of the team that shared a common dream, a devoted servant who had sacrificed for the ministry. Yes, the behavior had to be dealt with. But neither Bill nor the other elders could conceive of a ministry future without the entire team intact. True, the community spirit that had united us years earlier had begun to weaken, but beneath the surface tension, there still lingered the sense that we were in this together. Sure, there were ripples of frustration, even hostility. But we could work through that. In the end we would all ride off into the sunset together, as we had always planned. Any thought to the contrary was unimaginable.

To protect the privacy of the person involved, the elders decided against a public disclosure; neither staff nor lay leaders were informed of the problem. The individual was allowed to continue in ministry, with the understanding that he would seek professional counseling and submit to the accountability and monitoring of the elders.

This is bad, thought Bill, *but it'll all work out eventually. It'll blow over. We'll be back on track before we know it.*

TOO BUSY TO GRIEVE

Three weeks later tragedy struck on another front. On a produce-buying trip to Chicago, Bill's father had a massive heart attack; he was found slumped over the steering wheel of his truck, dead at fifty-three. Bill rushed into the city to face the most grievous loss of his life. An energetic, eccentric man, Bill's dad had always been a "bigger than life" character. He wore the same thing every day—black pants and a tieless white shirt—but in no other way was his life routine. At a moment's notice he would head across the globe, with little more than a toothbrush and passport in his bag. He once took Bill to the airport and said, "Let's get on the next plane that's leaving for anywhere." The next flight happened to be to Jamaica; they spent three days there.

Comfortably affluent, with his own plane, summer home, and seagoing yacht, Bill's dad often drove used cars and felt most at home in a stick-shift pickup truck. But he was more than an eccentric businessman; nearly every Sunday afternoon found him leading a hymn-sing for a group of mentally retarded women at the state hospital in Kalamazoo, Michigan, often with Bill or one of Bill's siblings in tow. He was also—and I can't overestimate the importance of this—Bill's biggest cheerleader, the person who believed in his potential and showed more confidence in his abilities than anyone else. When Bill left the family business to go into the ministry, his father had been disappointed, but he had come to respect Bill's choice and offered his unflagging support. Now, when things looked dark and Bill needed encouragement more than ever before, his dad was gone.

I wish I could say I was a tower of strength for Bill in the difficult weeks and months that followed, but I wasn't. I earnestly grieved with him, but being four months pregnant and extremely sick, with a toddler to care for, I was fighting my own battles. A month after his father's death, I ended up at my parents' home in Michigan, increasingly ill at midterm and unable to care for Shauna. One frantic call and a midnight drive later, Bill found himself hovering over a bed in the hospital he had been born in twenty-six years earlier. Our tiny little boy had died in the womb.

Loss had been added to loss. But grieving takes time, and that was one thing neither of us had. As Bill said later, "I just kept going. The church needed my leadership. It did not seem appropriate to sit and contemplate the condition of my heart." I too chose to "just keep going." An urgent request came into the church office: a marriage had broken up, leaving two young children unattended. Within days I became unofficial foster mom to a three-year-old girl and an eight-year-old boy, who stayed with us for nearly six months. Shauna was two. Life goes on.

WORKING TOGETHER OR DRIFTING APART?

This morning as I scanned Bill's office calendar from 1978 I noted one "minor" item I forgot to include in the fall events I just outlined. From mid-September through the end of October, Bill was involved in his second annual series of "home meetings." Six nights each week for six weeks, he held two meetings per night, in homes, with small groups of people from the church, to cast the vision for a church building and to present the financial needs associated with that. He believed it was essential to communicate the vision and the needs in an intimate question-and-answer setting in which people could freely voice their concerns. He also knew that in a more personal setting people would have a greater sense of ownership and be able to see more clearly the importance of their contribution. With nearly two thousand people attending at that time, it would have been easy for people to assume that their individual gift would be neither needed nor missed. In reality we needed everyone working together; Bill wanted to make sure people knew that.

After six weeks of home meetings, we held a fund-raising extravaganza at Woodfield Mall. On a Saturday night after store hours, we rented the entire atrium area of the mall, set up round tables for fifteen hundred people, catered a dinner, and presented a concert by the Willow Creek orchestra and vocalists. After Bill described again the many needs that the new building would meet, he challenged people to give. We raised $735,000. The notation on Bill's calendar for the previous week's New Community says simply, "Prayer." The following week's notation is, "Praise and Thanksgiving."

For Bill the next few months were a blur: meetings with architects; formalization of a board of directors, building committee, and camp board; continued personal discipling of men in the church (which included occasional ski trips and other bonding activities); staff restructuring; teaching at both weekend and mid-week services; performing weddings (in a growing church of young people, there were almost weekly weddings); and outside speaking and consulting commitments to youth ministries around the country.

Thrown into the jumble of an already-out-of-control schedule were numerous late-night elders meetings to resolve ongoing staff dissension. The staff member who had been confronted earlier had not made a clear break with the troublesome behavior and seemed increasingly resistant to accountability. Few staff members were aware of the cause of tension, but clearly they sensed it; some assumed it was

79

just a power play by Bill and the elders. This pushed those staff members back toward the extreme autonomy that had characterized behavior in previous years. Reporting structures, job descriptions, scheduled hours—these they considered unnecessary and unreasonable requirements.

Philosophical differences also surfaced among staff members. Where should staff resources and energy go? Into discipleship? Small groups? Adult education? Increased creativity in programming? Outreach through the arts? There was little agreement on such questions.

Personality differences added to the tension. The Willow Creek start-up team was stacked with mavericks who by nature hated to be reined in. They were bold, independent freethinkers—they had to be to start a church like Willow Creek— but now they were chafing under the increased accountability necessitated by growth and complexity.

Bill's shift to expository teaching at New Community, accompanied by a stronger call to commitment and righteous living, also fed dissension on staff. Some embraced the change; others felt betrayed by an approach that seemed "too extreme, too negative, too heavy-handed."

Still, the mounting staff tension was not enough to weaken our ministry to the unchurched in our community. Only a handful of insiders were really affected by it, and even among them their commitment to the cause was clearly strong enough to keep them going. In April over three thousand people attended our Easter celebration, which was exactly what it has always been: a moving blend of practical, biblical teaching and creative, high-quality programming. It was a prime illustration of God's wisdom in bringing together the gifts of an extraordinary team. As in the past, there was power. There was synergy. There was the obvious ministry of the Holy Spirit.

The transforming, empowering work of the Spirit was also evident on May 31, 1979, when seventeen members of the board of directors, most of them fairly new Christians, raised liquid collateral totaling $1.7 million in order to secure a $3 million construction loan for the proposed building. In other words, these individuals provided guarantees that if the church defaulted on the loan, they would personally cover it. They provided personal financial statements to the church and the bank, and literally put their homes on the line.

Of course Bill and I were extremely grateful for the commitment and generosity of the board. But as I look back I think we may have taken it for granted. We were young and naive. I don't think we realized how unusual it was for aggressive, dynamic, successful businessmen to put their wealth on the line. Many such people talk about giving, but when it comes right down to it, they often are unable to part with that which is their symbol of success. I look back with awe to that sincere, devoted group of men who met together on a Monday night in the back room of a local country club and signed on the dotted line. What moved them to do it? Why did they choose to sign on with a bunch of twenty-something dreamers?

Years later one of those men gave the only answer that can explain it: "Because it was so clear that God was in it."

FROM A DREAM TO A NIGHTMARE

On June 6, 1979, construction began on the future home of Willow Creek Community Church. On July 20 Bill and I moved into a home in the subdivision next to the church property so Bill could help to oversee construction. Also on that day our son, Todd, was born. I left for the hospital from one house and went home to another one. Chaos reigned, but after nine months of daily sickness, I was thrilled just to be healthy again. Repeatedly during those months, Shauna and I had gone to Michigan to stay with my parents; Bill's schedule did not afford him time or energy to deal with a sick wife and a toddler. Now at last we could be together. We could be a family.

But it wasn't long before I wished I were in Michigan again—not to get away from Bill but to escape the growing tension at church. The staff situation came to a head in early September when the elders confronted the erring staff member with his ongoing pattern of behavior and his apparently unrepentant spirit. Rather than discuss the situation, he opted to resign. The elders accepted his resignation.

The following morning an elder announced the staff member's resignation, citing "differing philosophies of ministry," and wished him well in his new endeavors. The elders assumed the congregation would accept the partial explanation given, but they clearly misjudged. By the end of the service, the core members of the church were in an uproar. "Give us the truth! Tell us what's really going on!"

The elders tried to explain in positive terms the philosophical and personality issues that necessitated a "parting of the ways." But in order to protect the privacy of the resigned staff member, they hid the real issue behind an opaque screen of secrecy. When people questioned the former staff member, he too avoided a straight answer.

Prior to this Bill's delineation of the staff structure had been imperceptible to the congregation: the team approach to ministry was still apparent and very real. However, at the staff level there was an increasing division between those who supported the new structure of accountability and authority and those who favored the autonomy of the past. As the latter discussed the sudden resignation with key lay leaders, unanswered questions gave way to assumptions. While many people trusted the elders' decision and chose not to demand further explanations, others filled in the information vacuum with an explanation of their own: Bill was after power. The elders were accused of being naive accomplices to Bill's misdeed.

While the congregation at large remained nearly unaware of the problem, the staff, board, elders, and key lay leaders were reeling. Overnight we became embroiled in a nightmarish round of accusations and mistrust, of betrayal and hostility. Years later it is undoubtedly hard for an outsider to understand why the elders continued to hide the real issue, given the intensity of misunderstanding that existed. If they had it to do over again, they would take a different—and more biblical—approach, but back then it seemed like a betrayal of friendship and an unnecessary injustice to innocent parties to publicize wrongdoings. So the confusion, the polarization, and the pain continued. At night our phone rang with people informing me of the selfish and evil actions of my power-mongering husband. The elders met night after night to try to save what appeared to be a dying dream.

"YOU DON'T KNOW THE WHOLE STORY"

But life went on. Ministry went on. The initial explosion over the resignation occurred on Sunday, September 9. We had previously scheduled for that evening an open house on the church property, where the foundation had already been laid for our new building. There was a big bonfire, and people divided into small groups to pray, but not about the fall fund-raiser and the progress of construction, because suddenly there were graver issues to pray for. Two days later Bill began his third annual round of home meetings. Answering questions about buildings and finances was easy compared to negotiating the continuing questions about Bill's apparent desire "to have the big pie all to yourself."

"You don't know the whole story," he would say, but that only brought up more unanswerable questions.

After one home meeting a large contributor said, "If you let this team fall apart, you're going to end up with a white elephant sitting out on that hill on Barrington Road." He was not the only one to share that sentiment. The positive energy of forward motion and growing momentum that had characterized our experience in ministry from the beginning had been replaced by the negative energy of swirling turmoil and increasing tension. On October 14 we celebrated Willow Creek's four-year anniversary, but the feeling was anything but celebratory.

There were, fortunately, many new people at the home meetings whose excitement about the future of the church was unmarred by the dissension that plagued the inner circle. Their enthusiasm buoyed Bill's spirit, but it wasn't enough to counteract the sense of doom that pervaded the October 20 fund-raising event. Months earlier we had scheduled rental of a Chicago and North Western commuter train to take almost fifteen hundred Willow Creekers into Chicago, where thirty CTA buses would ferry them to Navy Pier for a concert by Chuck Girard, whose music had so inspired us during our early Son City days.

We loaded the train, in which church leaders clad in railroad worker attire served box suppers. It was supposed to be a festive affair, and for the majority of people it was, but on a leadership level it was extremely uncomfortable. The elders didn't know who would give them a friendly pat on the back and who would take them into a corner and ream them out. Bill didn't know which smiles were sincere and which hid unspoken accusations. We were gathered together to raise funds for a common cause, but who was still on board? Who was really on this train ride?

DERAILED

Needless to say, our fund-raising efforts fell short of the goal. Many people Bill had been counting on were disillusioned, with growing uncertainty about the future of Willow Creek. Several board members had resigned. Our largest donor was in the process of leaving the church. At the 1978 fund-raiser he had given a quarter of a million dollars. At a time when staff members and young lay leaders were mortgaging their homes in order to give two, three, or four thousand dollars, losing a six-figure donor seemed like signing Willow Creek's death certificate.

Within six months nearly half our staff was gone. The team was destroyed, and we realized more than ever before that the dream had been not just to build a church but to build it *together*. I remember sitting alone at night while the kids slept and Bill attended another elders meeting and thinking, *This is not what God had in mind. This is not how it was supposed to turn out. Sin has ruined His plan. We have ruined His plan. This is wrong. Really wrong.* It all seemed so senselessly tragic. Why did it happen?

Included in the ranks of departing staff members were Dave and Sue Holmbo. Though I grieved the loss of every staff member and lay leader, I absolutely could not accept that Dave and Sue were gone. It had always been Dave and Sue and Bill and Lynne. Dave was Bill's best friend. Sue was mine. It was supposed to stay that way forever. During those early years when Bill and Dave had been "married" to the ministry, Sue and I had been each other's survival kit. Late at night we would walk to the neighborhood Dairy Queen and drown our loneliness in a hot fudge sundae and in the comfort of a friend.

Sue was lively and spontaneous, the life of every party—a contrast to my more subdued demeanor—but we complemented one another perfectly and loved to be together. I could not accept that she was gone. And every feeling I had about the loss of Sue was paralleled by Bill's feelings regarding the loss of Dave. Had we been able to see the future, we could have taken comfort in the crossing of our paths again in future years, but back then all we knew was the deep sadness of another loss.

FASTER ISN'T ALWAYS BETTER

What is going on? we asked, over and over again. *Why is this happening?* But as the pain became greater and our defenses of denial broke down, reality became clearer. Had we been older and more mature, in fact, we undoubtedly would have seen the crash coming. As a staff, we had been on a collision course since the church began.

One of Bill's goals during those early years was to get the church to the point where it would be self-sustaining, where there would be enough core people to cover leadership needs and provide an adequate financial base. He knew enough about business to know that in any organization there's a start-up phase during which leaders have to "go all out" for the cause. Bill was more than willing to go all out for Willow Creek, and so was every other staff member. The mentality was: *We'll do whatever it takes to get this church going. If it means living at an insane pace for a while, so be it. After all, anyone can handle a year or two of living on the edge. We'll survive.*

But a year or two turned into three or four. And we didn't survive.

First to die was the sense of community we had enjoyed in Son City. Years earlier we had worked together, played together, dreamed together, and prayed together. Personal accountability had grown naturally out of the intimacy of our relationships. The condition of our inner lives and the state of our relationships had been normal topics of conversation. But as the pace increased, the intimacy decreased. We barely had time to concern ourselves with one another's ministry responsibilities, let alone our personal lives. We just assumed we were all still on the same track spiritually. And that our personal lives and marriages were in order.

But both assumptions were wrong. For some, questions and doubts were beginning to weaken faith, and without a forum for authentic dialogue, faith fell by the wayside. Had we known, perhaps we could have joined in a collective pursuit of a deeper understanding of true Christianity. But we didn't have time to know. So doubters struggled alone, weary and disillusioned, and some lost the battle.

Others lost their marriages. Sadly, divorce followed on the heels of several staff resignations and lay leader departures. And how could it have been otherwise? What's harder to understand is how any of our marriages survived. Throughout those years I loved the church, as I always had; I wanted it to survive, and I hated the thought of doing anything to hinder its growth. But we and others were paying a higher and higher price in our marriages. Was God really demanding that price?

Today I would say that our sacrifice exceeded God's demand, but back then I didn't know what to think. Yes, Bill and I seemed to be drifting dangerously apart, and hostility seemed more at home in our hearts—in mine, anyway—than love. But how could I place my little dream of marriage up against the giant dream of the church? I felt as if I were fighting God. How could I possibly win? And did I want to battle God? Of course not. I wanted to be a spiritual woman, a godly wife, a devoted disciple. I wanted to pay whatever price the work of the kingdom demanded, just as Bill did. Just as we all did.

And so two by two we paid the price in our marriages. Bill and I were the models; others followed our example to the letter.

Bill and I look back at these years with deep sadness and regret. How we wish we had modeled a healthier pace. How different things might have been had we taken a long-term view of life instead of focusing entirely on the excitement and the urgency of the present. Bill's understanding of his own addiction to fruit-bearing would have served him and the entire core group so well back then. We lament that youth and immaturity led to such excesses.

Why our marriage survived when others didn't I don't fully understand. Having children surely made a difference; neither of us could tolerate the thought of making our kids pay for our frustrations or errors. Our leadership responsibility to the church also made a difference; we were both unwilling to jeopardize the work God was doing in our midst. Beyond that we have to claim the extraordinary power of prayer and perseverance, and the gracious protection of God.

THIS PIE IS WAY TOO SMALL

But the pace of our lives wasn't our only problem.

During those early years nothing caught Bill more off guard than the financial strain of starting a church. Weekly he would calculate what the Sunday offering had to be in order for the church to stay afloat, and invariably we would receive less than that amount. Somehow we always managed to keep going, but not without extreme measures. Once Bill severely chastised a staff member for ordering $8.50 worth of pens and pencils from an office supply store and billing it to the church without proper authorization. The church simply could not absorb expenses like that and survive.

There was constant tension about how to divide the resource pie between programs, staff salaries, and land and buildings. Because of our commitment to effective outreach through the seeker service, Bill tried to keep the program budget as full as possible. But he also believed it was important for us to acquire a permanent facility as soon as possible. Our increasing attendance and our subministry programs eventually brought us to the point where we had to rent five different facilities each week, which required the constant moving of sound and lighting equipment and created tremendous inconvenience and frustration. Our building-hopping also saddled us with a negative, fly-by-night image, which turned away many people in the community. And we constantly faced the threat of eviction. Consequently, we tried to pour as much money as possible into the land and building fund.

Who got shortchanged? The staff. Because of our zeal and willingness to pay any price, no one complained. Spouses worked and staff members moonlighted; we were able to make ends meet because most of us were single or newly married and were not burdened by mortgages or child care costs. But the lack of adequate salaries added even greater strain to our already overburdened lives.

Ultimately, excellent programming and permanent facilities enhanced the church's growth rate, which led naturally to a broader financial base, which eventually resulted in far more adequate staff salaries than most of us had even dared imagine. But by that time many staff members who had sacrificed to get us there were gone. We had been willing to pay the price, but had we been wise?

WANTED: ANYONE AVAILABLE

Our selection of lay leaders was another example of expediency winning out over wisdom. The downside of starting a church for the unchurched is that if you succeed, you end up with a church full of baby Christians. Don't get me wrong: that's wonderful and inspiring and exciting. But it creates a challenge when it's time to fill leadership slots.

We thought we had enough potential leaders in our start-up core, but we hadn't anticipated the rapid growth of our first two years. Suddenly we needed more musicians and more Sunday school teachers and more board members and more module leaders. Who did we have to choose from? A fresh crop of new believers. Well, no problem. They were enthusiastic and teachable and, above all, available.

So we made them leaders.

But few of them were ready for that. They were sincere and growing but, at best, spiritually immature. Generally in their twenties and early thirties, many of them were working through difficult issues in their personal lives or marriages and were totally inexperienced in leadership. They were willing to work hard, but they didn't have a solid core from which to be giving so much. By the time the staff tension became evident and difficult questions arose, many of these young leaders were on the edge of burnout and ill-prepared to respond to turmoil in a mature fashion. Some stayed and grew and are active members or key leaders at Willow Creek today. But many left the church hurt and disillusioned.

Some left the faith.

A QUESTION OF BALANCE

Bill grew up with a clear knowledge of certain critical biblical truths: God is holy. God is just. We are sinners. Hell is real. These truths were painted in thick dark colors on the canvas of his youthful mind. It wasn't until his conversion at age sixteen that he learned these truths: God is love. Forgiveness is available in Christ. Salvation is a gift of grace. Against the foreboding backdrop of God's holiness and justice, the brilliant reality of God's love overwhelmed him. It was life and light and freedom and hope.

This was the Good News that opened the hearts of hundreds of kids in Son City. *God is holy and just, and we deserve hell. But God loves us. Through Christ we can receive forgiveness and eternal life.* Always in Son City the message of God's love was flanked by the truth of His holiness and His justice. God was love, yes, but sin was sin, and God hated it, so we had to hate it, too. Bill's teaching was balanced; it drew kids to a God of love, yet it had a prophetic edge and a clear call to discipleship.

During the early years of Willow Creek, however, Bill found it harder to keep a biblical balance between God's holiness and His love. It was far more difficult for a twenty-three-year-old to question the lifestyle or values of a businessman twice his age than it had been to challenge the dating practices of a high school junior. It was hard to be a prophet when people greeted you with, "Hey, kid, how you doing?" Bill's insecurity as a teacher to adults dulled the edge of his challenges. He confronted less and comforted more.

"No matter who you are," he said, "God loves you. No matter what you do, God will forgive you. No matter how badly you fail Him, God will accept you back into the fold." Bill spoke confidently about God's love and trusted that the power of that truth would melt the hearts of his listeners as it had melted his.

But the unchurched people coming to our seeker services too seldom heard the truth of God's love the way Bill had heard it: against the backdrop of God's justice and holiness. Without the proper balance in teaching, Willow Creek became a breeding ground for spiritual carelessness. People said, "I can cheat a little here. I can play with that sin there. It's no big deal. God will forgive me." Grace became, all too often, a license to sin more.

Even certain lay leaders and staff members adopted this permissive, cavalier attitude toward sin. Some who discovered the moral issues at the core of the staff problems seemed to be little bothered by it. *Oh well,* they thought, *No one's perfect. We all have our flaws. Who are we to judge?*

HANGING BY A THREAD

All these factors together—insane pace of life, financial stress, immature leaders, and imbalanced teaching—created an environment ripe for disaster. Perhaps had the elders told the church body the whole truth about the staff member's behavior to begin with, in a biblical way that acknowledged the seriousness of sin but also opened the door for repentance and restoration, the damage may yet have been "contained." But their failure to do so started the dominoes falling, which led to what we have unaffectionately called the Train Wreck of '79.

Over the years, our elders have handled many other potentially explosive situations wisely and lovingly, and time after time they have protected our church body from division and deception. But the route to learning their gentle art was painful and frightening. Dr. Bilezikian, who had a broad range of church experience, was confident that the church would survive the Train Wreck, but those elders with less experience felt far less secure. It seemed to them, and to many of us in the core, that we were hanging by a thread.

Every week that went by without a mishap, we would build a little more strength. But then there would be another disclosure of sin, another staff resignation, another key leader leaving, and the bottom would fall out of our confidence again.

Then there were the continuing financial realities. As giving dropped, the board learned that the building would cost $1 million more than had been projected. We were already several hundred thousand dollars short of the original estimate. In 1979 prime rate was twenty-one percent, and our construction loan was two points over prime. While we were paying over $17,000 a month in interest, a collapsed beam in the building delayed us three months. Three months at $17,000 per month!

With a new wave of core members leaving and another tier of key donors on the way out, a board member approached Bill and said, "We have a $3.5 million loan. We're in a $6 million building program. There is no way we can make these numbers work if people keep leaving. I have $250,000 at stake for liquid collateral. If you let this team fall apart, I'm going to lose everything. I don't care what anyone has done, you keep this team together."

THE REMINDER OF A DREAM

That was the breaking point for Bill. *The dream is dead. I've ruined everything. Half the staff is gone, and the rest is burned out. There are wrong people in leadership positions. We're in a building program we can't pay for. It's hopeless.*

We're going down, and we're taking fifteen guys' life savings, and my own, with us. What have I done?

Our house on Alder Drive became a house of tears and prayer that night. Face-down on the gold shag carpet of our family room, Bill emptied his heart to God. He wept over his failure to organize and lead the staff properly and to be a better friend when he saw staff members starting to drift. He repented of the insane schedule he had modeled and of his imbalanced teaching. He confessed personal sins that he had not taken seriously. *Oh, God, how I have failed. Please forgive me.*

He laid facedown in a swamp of despair, hopeless but for one thing: the calling. Up through the murky waters of his failure bubbled the reminder of the dream. He couldn't shake the sense that Willow Creek was still alive in the mind of God, that Willow Creek was still under God's mandate to "be the church" and "reach the lost" and "produce fully devoted followers of Jesus Christ."

Earnestly Bill begged for a second chance. *If You will just do something to get us through this, I will never be so careless or sinful again. I'll teach the truth that's in Your Word, with painstaking attention to balance. I'll develop better accountability structures. I'll slow down the pace. I don't deserve another chance, but if You give me one, I'll try with all my heart to do it right.*

Late into the night Bill waited for an answer. Would God choose to extend His grace? Would He rescue us from our own sins and errors? Did He in fact want the dream to live? Eventually the answer came. A skeptic might call it nothing more than an echo of Bill's desire, but in his soul Bill believed it was a message from God: *Don't give up. Keep going. You've learned invaluable lessons. Now get up and apply them. Do the right thing. Move forward.*

Afterward Bill felt a sense of surrender: the situation was in God's hands. He would follow God's direction as best he could. The outcome was up to God.

Bill met with the board and apologized for the leadership mistakes he had made and for his imbalanced emphasis in teaching. "I failed to call people to holiness," he said, "and I was wrong. Sin has consequences. I need to stress that more. Grace is real, but it's not a license for sin." He also told them that he was going to move forward and he hoped they would join him. "This is going to be God's church," he said, "done God's way."

For Bill it was a horrible, excruciating time, but spiritually rich. He didn't have his dad to turn to. I could offer him little of the support he needed. It was between him and God.

chapter five

THE BUILDUP
1980–87

*Before the Train Wreck we were a bunch of young kids on a roll.
Humility wasn't high on our list of character qualities. We thought
we were pretty invincible. But the Train Wreck caused such
incredible brokenness. As painful as it was, it served a God-honoring
purpose. Real fruit can be born out of brokenness.*

LAURIE PEDERSON,
WILLOW CREEK ELDER

As we entered the decade of the eighties Bill wanted to make sure that he and every other core member at Willow Creek understood the dangers that threatened the church in general and Willow Creek in particular. In January he began a New Community series based on Revelation 2 and 3, called "The Fate of Four Churches." In February he taught "The Fate of Four More Churches." This was followed by a five-week series called "A Look at the Opposition." His 1979 study of 1 Corinthians had been an attempt to highlight God's attitude toward sin and the importance of righteous living. But the force of Bill's New Community messages in 1980 made the previous year's challenges sound like cheerful banter.

"There was no moderation," he admitted later. "I firmly believed the only way out of the mess we were in was to teach our way out. So I taught with a vengeance."

Vengeance, unfortunately, was what many people felt. "Who are you mad at?" they would ask after Bill pounded out one message after another on sin and deception and the need to live a life of integrity.

Within six months Bill had mellowed a bit, but his teaching was still focused almost entirely on holiness and sin. Understandably, this raised flags of concern

91

for many people. Most of these people could accept the general content of his teaching; it was the teaching balance that concerned them. The pendulum, it seemed, had swung from one extreme to the other.

Throughout that year Bill confided to me that he felt as if he were signing up for war every time he walked into New Community. Every time he preached, he felt as if he were on trial. As key staff members continued to leave throughout that year disgruntled members followed, saying, "We can see why these staff members are leaving. Bill is trying to turn Willow Creek into a traditional, fundamentalist, legalistic church—the kind we were trying to get away from."

Bill's weekend messages changed, too. He wanted to make sure that every attender knew exactly what Willow Creek Community Church stood for. The first service of the new year was a baptism service; Bill's message was called "Reflections of Christ." This was followed by four weeks of clear teaching on what it means to become a Christian. Then he taught verse by verse through the Beatitudes. He taught an eight-week family series, followed it up with a straightforward message on repentance, then ended the ministry year with a "Call to Discipleship" series about the great men in the Bible: Noah, Abraham, Jacob, Joseph, and David.

This change in the teaching menu was more than some people could stomach. They had cut their teeth on a steady diet of grace, and more than a few of them left as the teaching became more balanced and biblical. But many new people came and responded to the teaching. In fact, many people who are still strong servants and leaders at Willow Creek became Christians during that era.

Bill instituted other changes as well. It had become clear that the module small-group system was providing an opportunity for social interaction but was not producing what we needed most: spiritually mature leaders. Therefore as 1979 ended so did the module system. The new emphasis was on one-to-one discipleship and small discipleship groups. Bill and I had been informally discipling Quigley and Diane Fletcher throughout the previous year, but on January 27, 1980, we started our first Sunday night discipleship group, in our home with three adult couples from the church. Using the Navigator study *Design for Discipleship*, staff and lay leaders throughout the church started similar discipleship groups.

Bill's calendar for that year reflects additional changes. Joint staff meetings and meetings with individual staff members had high priority on his schedule. Many more hours for "Message Preparation" were blocked off on his calendar, as his new style of teaching demanded more disciplined study. Elders meetings were scheduled every week after New Community so elders could deal immediately with any problems that arose. And "HOME" was written across far more evenings than it ever had been in the past. In every area of Bill's life and ministry, he was making a conscious effort to achieve a more healthy balance.

FROM MOTOCROSS TO AMAZING GRACE

Balanced living also demands recreation of some sort, particularly when life is heavy with responsibility and stress, so Bill took up the "sensible" sport of motocross, which offered him the opportunity to vent the frustrations of his life at a high rate of speed on a bumpy track in the middle of a farmer's field. In July 1980 it also offered him the chance to spend some quiet time in the hospital, recovering from a bruised kidney and reflecting over the past ministry year. Though the forced slowing of his pace seemed ill-timed in terms of the pressures of the ministry, the time for quiet evaluation was invaluable. The following month Bill gave a talk at New Community called "Midcourse Corrections," in which he presented his rationale for the adjustments he had made throughout the church. Several weeks later he detailed for the New Community the current staff structure and emphasized the increasingly strategic role of the boards.

Though Bill and the elders had reacted to the crisis of 1979 by instituting necessary changes as quickly as possible, there was no dramatic overnight return to stability. There was still, during the early months of 1980, the sense that we were hanging on by a thread, still the fear that another major upset was right around the corner, still the overwhelming financial burden, still the elders' concern about another pattern of sin being uncovered, still occasional waves of people leaving.

But as spring turned to summer the tension clearly seemed to be easing. For the most part the congregation appeared to be in agreement with the teaching trends. Staff lines had been drawn, choices had been made, and those who remained seemed to share common values and goals. We began to breathe a little easier.

Then another bomb. We learned that the *Chicago Tribune* was planning to do a major article on Willow Creek. The *Sun Times* had previously published a slanderous story about us, likening us more to a cult than to a church. During the days when the Jonestown massacre had raised the fear of cults to a fever pitch, the article was horribly damaging. Now the *Tribune*. Why were they doing this? What was their slant? We were shaken by the thought of a public exposé of the turmoil of the previous year. For weeks we prayed about that article, fearing that another negative story would mean the final destruction of all that Bill and the elders had tried to salvage in the previous year.

Finally the publication date arrived. Fearfully we flipped through the pages in the special *Sunday Magazine,* only to discover a sensitively written account of an unchurched family's spiritual transformation, a moving description of a weekend service, and a thoughtful discussion of our motivation for ministry and our dreams for the future.

It was Sunday, September 13, 1980, a year and a week after the first staff resignation. Whether God intended this or not, the elders and many core people who had suffered through that horrendous year saw that article as an affirmation from God, a sign along the way that said, *Keep going. You're heading in the right direction. Stay close to Me and obey Me. Continue to seek truth and you'll find the light at the end of the tunnel.*

In keeping with that admonition to "continue to seek truth," Bill started October with a New Community series called "The Doctrines of the Christian Faith." On October 12 we celebrated Willow Creek's five-year anniversary, grateful to have survived the previous year. In November Bill started another annual round of home meetings, knowing that for the fifteen board members (including us) who still had their personal assets on the line, a successful year-end fund-raiser was crucial. December started with a two-week series called "Overcoming Anxiety"—a subject Bill had learned much about in the preceding months—then concluded with a two-week series called "The Day of Reckoning," which ended the year with one more reminder that life is short and hell is real and we'd better take God seriously in the here and now.

By December 1980 nearly half of the core kids with whom we had started the church were gone, along with a sizable number of the early lay leaders and half of the original church staff. But the New Community was beginning to stabilize, the weekend seats that had been vacated during the last months of 1979 had been filled by a new group of seekers, and the remaining staff had a renewed sense of unity. When the congregation gave generously and met the end-of-the-year financial goals, allowing us to continue work on our new building, we believed we had been visited by amazing grace.

THE IRRESISTIBLE CALL

Years later Dr. Bilezikian was asked to describe the clearest example of God's protection on Willow Creek during the Train Wreck era. "That Bill didn't buckle under the pressure," he said. "When I saw that he had the resources and strength to keep going despite enormous opposition, then I knew that the mettle of the man had been tried and that by God's grace we could go forward."

Though Bill didn't have his father to depend on during those difficult years, I believe he drew tremendous strength from the lessons his father had taught him about perseverance and hard work and taking risks. The "rotten potato" reminder that he only had to face life "one bag at a time" was invaluable during that era.

But there was far more to his endurance than that. There was God's call. Again, I wish I could find the words to adequately describe the power of the call that has surrounded Willow Creek since the beginning, but I know I can't. Even in my own mind there's something inexplicable about it. The call has seemed to exist on its own, and the only word that seems worthy of standing next to it is the word irresistible. I don't believe we were puppets on a string, forced to respond in a given way. But turning our backs on the call never seemed to be an option. It wasn't that every time the temptation to quit reared its ugly head we beat it down. It's more that the thought of quitting just never quite made it to the serious temptation stage.

Years later in an interview, Bill said that one thing which kept him going through that time was that my response to the call never wavered: I never asked him to quit, never suggested that perhaps the dream was dead. As I look back I don't know why I stood so firm. In many ways it was a miserable time for me. I was a young mother of a toddler and an infant. Grandparents were in another state, baby-sitters cost more money than we usually had, and Bill's time and energy were almost entirely consumed with the stresses of the ministry (even when he was home, he was usually home "in body only"). Also, as the only person in the core leadership group with young children, I often felt left out, isolated both from Bill's life and from the life of the church. Then there were the personal losses—the miscarriage mentioned earlier, and later twin boys also lost at midterm—which I had so little time to grieve. But it never crossed my mind that we should quit. Opposition, misunderstanding, accusations—even deep personal disappointment—seemed small when stacked up against the call. And then there was the fruit of changed lives that appeared constantly before us.

I am not trying to imply that there is never a time to quit. On the contrary, I believe that some endeavors, some subministries, even some church start-up ventures, need to be allowed a dignified death. Perhaps there was no divine call to begin with. Perhaps zealous leaders moved ahead prematurely. Perhaps strategies and plans were ill-conceived, because of ignorance or inexperience. Perhaps sin was given too much room. Perhaps the wisest choice, the Spirit-led decision, is to quit, regroup, and begin again later. Neither Bill nor I would ever say there is any particular merit in stubbornly hanging on to a dream that has died or a ministry that has proven ineffective. We would both say, however, that for those of us at the core of Willow Creek at the end of 1980, the call had surrounded us and captured us. We could not walk away from it.

We knew that God might choose to withdraw His blessing from Willow Creek, in which case it would die. But that had to be His choice; it would not be ours. And despite the mistakes, the frailness of our efforts, and the clever ways

Satan tried to shipwreck what we did, God intervened. He rescued us from our own sin and immaturity and from the sinister schemes of darkness.

TURNING POINT

On Sunday, February 15, 1981, we held our first service in the new building. The office area was not yet completed; in fact, we would remain in our Vermont Street offices for another six months, waiting for funds to buy needed materials so church volunteers could finish the office area. But there was no way we would let that completed auditorium sit empty while we waited for offices. On that memorable weekend, Bill gave a message called "Monument to a Miracle." He talked about Joshua crossing into the Promised Land and echoed the Old Testament leader's words when he said, "It is God who deserves all the credit for what we see today."

Euphoric is the only word to describe the mood in the auditorium that morning. Many of us who had helped start the church came early. Scattered throughout the auditorium, we wept, awed by the brick-and-mortar miracle God had performed.

But the acquisition of ninety acres of prime real estate and the construction of a spacious auditorium was not the only miracle we celebrated that day. We had survived a coup from the Evil One. We had been given a brand-new start in ministry, an opportunity to recommit ourselves to the basic values that had motivated us when we started Son City almost a decade earlier. We sat in the auditorium, looked across the snow-covered hills and the frozen pond, and thanked God for all He had done.

We moved into the new building, and into a new era, humbled. The Train Wreck had shattered the pride and the youthful naïveté that had been nourished by the explosive success of the Wonder Years. Never again could it be said that everything we touched turned to spiritual gold. Brokenness of soul and painful confessions had left us with a deep and lingering awareness of our weakness and our dependence on God. Grace was no longer a laughing matter to us. Reliance on the Bible was not just something we talked about. We had come face-to-face with our own vulnerability; we knew that just a few slips in judgment, in teaching balance, in relationships, could put us back into the furnace again.

Because we had learned what can happen to a church staff without the oversight of a group of godly, discerning people whose primary goal is to protect the overall vision of the church, the leadership of the church was passed from the staff to the board of elders, which added several new members at that time. While Bill continued as the point person for the staff, he came under the authority of the elder board, of which he remained a member.

The elders began to take a very high profile. Several times each year they went on two- or three-day retreats to discuss problems, needs, and future ministry plans. Prayerfully they evaluated the health and holiness of the church. Department by department they analyzed the direction and effectiveness of programs and subministries.

Past mistakes had taught them to deal with matters of church discipline immediately—and publicly when necessary. If members of the congregation fell into patterns of sin that impacted others in the congregation, or if they engaged in behavior that created dissension or division, the elders intervened, privately first and then publicly to whatever extent they deemed biblical. When leaders fell, those within their sphere of influence were told the truth. In the past, secrecy had been destructive rather than helpful in the restoration process.

The lessons of the Train Wreck era have served our elders well. Over the years they have confronted deception, resolved disputes, and handled many sensitive discipline cases with integrity and wisdom, thus protecting the church from heresy, division, and turmoil.

In 1980 the elders also began to oversee the teaching more closely. As discerning people devoted to the Word of God and in touch with the needs of the congregation, they began to meet with Bill and other teachers in the church to discuss upcoming teaching themes and series. They began to evaluate Bill's messages—as they still do—for content, tone, and balance, giving him written feedback after every message.

The elders also became responsible for making major philosophical decisions regarding the direction of the church. Does this proposed subministry fall within the scope of our purpose as a church? Is this approach to outreach truly biblical? Are we ready as a congregation to take on this responsibility? Does the Holy Spirit seem to be leading us in this direction?

Hiring new staff also fell under the domain of the elders. The entire elder board began to meet with each potential staff person to discuss their commitment to Christ, their integrity as a worker, the health of their family life, and the "fit" between their proposed job description and their personal gifts and passions. As the issue of personal purity came to the forefront in the church as a whole, so it did in the selection of staff. Giftedness and proficiency were not deemed unimportant, but character and godliness were now given top billing. Over the years many competent, gifted people have been "passed over" for staff or lay leadership positions or as musicians or actors, because their professional competence seemed to hold higher priority to them than their commitment to Christ.

The elders began to meet as an entire group at least monthly and in smaller groups as needs arose, and they began praying monthly with the sick. They also instituted a formal church membership procedure. They had previously considered formal membership unnecessary, but it had become apparent that we needed a means of identifying those who were serious about spiritual growth and discipleship, and of screening possible candidates for service opportunities and leadership positions. At this time the elders began meeting personally with each person who sought formal membership at Willow Creek.

LEADERSHIP AND WORSHIP

Under the elders' direction the church entered an era of consolidation. While weekend growth continued steadily throughout this era, the emphasis of the staff and elders was on assimilating those already in the church and building up the subministries of the church. An extensive ministry to singles was developed, as well as a more formalized women's ministry and an extensive range of pastoral care ministries. The youth ministries exploded with the addition of a junior high ministry called Sonlight Express and with the expansion of Promiseland, our Sunday school program, which had been hampered by the facility limitations in the old theater.

With the start of each new subministry came a new demand for leaders. Bill had learned during the early years that leaders are developed through discipleship, so a major emphasis of the early eighties was the expansion of the disciple-making small-group ministry that had replaced the module system of the theater days. Many of the lay and staff leaders who carried Willow Creek through the Buildup era were "homegrown" products of our two-year discipleship groups.

Bill continued teaching expositorially at New Community. The "pursuing purity" theme that characterized his response to the Train Wreck received a new burst of energy when Bill crossed paths with Dr. R. C. Sproul. During the spring and summer of 1982, Bill and I spent three separate weeks at the Ligonier Valley Study Center, then located in Pennsylvania, under Dr. Sproul's colorful and challenging teaching. Bill and Dr. Sproul nearly came to verbal blows over their differing views on evangelism, but it is no overstatement to say that R. C.'s teaching on the holiness of God was pivotal in Bill's spiritual development, both theologically and experientially.

Bill's theme for that year's annual Labor Day staff retreat grew out of his conversations with R. C. If God was as "high and lifted up" as Bill had discovered Him to be, then He deserved our worship. Bill spoke that week about our need to become a worshiping people and to present our lives, individually and together as a church, as a sacrifice to God with a fragrant aroma. Our assignment for the week was to each find a log and carve our name on it. The last night at camp, we all placed our inscribed logs on a huge bonfire and mingled our songs of submission and praise with the blazing embers that danced skyward and melted into the black night.

On Saturday, October 23, 1982, Dr. Sproul taught his entire "Holiness" series to the leadership body of Willow Creek. Bill followed with a New Community series based on R. C.'s teaching. "God's Intrinsic Worthship" was the first message of the series, and it instituted a new era of worship at Willow Creek. Since 1975 we had considered our New Community services to be our "worship services," but suddenly we realized that we had not even known the meaning of worship, for we had not known the greatness of God. New Community worship was to take another, even deeper, turn several years later when Bill fell (or was divinely thrown) under the influence of Dr. Jack Hayford and other godly men and women with a more Spirit-anointed approach to worship. But it was first through the ministry of Dr. Sproul that worship came alive at Willow Creek.

ACCOUNTABILITY

One of the major values that grew out of the Train Wreck era was the value of accountability. Before 1979 we had experienced community without accountability. Willow Creek started as a maverick church led by a staff of energetic racehorses ready to charge full speed ahead. Each prized freedom and independence. Each had a clear inner sense of where they wanted to go with their respective ministries and believed that the last thing they needed was someone looking over their shoulder. Growing up in legalistic churches where every step out of line was judged fed their desire for autonomy and freedom. The hectic pace of life made accountability impossible even if they had wanted it, and the arrogance and naïveté of youth made them feel invulnerable.

But as I mentioned earlier, that sense of invulnerability had turned into its opposite by the time we entered the eighties. Bill, the elders and board members, and the staff and key leaders all knew one thing well: we were vulnerable, as individuals and as a church. The primary antidote to our vulnerability was accountability. But what exactly did accountability look like? How could we live it out in our relationships?

God provided the answers to those questions through a federal judge from Eugene, Oregon. When Bill first met Mike Hogan through a mutual friend, he was caught off guard by Mike's relational intensity. "What's going on in your life?" Mike asked, and he wouldn't accept a superficial answer. Over time Mike showed Bill the potential of male friendships.

Among other things, Bill learned from Mike that he had grossly misjudged the amount and depth of communication required to sustain healthy relationships and promote accountability. He learned that meticulous truth-telling was the only answer to the inevitable friction that occurs when people live or work together. During the busy early years staff relationships had too often operated according to optimistic assumptions like *Time will heal this wound* or *If I pretend there's no problem, it'll go away* or *It's none of my business* or *I don't have time to ask, but I'm sure he's doing fine.* Mike taught Bill to invite and ask the hard questions and to receive and give the hard answers.

Shortly after meeting Mike, Bill began meeting regularly with three men from the board of directors—Don Albrecht, Rich Schmidt, and Quigley Fletcher. In October 1981 Bill took his first "men's only" sailing trip with them—an event that was repeated again and again. During the next few years, I watched God take four independent mavericks and mold them into a band of interdependent brothers. I watched the four of them challenge each other in regard to their marriages, their business practices, their stewardship, their future plans. I watched Rich, Quig, and Bill weep together as a brain tumor cruelly took Don's life. I watched throughout the years as Bill added others to his "inner circle" and allowed one after another to mark him, each in his own unique way.

The benefits of brotherhood that Bill learned through Mike Hogan and the guys in his first men's group deepened Bill's understanding of relationships, influenced the direction of our small-group ministry, and eventually became the subject for a series Bill taught at our weekend services.

Today the general concept of accountability is evident throughout the entire Willow Creek ministry, from the depth and intensity of elder interviews of potential staff to the checks and balances that permeate the handling of finances to the personal sharing that is a part of weekly management team meetings.

GAINING GROUND AND RESPECTABILITY

In January 1983 Bill started a weekend series on the Ten Commandments. Though he feared attendance would drop during ten weeks of "thou shalt nots," it actually increased from 4,100 to 4,600 during that series. Because Bill went beyond the "whats" of the commandments to explain the "whys" behind them, many unchurched people who were accustomed to seeing biblical mandates as harsh and repressive received a first-time view of the love and wisdom behind them. For many seekers, that series proved to be the catalyst for major life change.

While Bill focused on weekend teaching during 1982 and 1983 he filled the New Community calendar with names like John MacArthur, Stuart Briscoe, Jill

Briscoe, Warren Wiersbe, J. Allen Peterson, Ron Carlson, Dr. Bilezikian, and many others. Though these gifted teachers provided excellent messages, the New Community suffered without the consistent presence of a teacher who understood the unique needs of our church.

The elders decided Bill should be the primary midweek teacher, but his weekend teaching schedule and church leadership demands left him little time to devote to New Community. The answer to this dilemma came in the person of Don Cousins, a team captain during the youth ministry days in Park Ridge and our Son City director during the theater days. Don had already left the youth ministry and joined the church staff. He was ready and willing to assume additional leadership responsibilities so Bill could devote more time and energy to teaching, and he gradually emerged as Willow Creek's associate pastor. During the coming years Don oversaw the start-up of most of our new subministries, launched an expanded discipleship program, and established himself as an effective New Community and weekend teacher.

From the beginning of 1985 through the end of 1987, weekend attendance grew from approximately five thousand to over nine thousand, with a third week-end service added on Saturday nights, in October 1987. Annual end-of-the-year fund-raisers allowed the addition of an education wing and a chapel, enabling the church to handle the increasing size of subministry events.

As the complexity of the church organization and the responsibility level of staff positions increased, it became necessary to recruit more and more staff from outside the church in order to tap into a broader pool of experienced ministry experts. The expanding staff necessitated continual rearranging of reporting structures and department divisions. While Bill continued to teach and to provide overall leadership for the church, Don emerged as the day-to-day staff leader. Both Bill and Don felt increasingly challenged by the task of leading a church that was growing so rapidly, but as in the early years, it was exhilarating to see so many people becoming Christians and growing in their devotion to Christ.

What's more, Willow Creek finally seemed to have shed its image as the black sheep of the Christian community. Bill had been asked to speak at pastors conferences around the country and at retreats and conferences at respected churches. In fact, hundreds of pastors had begun attending leadership conferences at Willow Creek. More and more churches seemed to be espousing the value of reaching the unchurched. Clearly we were heading into an exciting new era of local ministry growth and national impact.

chapter six

THE WORLD DISCOVERS WILLOW
1988-91

It was as if someone had switched on a spotlight. One minute we were going about our business, doing ministry at Willow Creek. Then suddenly, it seemed, reporters converged on the church, and camera crews roamed the hallways. Now everything we did seemed to carry extra weight and responsibility—and no matter how much we did, it was never quite enough to keep up with the ever-accelerating growth of the church.

LEE STROBEL,
WILLOW CREEK TEACHING PASTOR
AND DIRECTOR OF COMMUNICATIONS

In the late eighties the national media discovered Willow Creek, and our recently gained respectability within the evangelical community gave way to an all-out fascination with the "megachurch" concept on the part of the secular media, from *Time* magazine to NBC's *Today Show*. More often than not we cringed as we read or heard analyses provided by reporters who used the language of business to describe what was happening at Willow Creek. The congregation became "consumers." Seekers became "potential customers." Our 1975 survey became a "demographic analysis." Finding effective ways to address people's needs became "marketing savvy." We were distressed when life transformation got less coverage than Bill's "natty business suits."

But many Christians and church leaders rightly concluded there was more to the story than the media were providing. As the coverage increased, the switchboard at Willow Creek buzzed. Informational packets about Willow Creek were sent to churches around the world, and attendance at our pastors conferences mushroomed. Major denominations eagerly sought teaching on "seeker-targeted" ministry, and Bill's ministry outside Willow Creek skyrocketed as he traveled across the U.S. and to Europe, India, and Australia.

Our elders wrestled with Bill's expanding role outside Willow Creek but ultimately sensed that God was leading them to affirm his ministry beyond our local church. I too agreed. Though I wasn't eager to have Bill away from home more frequently, it seemed clear to me that God wanted to use Bill's teaching and leadership gifts in a broader context. While Bill continued as the primary teacher both on weekends and at New Community, Don Cousins assumed more of the day-to-day leadership of the staff and taught periodically.

Meanwhile attendance at Willow Creek continued to climb and brought a new challenge. Since the beginning days of Willow Creek, seekers had come primarily "on the arm of a believing friend" who helped them become assimilated into the life of the church. Suddenly we had an influx of seekers whose only connection with Willow Creek was an article they read over their morning coffee, or a "human-interest spot" on the evening news. We were delighted to have them; unfortunately, we had no mechanism for assimilating them. All our points of entry were big. Big weekend services. Big New Community. Big subministry events.

The only small-group opportunities we offered were discipleship groups, which required a two-year commitment to an intensive study program. Most newcomers were hesitant to make such a long-term commitment when they knew so little about God, Christianity, or Willow Creek. Those brave souls who *were* willing to jump into such a commitment had to go on a six-month waiting list, due to our severe shortage of trained group leaders.

It became obvious that in order for Willow Creek to continue to grow larger, it had to grow smaller. We had to begin to emphasize smaller events and smaller classes in which more personal interaction could be encouraged. As the eighties flew toward the nineties the problem of how to grow smaller became a pressing concern, and we began to prepare for a total transformation of our small-group ministry.

But finding a way to grow smaller was not the only concern prompted by our mushrooming attendance. Suddenly we were short on classroom space for kids, office space for staff, and video overflow areas for weekend attendees. So in the spring of 1989, we kicked off a $23 million building program that the board and elders believed would address both the challenges of growing bigger and the need to grow smaller.

The 210,000-square-foot addition would include a gymnasium for our youth ministries and for sports outreach activities, classrooms for children and adults, conference rooms for seminars and workshops, "breakout" rooms for small-group meetings, and a central atrium filled with tables, chairs, and a complete food service area. This inviting, sunlit room, where people could come throughout the day or before and after ministry events, would be ideal for small-group meetings, Bible studies, or sharing meals together. It would be the "great room" of Willow Creek, the place where people could connect, linger, relax, and be "part of the family."

A GROWING STAFF, CHURCH, AND SCHEDULE

While the new building would address some of Willow Creek's growth challenges, there were certain frustrations that no amount of brick and mortar could address. The reorganization of the staff to accommodate Bill's more frequent absences slowly eroded staff morale. Staff members who had been at Willow Creek since the beginning—"the old gang that had sat around Bill's campfire for years"—suddenly had virtually no access to him.

The rapid addition of new staff members, most of whom were hired from outside Willow Creek and often without Bill's direct involvement, added to the sense of upheaval. Suddenly there seemed to be two separate staffs. On one side were those who shared almost twenty years of ministry memories. These Willow Creek veterans had sacrificed time and money and energy during the difficult start-up era, when every ministry move was an exercise in faith. They knew how it felt to be treated like the "misguided child" of the Christian community; they had persevered through the Train Wreck; they had "grown up" as servants and ministers throughout the Buildup years; they had "owned" the calling for nearly two decades.

On the other side were the newcomers, the highly trained specialists who had been offered good salaries to join a nationally renowned team. With tender hearts and sincere zeal for God and ministry, these newcomers provided the "fresh legs" and "new insights" Willow Creek needed to enter the next era. But it wasn't easy for the "old gang" and the "fresh legs" to work together. It took time to discover the common points of their differing perspectives and to develop a mutual appreciation of the unique and necessary contributions of each group.

While individual staff members struggled with the relational dimension of a rapidly growing staff they also had to deal with radical operational changes. The comforting bond of a shared history and the ease of familiar patterns gave way to new people, new reporting structures, new procedures, and an unwelcome maze of memos, logistical hoops, and official policies. Suddenly what had seemed very personal became, by contrast at least, impersonal. The all-staff Christmas party that had been hosted for years by a beloved board member and that always ended with the staff singing Christmas carols around a piano gave way to a carefully programmed Christmas event for three hundred near-strangers in a conference room at the church. The all-staff retreat at Camp Paradise, where staff members water-skied with Bill and literally sat around the campfire together, gave way to one-day retreats at a local lodge, where staff members met with their department heads. For the veterans of the early years, the move from a small staff to a megastaff felt almost like "losing family," and many went through a period of grief.

What complicated these changes was that while the staff continued to grow and become increasingly complex in its operation, Bill's travel schedule accelerated and he progressively became more inaccessible. Day-to-day staff leadership was handled very ably by Don Cousins, but many staff members felt unsettled—and justifiably so—without the unifying vision-casting role that Bill had filled since the beginning.

Bill felt the weight of this frustration but was torn. His primary commitment was to Willow Creek, but God seemed to be blessing his expanded ministry. He tried to juggle both. Hardest to "fit in" was his teaching ministry at Willow Creek. Little preparation was required for his outside speaking, but he had to keep coming up with new messages for weekend and New Community services at home. It was not uncommon in 1989 for Bill to speak at New Community on Wednesday night, speak at a two-day conference somewhere in the U.S. or beyond on Thursday and Friday, prepare his weekend message at 4:00 a.m. in a hotel room or at midnight on an airplane, then speak at Willow Creek on Saturday night and twice on Sunday. On Monday morning he would begin working on his next New Community message. This schedule crossed the line of insanity when growth necessitated the addition of a second New Community on Thursday nights. Don Cousins taught at Willow Creek when Bill scheduled longer trips and missed a midweek or weekend service, but Bill continued as the primary teacher.

CRASH!

By December 1989 Bill was working seven days a week, coming home only to recuperate enough to get back to work. But he had reached his breaking point. One Saturday, just a few hours before the evening service and a few minutes before he had to officiate at a friend's wedding, Bill laid his head down on his desk and sobbed uncontrollably, entirely depleted of physical, emotional, and spiritual strength. As he said later, "Something broke inside me that day. I didn't know what it was, but it scared me. I felt as if I were coming apart at the seams."

Somehow he made it through the coming weeks, spoke at six Christmas Eve services, then left with us for a family vacation. We had been offered a quiet place in the sun by some dear friends, but the quiet was broken by holiday crowds, and we did not receive the refreshment we needed. By the time we returned home, Bill was in worse shape than when we left. He called the elders and said, "I don't know what I'm going through, but clearly I've not reached the end of it. I need to get away again." I had seen Bill stretched beyond the limit many times—his need to "recuperate" was a common topic of conversation in our family—but I had always been amazed by his ability to reenergize quickly, to bounce back almost overnight. I had never before seen him depleted to the point where he could not get himself recharged.

As the kids headed back to school Bill left for three days of solitude at a lodge in Wisconsin. He moved through those three days slowly, enjoying leisurely meals in small-town restaurants and ambling down quiet, tree-lined streets. He got a haircut and said, "Take your time. I'm in no hurry." For years a friend of ours had come to our home and squeezed in Bill's haircut between ministry events; it was so refreshing for him to be "in no hurry" for a change.

But the relaxed pace ended abruptly. The weekend teaching series he returned to in January 1990 was called "Negotiating the Maze of Life." If ever a series grew out of Bill's own struggle, it was that one. The month continued with the usual round of board meetings, staff meetings, administrative responsibilities, and New Community teaching, with a speaking trip to California thrown in. By the end of the month, Bill knew he was "not making it."

He left for a weeklong stay at a friend's home in a southern state, hoping to recuperate enough to face the February blitz: January responsibilities that he'd put off, fund-raising decisions for the new addition, a three-day Willow Creek pastors conference, separate speaking trips to California, Oregon, and Texas, and a driving trip with our son from California to Chicago. The weekend series that month was called "Christianity's Toughest Competition." The third week of that series, with a message called "Moralism," brought Willow Creek's highest regular weekend attendance to that point: 15,200. As the excitement and energy level at Willow Creek peaked, Bill slid farther into exhaustion and despair.

As he moved from February to March and April he had less and less energy for personal relationships or staff interactions. Decision making, one of his past strengths, had become a burdensome chore, and on more than one occasion he walked out of meetings prematurely, overwhelmed by the challenges of growth and change. Most distressing of all, teaching was becoming nearly impossible. More and more frequently he called on Don Cousins, Dr. Bilezikian, and other Willow Creek teachers to cover for him, though he tried to continue as the primary teacher.

A RADICAL SOLUTION

Clearly Bill was suffering from extreme exhaustion, but what exactly did that mean? Why had he gotten to that point? As he looked at his life more carefully one thing became clear to him: he was teaching way too much. Bill's top three gifts, in order of strength, are leadership, evangelism, and teaching. But he had allowed his ministry to become structured in such a way that he poured far more time and energy into teaching, which drains him, than into leadership or evangelism, both of which energize him. He was always two or three days away from his next teaching assignment, always trying to pump out new messages.

Emotionally Bill had begun to feel like a soldier. The next battle was always just around the corner. The adrenaline was always pumping. Spiritually he felt his heart and soul shrinking. He felt as if he were under orders more than under grace. He knew the duty of servanthood, but he experienced little of the joy of sonship. He felt unmotivated and depressed; he faced each new day simply because he had to. It was becoming clear that if he didn't learn to minister in a manner more consistent with who God created him to be, he was going to self-destruct. Somehow he had to reorder his ministry so he could teach less.

His solution? Team teaching.

When Bill came up with the idea of hiring another teacher to share the primary teaching responsibility with him, Christian leaders from all over the country counseled against it. "It will divide the church." "It will give rise to personality-based factions." "It will destroy everything you've tried to build during the past fifteen years." But Bill felt he had no choice. As he put it, the way he was doing the work of God was destroying the work of God in him. He had to find a different way to do it.

In June 1990 the elders hired Jim Dethmer, a senior pastor from Baltimore, to "team teach" with Bill. Bill was ecstatic. As we left on our summer study break in July, Bill could see the light at the end of the tunnel. He began to relax. He felt as if he had broken a destructive pattern, and he began to feel the softening presence of the Spirit at work in his life again.

CRISIS MODE

That summer during quiet mornings away from the demands of ministry, Bill examined more deeply the patterns of his life. It became obvious that overuse of his teaching gift wasn't his only problem. The general pace of his life, which had escalated dramatically during the latter half of the eighties, had forced him into a chronic condition that he later described as "crisis-mode living." That's when you spend every waking moment of every day anxiously trying to figure out how to continue juggling the fiercely competing demands of life. Everyone has to do this occasionally, but when it becomes an ongoing pattern of life, it becomes destructive. There's no time for quiet reflection. No time for recreation. No time to recharge one's emotional batteries. No time to deal with root issues. One skims across the surface of relationships, puts Band-Aids on gaping emotional wounds, and finds a stone-cold core of impatience where compassion used to be.

A passage in Dallas Willard's book *Spirit of the Disciplines* held Bill's attention in a vice grip during that time:

> How many people are radically and permanently repelled from The Way by Christians who are unfeeling, stiff, unapproachable, boringly life-less, obsessive, and dissatisfied? Yet such Christians are everywhere, and what they are missing is the wholesome liveliness springing from a balanced vitality within the freedom of God's loving rule.
>
> Such failure to attain a deeply satisfying life always has the effect of making sinful actions seem good. Here lies the strength of temptation. This is no less true if the failure is caused by our efforts to be what we regard as "spiritual." Normally, our success in overcoming temptation will be easier if we are basically happy in our lives. To cut off the joys and pleasures associated with our bodily and social existence as "unspiritual," then, can actually have the effect of *weakening* us in our efforts to do what is right. It makes it impossible for us to see and draw strength from the goodness of rightness.[1]

By no stretch of the imagination could Bill describe his frantic life as "satisfying," and though he had not become involved in the visible sins that had sidelined so many Christian leaders, he could not deny his increasing struggle with sinful attitudes of bitterness and resentment. More and more he felt that his life was unfair. When he heard of people enjoying life, he felt an anger building inside him that he could neither explain nor justify. When friends told stories of fun vacations, he fought vainly to beat down feelings of jealousy. He didn't like the life he was living. He didn't like the sins he was battling. He didn't like the haunting juxtaposition of his growing church and his shrinking heart.

Breaking these unhealthy patterns became Bill's summer goal. He spent time alone, replenishing himself emotionally; he read for pleasure; he engaged in fun, relaxing activities with the kids and me; he enjoyed lighthearted conversation with close friends; he lived slowly. It paid off. He began to feel refreshed. He knew he had only begun the process of healing, but already he was feeling healthier—as a husband, a father, a Christian, a pastor.

In September 1990 Bill started a new weekend series called "Building Bigger Hearts," which flowed out of the mounting sense that his own heart had begun to grow again. Jim Dethmer began teaching at New Community, and the congregation welcomed a new voice with a fresh perspective. In October we celebrated Willow Creek's fifteenth anniversary with a joyous outreach event called "What a Ride!" For Bill the anniversary was an authentic celebration, not just of fifteen years of God's blessing on Willow Creek but of his personal survival during a frightening year, of the apparent success of team teaching, and of his hopeful attitude toward the future.

REDEFINING COMMITMENT

That is not to say, however, that Bill's personal struggles were over. Though team teaching continued to be a tremendous help and though Bill was trying to incorporate more fun activities into his schedule—he went to "Barefoot Ski School" and took several rejuvenating trips with friends during the next year—his ministry schedule was still overloaded with past commitments he had to keep. Ministry opportunities outside Willow Creek kept him on the road more than at any time in the past, and while he had gotten beyond the panic points of the previous year, he was still battling exhaustion and a waning enthusiasm for ministry. During our spring vacation, in fact, he talked of leaving the ministry. "Perhaps it's time for a different kind of challenge. Perhaps I need to go back into the marketplace."

During our summer break of 1991, a friend loaned us a sailboat, and Bill was able to renew a youthful passion that had been crowded out of his life by the pace and financial limitations of ministry. For years we had rented a tiny summer cottage in a resort town on Lake Michigan, and there Bill would walk along the harbor, looking at boats and remembering the quiet hours he and his father had spent on the water. Now finally he could recapture that pleasure from his past. Our friend's boat was named *Blessing,* and for three summers it proved to be one—for the kids and me and especially for Bill. He spent long afternoons at the helm, letting the wind and waves renew him as they had in years past.

Much of Bill's summer reflection centered on one question: what does healthy commitment to the cause of Christ look like? He had concluded that his commitment to Christ had long ago ceased to be healthy, but he wasn't sure how or why that had happened. He began searching for an explanation by reexamining the verses that had shaped his concept of commitment during the early days of his Christian discipleship.

He recalled how he had been pierced by "self-denial" verses like Luke 9:23: "If anyone would come after me, he must deny himself and take up his cross daily and follow me." He remembered the impact of Acts 20:24, where Paul said, "I consider my life worth nothing to me, if only I may finish the race and complete the task the Lord Jesus has given me—the task of testifying to the gospel of God's grace." Prior to being challenged by these verses, Bill had only one intention: to live life *his way*. He had laid his plans and identified his goals, and they had little to do with God. So he had needed a radical call to commitment in order to break his "strong streak of selfish ambition" and to get him to consider what Christ might want him to do with his life.

Then there were the "serve others" verses. To someone as "hopelessly self-centered" as Bill admits to having been, Mark 9:35 was a jolt: "If anyone wants to be first, he must be the very last, and the servant of all." For Bill this was a new world order. And Jesus' words to Peter in Matthew 4:19, "I will make you fishers of men," sent him a clear and challenging message. While Bill had been almost totally consumed with commercial business, what really mattered, Jesus said, was people business. Slowly verses like these began to chip away at the self-centeredness in Bill's life.

Finally there were the "spiritual growth" verses. "Continue to work out your salvation with fear and trembling," Bill read in Philippians 2:12. "Train yourself to be godly," he read in 1 Timothy 4:7. Verses like that challenged him to assume responsibility for his spiritual growth. He realized he needed to devote himself to spiritual disciplines that would help him root out the sinful patterns in his life and strengthen himself for service.

I knew Bill in those days, and I knew how deeply those verses had changed him. I saw the transformation. How, in fact, could I *help* but see the transformation? Bill had always pursued his goals with intensity, whatever they were. Had he chosen to be an athlete, he would have pursued physical strength and stamina with intensity. Had he chosen to be a criminal, he would have pursued crime with intensity. Had he chosen to become a millionaire, he would have pursued money with intensity. When he chose to follow Paul's path of running a race for God, he knew of only one way to do it: to run with intensity. So at seventeen he put on his running shoes and headed out.

SAME VERSES, NEW PERSPECTIVE

As Bill began to run the race for God he discovered something wonderful: the joy and fulfillment of responsible Christian commitment. But after twenty years of ministry Bill began to understand that the very same verses that God had used so constructively in his life had, over time, been used by the Evil One to push him past responsible commitment into an unhealthy form of commitment that had almost sidelined him. He thought of Paul's words in 2 Corinthians 11:3: "But I am afraid that just as Eve was deceived by the serpent's cunning, your minds may somehow be led astray from your sincere and pure devotion to Christ." He began to see how he had been craftily lured from a simple and joyful love of God into a guilt-driven, anxiety-producing pattern of overwork "for the cause of Christ."

Those "self-denial" verses that had been so wonderfully used to break the back of selfish ambition in Bill's life had never been adequately explained to him. No one told him what it meant to "deny himself," so he applied his own interpretation: deny feelings. Seeing Bill's increasing exhaustion, an elder once asked him if he still enjoyed leading the church and teaching. Bill's immediate response: "Don't ask me that question. I can't afford to think about how I feel. I just have to get the job done. I just have to keep going."

Along with dying to honest feelings, Bill died to a host of wonderful, God-given desires—like recreational opportunities and replenishing relationships and ministry endeavors that genuinely excited him—because they seemed too fun and exciting to be "legal." He thought he had to just keep pounding away at the task at hand, and the more miserable it made him feel—the more it felt like "taking up his cross"—the better it was.

Eventually he came to a new interpretation of Luke 9:23: Die to the sinful aspects of your life that pull you away from God. Die to distorted thinking patterns and impure motives. Die to lust. Die to greed. Die to selfishness. Die to envy. But don't die to the "self" inside you that God created. Don't deny the passions and dreams he has given you. Don't assume that every desire is sinful and every personal aspiration is bad. Don't dismiss legitimate needs for rest and recreation, pleasure and friendship.

Bill learned how destructive it can be to ignore—as many Christians do—the smiling whisper of God that says, "You can enjoy this pleasure. You can live to this dream. You can experience this rest. You can taste this joy. You have my blessing." If we become embittered in our spirits and resentful of what it means to follow Christ, it may well be that we have denied more than God asks us to.

Bill also looked again at the "serve others" verses. So often they were backed up with the challenge of the Good Samaritan: as the Samaritan took the beaten Jew to an inn, bandaged his wounds, and paid for his lodging, so we must care for the needy people in our world. Time and again Bill, myself, and other staff members heard this story and recommitted ourselves to serving others. But we never considered the unanswered questions the story raises. What about the obvious limits to the Samaritan's mercy? He didn't take the beaten man home with him and say, "You can move into my house for the month it takes you to recuperate." He didn't cancel his business trip in order to care for the wounded man.

And what about the scope of the Samaritan's mercy? What if there had been forty-five beaten Jews on the road to Jericho? Would the Samaritan have rescued them all? Would he have loaded them on a donkey one at a time? Would he have gone back for load after load? Would he have filled the hotel? Or emptied his bank account?

We never asked these questions during the early years of our ministry. But the reality of Christian leadership is that we are surrounded by overwhelming needs. How many of them should we try to meet? How often should we try to meet them? To what extent should we go? When is enough enough? There are no easy answers to these questions, but when one serves past the point of exhaustion and bitterness, he has probably gone too far.

As Bill began to see the distortion in his attitude toward service he began to focus on the serving patterns of Jesus, God in the flesh. Jesus was undoubtedly the most empowered, inspired, and energized Christian leader the world has ever known, yet He often said, "That's it for today. No more healings. No more feedings. No more counseling. No more teaching. My coworkers and I need to get in the boat and cross over to the other side and camp out for a night or two. We need to get refreshed." Jesus knew where the limits were. He knew when giving became self-destructive, and He refused to push Himself or His disciples that far.

Bill realized he had pushed himself to the point where his devotion to God had lost the sweetness of earlier years and his service to others had lost the spirit of love that should motivate it. Clearly it was time to take a lesson from Jesus.

It was also time to reevaluate his long-term response to the "spiritual growth" verses that had motivated him so powerfully for years. Bill has always been one to thrive on challenge and to enjoy challenging others. Therefore the environment at Willow Creek has generally been a "high challenge" environment. Keep growing. Set high standards. Strive to achieve them. All well and good—except when we take on too much of the responsibility for our spiritual growth or when we begin to see growth as a means of earning God's favor. Slowly Bill had moved away from a daily awareness of the ongoing work of the Holy Spirit in him and toward a growing dependence on his own efforts to grow spiritually. But that was becoming a burden. He had to slow down, let go of his anxious and driven pursuit of growth, and learn to trust more in the work of God in and through him.

As Bill began to adopt a healthier perspective on commitment he gradually began to feel refreshed. He felt the warmth of compassion seeping into his soul again. He felt himself relaxing in his relationship with God and feeling again the unconditional love that had so moved him as a teenager.

UNSEEN WOUNDS

I was grateful for the changes taking place in Bill's life. But his journey toward those changes had taken its toll on me. For over fifteen years I had been working conscientiously behind the scenes to protect the stability of our home against the pressures of frantic schedules, unrealistic expectations, and loss of privacy. In order to alleviate the stress in Bill's life and in order to allow him to devote whatever free time he had to our children, I had taken nearly full responsibility for the practical demands of home ownership and child rearing. I had also edited several books for Bill, which had left little time for my personal involvement in Willow Creek ministries, though I had begun to find a writing and speaking niche through our women's ministry and outside Willow Creek. But the added time demands and emotional pressures associated with Bill's recent "crash" had drained me. For years I had battled depression. As 1990 came to a close I felt I was losing the battle. In January 1991 I walked into a Christian counselor's office.

The choice to take that walk was one of the wisest I have ever made, but it was also one of the most difficult. And it only became harder as the weeks and months went on. As I discovered unseen wounds deep inside me that had for years undermined my pursuit of meaning, joy, peace—and God—I became angry. As I began to unravel the tangled knot of my own feelings about my life I sank into a dark place of sadness. It ended up being a place of healing; I came out of that era with a far more intimate relationship with God, a clearer understanding and a healthier acceptance of myself, a less driven yet more passionate approach to ministry, and a stronger, more joyful "self" to bring to my husband and children. But for a time life was extremely painful. I withdrew from public life, from friendships, and sadly, from Bill. I wanted to be a good wife to him. I wanted to support him as he faced the demands of ministry. But I couldn't do it.

Bill was already nearly overwhelmed with the challenges of life. How could he add one more burden? How could he handle "a broken wife"?

It was this challenge—of coping with my brokenness—that finally pushed him into a Christian counselor's office as well. He had already tried to "fix me" by applying to my wounds the same balms that had seemed to heal him, but his efforts had failed; in fact, they had pushed me farther into despair. Finally he realized that he could not solve my problems. The most he could do for me was be patient and accepting of my earnest though faltering attempts to find wholeness. Lovingly he committed himself to that.

But he needed, for his own survival, to find a way to cope with my ongoing struggle. Ministry was moving as fast as ever; somehow Bill had to keep up with it, regardless of the drama unfolding at home.

THE GOOD SHIP *CRISIS MODE*

The counselor suggested first that Bill continue the process he had already begun, that of reorienting his relationship with God. For years Bill had looked to God for strength and power and wisdom. Now he had to learn to look to God for tender, nurturing love. Bill began to focus on Scripture passages and Christian books that emphasized this aspect of his relationship with God. Gradually his prayer life began to change. As he opened himself up to a gentler side of God he began to experience grace and divine love in a new way. During those times when he grieved my inability to offer him the nurturing love he desired, he was able to find comfort in this softer side of his relationship with God.

The counselor also suggested that Bill seek nurturing care and kindness from a few safe, mature friends who had high integrity. "Go to them," he suggested, "and tell them you are going through a difficult era and you need an extra dose of love and encouragement."

Asking for help in areas of personal or emotional life did not fit Bill's normal way of operating. "I hate to be needy," he told the counselor. But he knew he had reached a point in his life where he could no longer afford to hide behind an image of self-sufficiency. Gradually he allowed a few close friends to see and respond to the sadness and loneliness in his life.

Next the counselor encouraged Bill in his ongoing attempts to "lighten up" at work. "Don't let your job add to the sorrow in your life," he said. "Eliminate as many of the draining, joy-killing aspects of your work as possible." For so many years Bill had been "pounding," working as fast and pushing as hard as he could. It was time to try to create a job description he could enjoy more, one that made him look forward to getting up in the morning. With the increasing pain in our relationship, he had to try to create a work environment that was as pain-free as possible.

The counselor's fourth suggestion, to pay careful attention to his physical well-being, was not hard for Bill to hear and apply. For health reasons he had already become conscientious about diet and nutrition, and as he quit pounding so hard at work and eased the flow of adrenaline he naturally developed healthier sleeping patterns.

But the counselor's final suggestion was one Bill could not so easily incorporate into his life. "You need to develop some energizing, heart-filling form of recreation," he said. "And you need to pursue it to the point of satiation. You need to have raucous fun!" It wasn't that Bill didn't know what to do for fun; his buried love for sailboat racing had resurfaced even before the counselor finished speaking. But sailboat racing was out of the question. Years earlier Bill had given up the dream of ever owning a boat. It was part of the decision we had made together: to avoid anything that might provide "scandal material" to anyone attempting to discredit us or Willow Creek. We could envision a less-than-honest journalist photographing a sailboat in such a way that it looked like a two-hundred-foot yacht and claiming it had been purchased at church expense or some such outrageous lie. Boats, we had concluded, fit in the "dangerous" category; we could never own one.

"I wish I were a golfer or a gardener," Bill complained. But he wasn't, and the deeper the pain in our personal life became, the more he wished he could enjoy the exhilarating fun of racing. In the spring of 1993, we followed what seemed to be the tender, gracious leading of God and did the unthinkable: using income from book royalties, we made a low offer on an eight-year-old, thirty-five-foot race boat. A month later the desperate owner accepted our offer. As Bill signed the check he thanked God for granting him the "internal permission" to pursue good old-fashioned fun and prayed that God would use the boat to accomplish His purposes.

Bill named the boat *Crisis Mode*, put together a crew of nine unchurched racing fanatics, and sketched out a racing schedule. For Bill the racing program combined three energizing factors: fierce competition, coalescing and building a team-crew, and personal evangelism. During the summers of 1993 and 1994 *Crisis Mode* won more races on Lake Michigan than any boat in its class and won second place in national competition, and Bill's crew reached extraordinary levels in terms of both skill and enjoyment of the sport. However, the highlight of Bill's racing career came on June 26, 1994, when he baptized the captain of his racing crew.

Crisis mode as a way of life has for the most part become a thing of the past. *Crisis Mode*, the boat, may soon pass on to a new owner. But the summers Bill spent at her helm—or during races, stationed in the companionway doing "runners" or "grinding"—helped offset the growing sadness in our personal life. It provided exactly what the counselor had suggested: acceptable but raucous fun. As Bill said recently, "That boat has brought me such joy that I'm almost ashamed to admit it."

The suggestions given to Bill by his counselor were basic, practical ways of dealing with pain. I include them here because I suspect that some of you reading this book may be carrying high levels of pain in your lives as well. The reality, for most of us, is that life is hard. And the sad truth is that it might not get any easier. So what do we do? Pretend that the inevitable disappointments, losses, and heartaches of life don't really hurt that much, and live with a buried despair that forces us into a state of emotional deadness? Or acknowledge the difficulty of life and find acceptable and spiritually sound ways to compensate for the sadness? Far better, I think, is the second option, which allows us to experience life authentically and to discover joy in the midst of pain.

TOUCHING THE SOUL

Bill was exceedingly grateful for the wise counsel he received. It kept him from being consumed by the sad state of our relationship, which had been thrown into such chaos by my inner struggles. But the counselor was not content to let Bill focus entirely on coping with *my* problems. Just as Bill was leaving a counseling session—confident that he could stay strong enough to continue the work that gave his life meaning, regardless of how long it took me to "fix myself"—the counselor asked one more question: "Have you ever considered looking inside yourself?"

Bill was not pleased. He had never been accused of being overly contemplative, and he was not about to enter the realm of the "navel gazers." Discussions about whether or not his diapers had fit properly or whether his nursery had been painted the right color had not earned a place on his "to do" list.

But the counselor probed. "Describe three times during your growing-up years when a person or an event touched your soul."

"Define 'touching the soul,'" said Bill.

"I shouldn't have to," said the counselor.

Bill had grown up in a staunch Dutch subculture in which the highest values included hard work, autonomy, self-sufficiency, frugality, and an unquestioning submission to the sovereignty of God. They were good values, noble values, and many of them had served Bill well, but some of them, when pushed to excess, encouraged the repression of honest emotion and discouraged the expression of legitimate needs. "Buck up" was the proper response to nearly everything.

As a child Bill learned well how to buck up. He learned to work hard, to be independent, to get tough, to follow the rules, and to perform in ways that would assure him a "head nod of approval" and a "smile of recognition" from those around him. Though his parents loved him and expressed that love in every way they knew how, the messages of his subculture had confused him. It was hard for him to separate love from approval and recognition. He knew he wanted love; he concluded that performing well was the way to get it.

Excelling in sports and distinguishing himself in student government were two ways to get the "love" he wanted. But when he became a Christian and discovered that serving God faithfully on earth would earn him a "well done" in heaven, he believed he had discovered the ultimate pathway to love. He committed himself to doing whatever it took to get that kind of approval and recognition from God.

As the counselor continued to push him deeper into the realities of his inner life Bill began to be flooded by two different yet entwined feelings: sadness and shame.

He tried to hold the sadness at bay, but it unexpectedly erupted one day as he drove to Detroit for a speaking engagement. For ninety minutes he wept while he drove, swept into grief by the stabbing realization that he had spent over thirty years of his life working and striving and pounding and pushing himself to the point of collapse—in part, to satisfy his longing for love. When his counselor had told him that each of us ought to receive love "just for showing up," Bill had laughed: love, he knew, was something you had to work for. Now he realized, with intense sadness, that he had been wrong. In his mind he watched a year-by-year documentary of his lifetime search for love, and he grieved.

The shame filled him when he faced the unsettling reality that while the Holy Spirit had fueled much of his drive for ministry, he had also been driven by his unmet emotional needs. He realized that as Willow Creek had grown bigger the increased approval and recognition he received felt remarkably like love to him. So in subtle ways—pushed by an unconscious drive—he had sought more and more success. He realized that part of his earlier concern about my "struggles" had been his awareness that it was not advantageous for a Christian leader to have a broken wife; he feared that he could not be as successful without my help or that I would somehow jeopardize the image that had earned him approval and recognition. He hated seeing the truth of that.

Bill didn't want that pain-driven pattern to continue. Through conversations with his counselor and with trusted friends, he pursued a deeper understanding of his emotional needs and committed himself to dealing with those needs in appropriate and direct ways so they would exert less control over his relationships and work habits. As he learned more about his own emotional and behavioral patterns he began to see more clearly the havoc wreaked on churches by "pathological pastors" who fail to understand the unconscious needs that drive them.

"Many of us," he says, "are crippled more than we realize by wounds and distortions we don't even know we're carrying, which cause us to behave destructively in relationships and in ministry. We may be harboring anger that leads us into harsh preaching or a controlling style of leadership. We may be filled with fear that makes us hesitant to walk out on limbs of faith. We may be shame-based and unable to stand up against criticism. We may be so hungry for love, as I was, that we will work ourselves nearly to death to try to get a poor substitute."

I am finishing this chapter at the desk in front of the window in my home office. Powdery snow just covered the grayness of our weathered backyard deck with a blue-white foam. Bill just walked in to see if I would finish my work in time to greet the friends who will be joining us soon to watch a Chicago Bears play-off game.

It is January 1, 1995. In the next chapter I will move the story back into the proper chronological sequence, but please excuse me as I wander off the timeline for a paragraph or two.

As Bill and I watched the year-end countdown televised from Times Square last night we were not sorry to bid farewell to 1994 or to an era of our lives that we seem, thankfully, to be leaving. In December 1989 Bill crashed in an explosion of tears in his office on a Saturday afternoon, and in December the following year, I was overwhelmed by the depression that had tormented me for years. For the past five years our personal life has been in turmoil as we have tripped over one another's pain and stumbled over one difficult lesson after the next.

But we enter the new year hopefully. We both believe that the hard work of the past five years has rewarded each of us with a firmer foundation on which to build the future. We have both looked deep inside, discovered previously unseen wounds and the hidden agendas issuing from them, repented of ugly sins, broken destructive patterns, and learned new ways of relating to God, to our friends and family, and to each other. We think we have grown in ways that bode well for our future as individuals and as a couple, both in ministry and in our personal life.

But neither of us anticipates a problem-free future. We move into 1995 with a new appreciation for the complexity and sadness of life. As long as we live in a world infiltrated by evil, we human beings are going to take our hits. Until God redeems the church, we're going to know pain and heartache. Sometimes when we look at our lives, we will see a black hole of despair, and the only comfort we will find will be the promise that things will be different in heaven. On this earth, we follow a Savior who was "acquainted with grief," and unless we live in denial, most of us will experience a measure of the grief he knew.

Hours ago I sat by the hospital bed of a friend whose hip had been broken in an auto accident caused by a drunk driver. Thankfully, her young children sustained physical injuries no more severe than bruises and broken ribs. But the terror of their second serious car crash in three years will not soon leave them. Vacillating between gratitude that their lives were spared and anger at the driver who hit them, she said to me, "Why are we so surprised when these things happen? Why do we so quickly forget that disappointments and losses and tragedies are a part of life?"

It's true. For most of us the good times, the pleasures, and the successes will be experienced alongside pain and loss and sorrow. Life is, after all, a tangled web. Our great challenge, then, as Christians, is to discover in our God a peace, a comfort, and a joy that is deep and strong and real enough to thrive in the sin-touched reality of our human lives. That has been the most significant focus of the past few years for Bill and for me. Building Willow Creek for almost twenty years has been extraordinarily challenging. But far more demanding has been our effort to build "the church in our hearts." Far harder it has been to create that quiet sanctuary within us where faith is strong enough, and God is near enough, to make an authentic difference in the way we live our lives.

NOTE

1. Dallas Willard, *The Spirit of the Disciplines* (San Francisco: Harper & Row, 1988), 80–81.

chapter seven

THE IDENTITY CRISIS
1992–94

*In the early eighties, fresh from the trauma of the Train Wreck, Bill
and other church leaders were asking serious questions about the
values and the identity of Willow Creek. In the early nineties, though
for different reasons, we were asking those same questions again:
Who are we? What is our mission? What does the future hold? It was
a difficult era of evaluation and sometimes-painful change.*

BETTY SCHMIDT,
WILLOW CREEK ELDER

Unfortunately, Bill and I weren't the only ones struggling in the early nineties. The demands of ministry, radical staff changes, the pace of life, family responsibilities, and accumulated exhaustion seemed to be catching up with many of the staff and lay leaders who had been at Willow Creek since the beginning. Some had been running full steam ahead since the Son City days. Now, without the energy of youthful idealism, life wasn't working quite so well. Many felt, as I did, that the "Willow Creek phenomenon" had forced us to grow up too fast. In our twenties and early thirties life had been so serious; we had carried such heavy responsibilities. Now, though barely on the brink of midlife, many of us felt worn down and weary; we dreaded the thought of a future rolling along at the same pace as the past.

The next two years (1992–93) saw many staff members and lay leaders reassess their gifts and redefine their job descriptions. They realized that after ten or fifteen years of doing the same thing at the same place, they were ready for a change. Some pursued new forms of ministry elsewhere or entered the marketplace. Others transferred to different departments within Willow Creek, where they assumed new responsibilities with renewed enthusiasm. Many continued in their same position but lightened their ministry load; after "hitting it hard" for so many years, they needed to work—and live—at a slower pace. To honor those who had offered years of uninterrupted service, the elders granted a number of short sabbaticals and provided educational and travel opportunities for restoration and refreshment.

In order to move away from leadership patterns tainted by what became affectionately called "your junk and my junk," many key leaders of Willow Creek entered, as Bill had, an era of increased attention to personal issues. Since the aftermath of the Train Wreck over a decade earlier, Bill and other members of the Willow Creek leadership team had made valiant attempts to live with greater balance in their lives. For too many the attempts had been in vain. For them the time had come to ask tough questions and face hard truths. Many began painful inward journeys; some entered counseling. An intern at Willow Creek during that era bemoaned that he had come to learn how to start a church, "but you guys have muddied it all up with all this talk about 'discovering your issues and working on your stuff.' How in the world am I supposed to start a church if I can't be a flat-out workaholic?"

This emphasis on emotional authenticity and healing made its way into the weekend and midweek services. While it was not the dominant theme of the teaching ministry, series such as the winter 1992 series called "Hunger for Healing" (based on the twelve steps of the recovery group movement) beckoned Willow Creek attendees to emotional as well as spiritual growth. Though such teaching was beneficial for many people in the church, it was probably most reflective of and responsive to the needs of many staff and lay leaders during that era. It offered a necessary midcourse correction for a group of hardworking servants of God who had for too long lived in crisis mode, held distorted views of Christian commitment, and ignored legitimate emotional needs. For many it was a painful era but also a time of healing, renewal, and positive change.

ORGANIZATIONAL BREAKDOWN

Unfortunately, it was a time of chaos for the church. With Bill and so many key leaders going through personal transitions, there developed a subtle sense of insecurity throughout the church. Numerous staff changes, Bill's frequent absences, and the positive yet disorienting dynamics of team teaching all contributed to a sense of uncertainty about the leadership and future of Willow Creek.

Also, it was becoming increasingly apparent that the infrastructure of Willow Creek, which had been built up during the eighties, was no longer adequate to handle the size and complexity of the ministry. Our rapid increase in attendance between 1988 and 1991 had created a demand for ministry services that we could not keep up with. We had no effective way to assimilate new people. Our procedure for formalized membership had created a bottleneck. Hundreds of people were on small-group waiting lists. People who had discovered their spiritual gifts and were eager to serve found it increasingly difficult to connect with service opportunities. Our information system—which had jumped from 30 computers to 130 in a matter of months—was caving in. Our pastoral care department and counseling center were swamped. Our weekend children's ministry, with its hundreds of volunteers, had become an organizational nightmare. Our church relations department was overwhelmed by demands from churches worldwide. New Community attendance had begun to drop as it became harder and harder to address the diverse educational needs of such a wide spectrum of people.

The list of "breakdowns" could go on and on. Throughout the Buildup years, growth had been steady and change had been manageable. When something needed to be fixed, the staff took care of it. If something wasn't working optimally, they tweaked it. But suddenly the infrastructure needed a lot more than a tweak. It was as if we had a twenty-story building resting on a foundation built for ten stories. As the foundation started shifting, the tremors were felt throughout the entire building.

It was becoming evident to more and more people that something was seriously wrong. Attendees were asking: How can I get to know people? How can I get involved? Lay leaders were asking: Why does everything suddenly seem so disorganized? Why aren't the systems working anymore? Staff members were wondering: How can we be expected to meet so many people's needs?

Bill used a different metaphor when he said later, "It wasn't as if a spark plug misfired. It was as if the crankshaft melted down. So we couldn't just go in there with a little wrench. We had to tear the motor apart."

It was clear we needed a major department and management restructuring, but the timing was terrible. Bill had not completely recuperated from his recent exhaustion and was becoming increasingly confused by the conflict between his growing national role and his responsibilities at Willow Creek. The elder board was in a state of flux, with several long-term and well-loved elders retiring and new members joining the board. A number of senior staff members had recently left, and others appeared to be heading in that direction as they reevaluated their gifts, passions, and calling.

A TOUGH TRANSITION

In October 1991 we added a fourth weekend service to handle increasing attendance, and by February 1992 we hit our highest nonholiday weekend attendance ever: 17,010. But the attendance peak proved to be a false high. Many of these new people entering Willow Creek's front door appeared to be exiting out the back. We could draw people in as effectively as ever, but we could no longer provide the personal, nurturing ministry they needed. As attendance began to drop steadily the questions about Willow Creek's future and its restructuring had condensed into one: Can the megachurch survive? It had become apparent that the structures that had worked for 10,000 people didn't work for 12,000 or 14,000 or 16,000. Was there another option? Could we discover it before it was too late?

It was obvious that unless we intended to add hundreds of new staff members, we needed to transfer more of the hands-on ministry of the church from staff personnel to lay leaders than we had done in the past. We also needed to develop a ministry structure that would facilitate assimilation of new people, offer church attenders more personalized care, provide increased discipleship opportunities, expand service options, and produce new leaders. Central to accomplishing these goals was to create more realistic spans of care throughout the ministry, which meant that each staff or lay leader should have a realistically limited number of people to lead and serve. Bill and the elders believed this could be done through an adaptation of Carl George's metachurch model of small-group ministry. Jim Dethmer was given the task of shaping the basic model into a form that fit the unique Willow Creek ministry. His goal was to help "grow Willow Creek smaller" by bringing a new small-group emphasis to every department of the church.

With staff morale already sagging, Jim's job of transitioning to a new ministry model was nearly impossible. Many staff members were asked to shift from "doing ministry" to "utilizing volunteers." Some could make the shift, but many couldn't; in almost every department there was huge staff turnover and a growing sense of insecurity among remaining employees. By the fall of 1992 when we created a long-overdue human resources department, staff morale had reached a new low. In meeting after meeting, elders, management team members, and human resource representatives met with department heads and other staff members to work through conflicts and misunderstandings and to revise numerous job descriptions in an attempt to meet the needs of the growing ministry while protecting the interests of hardworking, faithful church employees.

It was an extremely difficult era—the kind in which solutions seem clear in retrospect but nearly impossible to discern at the time.

POSITIVE CHANGES

But despite these growing pains, we were clearly headed in a positive direction. In March 1992 we celebrated the opening of our new building addition. As with the opening of the original auditorium in 1981, this move seemed to signal our entry into a new era. The leadership body of Willow Creek had realized the need to grow the church smaller, new ministry structures had been set in place, and now we had a physical structure that facilitated the shift to a more personalized form of ministry.

I remember overlooking the atrium area from the second-floor balcony, listening to the hum of hundreds of conversations being enjoyed by families and small groups gathered around the tables of our "great room." Then I walked through the hallways of Promiseland, peeking into breakout rooms filled with groups of eight to ten kids learning Bible truths from a volunteer leader. During the week there were small groups of women scattered throughout the building in Bible studies or service groups. Members of the dads ministry met for breakfast and joined in prayer around tables in the atrium before heading off to their jobs in the marketplace. After attending the aerobics classes taught in the new gymnasium, men and women from the church, often with unchurched friends from their neighborhood, met in groups for study and personal sharing. Clearly we were heading in the right direction.

In other areas too, problems were slowly being faced and solved. In the fall of 1992, we launched the New Community Institute to provide a broader range of teaching options at the midweek services. Three times each year, the institute offers four-week classes on Wednesday and Thursday nights. New Community attendees gather together for corporate worship, then divide to attend one of fifteen to twenty classes offered, including Bible studies, marriage and family workshops, leadership training classes, doctrine and theology studies, and more.

Also in the fall of 1992, the Willow Creek Association (WCA) was formed as a ministry separate from the church to respond to the needs of seeker-oriented ministries worldwide. The WCA lifted a tremendous burden off Willow Creek staff members by assuming responsibility for Willow Creek's church leadership conferences and for the publishing and distribution of curriculum and training materials. In less than two years there were fifteen full-time employees working with nearly a thousand churches worldwide. It has been exciting to watch the WCA cross denominational, racial, and cultural barriers and encourage a spirit of cooperation, encouragement, and mutual benefit between diverse ministries that share the common goal of turning irreligious people into fully devoted followers of Jesus Christ.

A major restructuring of the pastoral care department was also completed, creating a system that not only meets people with dire needs at their point of breakdown but also assists them in "mainstreaming" back into the ongoing life of the church. Our counseling center, which had become unwieldy because of the number of both counselors and counselees involved, was transitioned into an assessment and referral center, more effectively utilizing the talents and expertise of godly and proven Christian counselors in our community. Our formal membership procedure was revised to eliminate the bottleneck inherent in the old system. Our department of Single Adult Ministries (SAM) shifted its emphasis from large-group gatherings to medium- and small-group experiences in order to enhance the processes of assimilation and spiritual growth; SAM now produces hundreds of mature leaders and servants who are critical to the ongoing local ministry of Willow Creek and to our ministry efforts worldwide.

These changes, and many others throughout various departments, did not immediately reverse our sinking attendance trends. In fact, by the end of 1993 our fourth service had been discontinued and weekend attendance had dropped by thousands—the first time since the Train Wreck that we had experienced a long-term drop. But the infrastructure of the church was "working" again, and thousands of people were discovering Willow Creek to be a place where they could feel both challenged and cared for.

GAINS AND LOSSES

At a recent staff Christmas party I was ambushed, as I often am, by an almost maternal feeling of love and appreciation for various staff members. That night I talked with Scott Pederson, who became friends with Bill when they were teenagers, moved with Bill to Illinois in 1972, became one of the original Son City team captains, then later started Sonlight Express, Willow Creek's junior high ministry, which he led for over a decade. I saw George Everding and Scott Troeger, both of whom became Christians in the early seventies—Scott through Son City and George through Camp Paradise; years later, they headed up the construction of both our major building additions. I visited with Scott's wife, Jan Troeger, a faithful servant since the Son City days, who is now on Willow Creek's board of directors. I talked with staff members who had moved their families halfway across the country (we seem to have a disproportionate number of displaced Californians!) and others who had been called by God to Willow Creek against all rational thought.

Though I can no longer be personally acquainted with every staff member, many I have known through the years have inspired and encouraged me tremendously. And when I see them collectively, united by their shared vision and gathered together by a divine orchestration, I feel awed and grateful and protective. Each time I meet a new staff member and hear their story and capture their vision, I feel again that old sense of being caught up in a miracle.

In the early nineties many new staff members joined us, and almost every time we ended up saying, "This is amazing. God brought the perfect person just in the nick of time." But for nearly every person who joined us another person left, and the exhilaration of welcoming new staff members was more than matched by the disappointment of saying good-bye to those leaving. In fact, the departure of staff members has been one of the hardest things for Bill and me to deal with since the beginning of Willow Creek.

In September 1992, after nearly twenty years of faithful, effective service to high school students and to adults, Don Cousins decided to leave the Willow Creek staff and pursue an independent teaching-consulting ministry. Few people will ever understand the kind of working relationship Don and Bill enjoyed for so many years. Don was just sixteen and Bill twenty when they met. Don had grown up at South Park Church. When Bill began teaching the Wednesday night Bible study that eventually became Son City, Don responded with a spiritual intensity that Bill could relate to. Don was disciplined, aggressive, and goal oriented. When Don became the captain of Son City's Red Team, his natural leadership gifts also became obvious. As Bill mentored Don in spiritual growth, leadership, and teaching, their friendship grew, as did Don's potential for ministry. By the time he was thirty-five, Don had built up a ministry infrastructure that responded to the needs of thousands of people.

But Don had been "pounding the same nail"—at a frantic pace—for almost twenty years. Like many of us, he felt it was time for a change. His decision to leave was a difficult one, both for him to make and for others to accept. After extensive conversations between Don and Bill and the elders, there was a consensus that Don's decision was indeed in line with God's leading. Still, for Bill and many others, particularly the veteran staff members who had served with Don since the beginning, the thought of moving into the future without their friend and colaborer was darkened by a sense of loss and sadness.

With team teaching easing much of Bill's teaching burden, Bill had been able—even before Don's departure—to reengage with the staff and provide some of the leadership direction he had offered in the past. Now, with Don's absence, Bill was prodded into even greater staff involvement. He welcomed this; in fact, this hands-on leadership role was what he enjoyed most about his job. He had not yet regained his "full strength"—emotionally and physically—but he was clearly feeling healthier all the time. By the early months of 1993, he was actually beginning to enjoy ministry again.

Then in March, during an indoor soccer game with a group of unchurched friends, Bill ruptured an Achilles tendon. Surgery and painful complications kept him in the hospital for nearly a week. Two weeks on his back with his leg elevated put him out of commission for our Easter services. It is an understatement to say that Bill was deeply grateful for Jim Dethmer's partnership in the teaching ministry. Jim willingly taught at six Easter services and eased Bill's load in numerous other ways while Bill recuperated.

Crutches and a full-leg cast slowed Bill down for many months, but the forced "cutback" sparked a time of personal reflection and reevaluation that yielded a valuable reward. By the fall of 1993, Bill felt genuinely excited about ministering at Willow Creek and had come up with a simplified vision of his role outside Willow Creek, through the Willow Creek Association. It had been years since I had seen Bill living so sanely and feeling so positive about ministry. It had taken over three years for Bill to work his way back from his "crash" in December of 1989, but he entered the 1993–94 ministry season feeling strong spiritually, emotionally, and physically.

It was a good thing Bill was feeling so strong. Team teaching, which had been his ticket to survival throughout the struggle of the previous years, had just suffered a devastating setback. During the summer months Jim Dethmer had decided to leave the staff to also pursue an independent teaching-counseling ministry. The decision had been agonizing for Jim. Sitting in a sailboat on Lake Michigan, Bill and I listened as Jim discussed his reasons and his options. We couldn't disagree with his decision, but we had a hard time accepting it. Though Jim had been at Willow Creek for only three years, he had made a tremendous contribution. He had helped to prove the viability of team teaching. He had started our small-group "revolution." And even more important, he had become a close personal friend to Bill, to me, and to many other staff and lay leaders. At the small-group leaders retreat that fall, Jim gave his final messages to the leaders he had built up and inspired. As he concluded his remarks several close friends, myself included, joined him onstage to offer formal farewells. Then over a thousand people surrounded us in concentric circles, and together we joined in a community embrace, which was deeply symbolic of the legacy Jim was leaving us. He had become greatly loved and would be greatly missed.

There had previously been five members of the teaching team. Bill and Jim had been the primary teachers, with supplemental teaching offered by Don Cousins, Lee Strobel (Willow Creek management team member and director of communications), and Dan Webster. Dan had effectively led Willow Creek's high school ministry, Student Impact (formerly Son City), since the early eighties, but he had recently decided to move out of youth ministry, and new ministry opportunities had taken him out of state. The loss of Don, Dan, and now Jim left Bill once again carrying an enormous teaching load. Lee could help with the weekend teaching, but Bill immediately began looking for a primary New Community teacher. In July and August he contacted several potential teachers; each considered the call but in the end felt led to stay where they were.

It was a huge disappointment for Bill. He was eager to devote himself more fully to Willow Creek than he had in recent years, but he feared the teaching burden. What did God have in mind? Why didn't God provide a teacher to share the responsibility? There seemed to be only one recourse: prayer. And pray we did—that God would either provide a teacher or give Bill the energy he needed to handle the burden.

In September 1993 Bill began a twenty-five-part weekend series on the Sermon on the Mount called "The Greatest Sermon in History." By the time the series ended, it was clear that God had indeed given Bill the energy he needed. The series proved to be a rallying time for the church. It carried that sanctified blend of grace and challenge that had marked the early years of Son City and the Buildup era of the early eighties. It showed seekers the relevance of Jesus' words about morality and relationships and priorities, and called believers to commitment and discipleship. There was a renewed sense at the weekend services that, as individuals and as a church, we were moving forward. At our December baptism service, hundreds of adults gave public witness of their personal decisions to become followers of Christ. As we moved into the early months of 1994 declining attendance trends reversed.

But while the weekend services enjoyed a growing sense of stability and momentum, the midweek services were suffering. Bill had adequately scheduled them through March 1994 by using the New Community Institute and outside speakers, and by speaking himself when necessary. But the New Community was getting everybody's leftovers. Nobody owned it. Nobody could provide consistent worship leadership and teaching. The situation was becoming critical. Prayer groups throughout the church put "a New Community teacher" at the top of their lists. The elders reintensified their search. It became Bill's single greatest concern.

In March, Dieter Zander, a senior pastor from California who had filled in as a worship leader at New Community the previous December, returned to Willow Creek as a possible candidate for a worship leader and teacher. For the congregation it was love at first sight. When Dieter returned the following week, God's design seemed obvious. Shortly thereafter Dieter joined the staff. In keeping with the unpredictable blessing of a God "who is able to do immeasurably more than all we ask or imagine," Dieter was not the only addition to our teaching team. Several months later John Ortberg, another outstanding senior pastor from California, joined the Willow Creek staff as the primary New Community teacher and supplemental weekend teacher. Once again God had provided the people we needed.

COMING BACK FULL CIRCLE

By the fall of 1994, Willow Creek had clearly entered a new era. Bill's enthusiasm for leadership was sky-high. A strong teaching team was in place again. Numerous subministries and departments had been restructured and seemed to be working optimally. Major staff tensions had been resolved, and a system was in place to deal with inevitable new challenges as they arose. And most dramatically, small groups had "infiltrated" nearly every area of ministry, just as we had hoped.

The small-group transition, which had been so excellently begun by Jim Dethmer, was completed under the leadership of Jon Wallace, a two-year "loan" to Willow Creek from another ministry. By December 1994 there were 7,500 people in 1,000 small groups, with a strategy in place to double—even triple—that number. Willow Creek attendees can choose from five different kinds of groups. Disciple-making groups are for believers who desire a structured discipleship process. Community groups are common entry points for believers new to the church who want to get to know people and learn more about what it means to follow Christ. Service groups provide care and accountability for all people involved in areas of service at Willow Creek. Seeker groups are designed for nonbelievers who want to learn more about what it means to become a Christian. Support groups offer encouragement and help to members going through personal difficulties. Small groups normally have from four to ten members, with an "open chair" policy that allows them to grow until they are ready to birth new groups. Leadership for new groups is provided by apprentice leaders, who have been trained in existing groups.

As groups become more pervasive throughout the entire structure of the church they provide an intimate setting for various kinds of training that used to be offered only in large-group settings, such as spiritual gift identification, evangelism training, and stewardship instruction. Also, the formal membership procedure, which used to be handled by the elders, is now conducted through small groups.

We have concluded that without a pervasive infrastructure of small groups, the megachurch concept is vulnerable and limited. Creative, moving programming and dynamic biblical teaching are essential elements of growth, but lasting life transformation seldom occurs without the love and personal accountability that can only come, face-to-face, in a small-group setting. One of Bill's greatest regrets is that he didn't move Willow Creek toward this type of small-group approach years earlier. The WCA encourages all new start-up churches to seriously consider such a program as their starting point for ministry.

I believe this renewed emphasis on small groups brings Willow Creek back full circle to the community feeling that so characterized the early Son City years.

Back then unchurched kids "wanted to be loved the way the Son City kids were loved." I long for the day when unchurched adults in our community regularly say that about Willow Creek.

If my own experience is at all representative, I believe that will happen. The women with whom I meet in a small group are slowly becoming extended family to one another. We are experiencing the support and encouragement and loving challenge that happen naturally when women shed their images and expose their souls to one another. I know what it's like to live without community; for years I handled the struggles of life in isolation. But recently I've discovered what it means to live in community, to walk through life with "sisters," and I can say without reserve that it's a whole lot better than walking alone.

In Bill's introduction to this book, he talked about what it means to "be the church" to one another. This is what it means. And it's happening throughout the Willow Creek body.

chapter eight

1995 AND BEYOND

It is hard for me to imagine a more exciting place to be than this place, or a more compelling time to be here than right now. There are times—maybe most times—when the work of the kingdom is largely underground: retooling, repairing, adjusting the sails, setting the stage. But there are times—given by grace—when the work becomes a kind of joyous rush, and for a moment we can see the power that usually remains hidden. . . . For me this is such a moment.

JOHN ORTBERG,
WILLOW CREEK TEACHING PASTOR

If an organization can be said to go through the same developmental stages that we humans go through, it seems reasonable to say that Willow Creek has reached a point of relative maturity. We spent our infancy and rocky adolescence in a rented movie theater. We progressed steadily through our young adulthood during the fairly smooth decade of the eighties. We dove into midlife crisis in the early nineties. And now, having emerged from that time of upheaval and exhaustion, we feel rested, settled, and prepared for a new era of ministry.

When we began Willow Creek, our vision was to become a biblically functioning community, and our mission was to turn irreligious people into fully devoted followers of Jesus Christ. We believed that lost people mattered to God and that the church was called to reach out to them. Early on we developed an effective outreach ministry—our weekend seeker service—as a tool to assist our believers in their personal evangelistic efforts. Other subministries of the church, such as our junior and senior high ministries, our ministries to singles, our ministries to women and moms, our ministries to men and dads, and now our seeker small groups, join the weekend services in providing opportunities for unchurched people to discover what it means to become a Christian. This is how we accomplish our goal of reaching out to the lost.

Discipleship, the process of helping new believers become fully devoted followers of Jesus Christ, has been a tougher challenge for us. We went from modules, which offered little in terms of true discipleship, to one-on-one discipleship programs and two-year discipleship groups, which were effective but narrow in scope because of our limited supply of qualified leaders. Now, with a small-group system in place that constantly produces new leaders, we have an effective, self-perpetuating discipleship system that also provides the nurturing pastoral care that can only be offered in a small-group setting.

For the first time in twenty years, we feel we can adequately address both ends of our mission: we can introduce the lost to Jesus Christ *and* help them become His fully devoted followers. In addition we finally have a membership process, carried out through our small groups, which provides a forum for discussing and evaluating an individual's progress along the path of discipleship. Through individual and group study of our Five-G membership materials (explained in Chapter 13), potential members are assisted in evaluating (1) their personal response to *Grace*, (2) their *Growth* toward conformity to Jesus Christ, (3) their submission to the life-changing ministry of *Group* experiences, (4) the development and deployment of their spiritual *Gifts*, and (5) their commitment to *Good Stewardship*.

Through an extensive reorganization of our community care ministry, we also feel more prepared than ever before to respond to hurting members of our congregation whose needs go beyond the pastoral care that they can receive in small groups. The community care ministry is prepared to help those who have deeper theological questions or prayer needs, suffer from chronic or terminal illnesses, have lost a loved one, are in the midst of marital breakdown or divorce recovery, are alone and pregnant, need a counseling referral, are facing financial crisis or unemployment, are living with a disability, have a family member who is incarcerated, or struggle with addictive behaviors.

We have also recently clarified a number of principles and strategies that have been operational at Willow Creek for years but were never clearly articulated. For example, in the next few chapters Bill will explain the ten core values of Willow Creek Community Church. Like the seven-step strategy, which Bill jotted on a paper napkin to describe a process that had developed almost by accident under the guidance of the Holy Spirit, the core values define the biblical concepts that have provided the foundation upon which we built Willow Creek. Having these values clearly articulated provides us with a tool for future evaluation. We can safeguard the direction of our church by making sure that any future ideas, options, or emphases align with our God-given vision, mission, strategy, and core values.

For Bill in particular, and for the leadership of Willow Creek in general, the concise articulation of the ideas presented in the second half of this book—combined with our increasingly successful adaptation to a pervasive small-group approach to discipleship, and our timely reorganization of various subministries of the church—symbolizes a line of demarcation for Willow Creek Community Church. There is a sense that for the past twenty years we have been students in God's divinity school, learning slowly and methodically—and sometimes painfully—what it means to be the church. Now, on the verge of graduation, we look forward to finally beginning the ministry for which God has been preparing us.

A NECESSARY FOCUS

As a preface to what Willow Creek's future might look like, let me take you back to 1975 and the parking lot of South Park Church, home of the original Son City. . . .

Bill paced the parking lot as he mulled over in his mind Dr. Bilezikian's vision of the church. *The church is God's redemptive tool in* **the world.** *The church can impact* **the world.** *The church, and the church alone, can transform* **the world.** Bill knew his heart, mind, and soul had been captured by that vision, but he also knew he could never be a part of God's vision to redeem and impact and transform "the world" if he limited his ministry to kids. Kids have the zeal and sincerity, but they lack the depth, the leadership skills, the life experience, the resources, the leverage, the power, to impact the world. With each step he took, he became more sure of his calling: to start a church and to help grow it up as best he could. In his mind he saw a picture of a church so strong, so biblical, so well resourced, and so alive with the reality of Christ that it could be a major player in the drama of God's worldwide plan. Six months later Bill started Willow Creek Community Church, with a very clear purpose in mind: to build a biblical community that could someday carry out God's redemptive purposes in the world.

The only problem was that starting a church proved to be about a hundred times harder than Bill thought it would be. Life transformation occurred far more slowly than he had anticipated. The demands of the corporate side of establishing an organization were far greater than he had anticipated. Over time, concern about "God's redemptive purposes in the world" became nearly buried under the incredible challenge of fulfilling God's redemptive purposes in our own community. How could we devote time and energy and money to "reaching the lost people across the ocean" when we were barely able to respond to the numbers of lost people walking through our doors? How could we, as a church, devote ourselves to "ministering to the needy of the world" when we hadn't come up with an effective way to embrace the needy people in our own congregation?

Throughout the years some people have questioned Willow Creek's commitment to "world redemption," because we have not sent massive amounts of money overseas or sent out missionaries to foreign countries. In reality our International Ministries department has been involved in partnerships with evangelical ministries in inner-city Chicago, in third world countries, and in Europe for years. Representatives from our women's ministries have led Bible studies and planned birthday parties for homeless women in Chicago. Men, women, and children pounded, scraped, and painted a rat-infested warehouse into a shelter for the homeless that is run by an African-American inner-city church. Willow Creek volunteers served as counselors and provided scholarships for inner-city kids to attend a Christian camp. Fathers and sons poured cement and replaced kitchen floors for the Appalachia Reach Out ministries in eastern Kentucky.

Children in Promiseland (our Sunday school program) have gathered clothes and donated them to an orphanage in Kenya. Hundreds of singles from our Operation Single Serve have gone on short-term mission trips to Mexico, where they have built houses for a church-based organization and ministered at a Christian orphanage. Contractors and carpenters constructed an orphanage in Jamaica. Nurses and doctors have treated the sick, in Jesus' name, in the Dominican Republic, Haiti, and Africa.

I was on a Willow Creek team that met with government leaders in Bulgaria, where we partnered with Prison Fellowship to provide medical supplies for prison hospitals and to send Christian literature to prison officials, for use in prison rehabilitation programs. We also met with Christian leaders in Croatia, where we provided financial help to a refugee center presenting the love of Christ to Moslem refugees from Bosnia.

I could add many similar examples. Still, I cannot deny that our involvement in such endeavors has been limited—but not because we have been disinterested in missions or worldwide outreach. We have been hindered in our ability to become highly engaged in a broader context by the nearly overwhelming challenge of responding to the extraordinary work of God through the evangelistic "mission" of our seeker services.

Repeatedly through the years, Bill and the elders have discussed their desire to be part of God's redemptive plan worldwide and have prayed for God's guidance regarding Willow Creek's involvement. Repeatedly they have sensed God's leading to focus primarily—not exclusively but primarily—on our local mission. Over and over it seemed God was saying, *You're not ready yet. You're not settled enough at home. You don't yet have an infrastructure in place that could facilitate a major thrust beyond the local unchurched community.*

A GLOBAL OUTREACH

But one of the gifts of maturity, it seems, is that it gives a person or an institution the ability to do two things at once. For Willow Creek relative maturity means we have finally reached a developmental point that allows us to enter a new era of worldwide extension without jeopardizing our God-ordained local ministry. With Bill's reenergized leadership, with many new and energetic staff members, with increased clarity of vision, mission, strategy, values, and desired results, and with the knowledge that we will be debt-free as a church by the end of 1995, the elders, board, and management team are confident that we are ready to aggressively extend our involvement to a more broadly defined "Jerusalem," to "Judea" and "Samaria," and to "the uttermost part of the earth" (Acts 1:8 KJV).

Our motivation for expanding into a more global ministry is twofold. First, of course, we want to minister to the needy: We want to extend the love of God in tangible ways to address the spiritual, emotional, and physical needs of the poor, the destitute, the oppressed, and the forgotten throughout the world. We want to offer a cup of cold water in Jesus' name and also to present the message of the Gospel to the lost beyond our local community. We want to be brokers of the extraordinary blessing God has lavished on our church. But also, we want to encourage spiritual growth in our congregation: We long to see Willow Creek attendees transformed as they offer their time, their talents, and their treasures to God in a new way. We want their hearts to be broken by the injustices and heartaches and tragedies that break the heart of God. We want their souls to be enriched as they see, firsthand, how the ministry of the Holy Spirit crosses racial and geographical and cultural boundaries. We want their devotion to Jesus Christ to deepen as they become, in a very practical way, part of His church worldwide.

This aggressive expansion of International Ministries was launched in November 1994, when Bill announced to our congregation that the entire amount gathered through our end-of-the-year giving would go to help the poor and the lost worldwide.

As Bill explained this new direction for our church at a weekend service he pointed out that the initials for International Ministries, I. M., are also the first two letters of one of the most powerful words in the English language.

"It's the word *imagine*," Bill told the congregation. "Martin Luther King challenged people to imagine a nation in which individuals would not be judged by the color of their skin but by the content of their character, and a culture, though still faltering, began taking its first tiny steps in the direction of that glorious picture. John Kennedy looked at our moon and imagined a person walking on it, and soon the footprints of a man brought science fiction into the realm of reality. Jesus challenged His followers to imagine a church strong and alive and dynamic, like a city perched on a hill, radiating the light of truth into the darkness of night. His followers imagined a beacon of hope, a lamppost of love, a torch of transforming power—and the church was born."

As we listened to Bill we, the congregation of Willow Creek, imagined too. We imagined food being offered to hungry kids in Chicago, and shelter being offered to the homeless, and money and training and personnel being offered to inner-city churches. We imagined clothing, medical assistance, and economic development programs being provided for families in third world villages. We imagined earnest church leaders who battle restraints both financial and political receiving encouragement through our resources. We imagined Willow Creek members working side by side with African-Americans and Hispanics in Chicago and with indigenous leaders and ministries throughout the world.

The needs presented to us were the needs of a desperate world. I. M.— International Ministries.

The challenge presented to us was to picture in our minds the difference we could make. I. M.—Imagine.

The question presented to us was, Are you willing? For many the response was, I. M.—I am. I am willing to see the need. I am willing to imagine a solution. I am willing to give of my time, my talents, and my treasures.

By January 3, 1995, we had exceeded our goal of $1.5 million and had established partnerships with local and international ministries with which hundreds of Willow Creek attendees would become personally involved in the coming months. We had done more than raise money; we had launched a new emphasis in the ongoing ministry of Willow Creek.

"JERUSALEM"

This new ministry emphasis is three pronged. The first area of focus is our "Jerusalem": Greater Chicago. Our ministry partner is Vision Chicago, a joint venture of World Vision and MidAmerica Leadership Foundation. Vision Chicago's goal is "to call and equip churches to effective outreach ministry in their own neighborhoods; to form new ministry partnerships which bridge [denominational] and cultural barriers; and to increase community support for metropolitan ministry."[1]

Central to Vision Chicago's mission are organized coalitions of neighborhood churches that bridge historical racial and cultural barriers by drawing together churches from both African-American and Latino communities. In many inner-city communities the neighborhood churches are the only institutional resources left—spiritually, and in more tangible ways, they are the city's last hope. Yet too often the impact of these churches has been minimal, because they have operated in isolation. The coalitions sponsored by Vision Chicago have provided avenues for racial reconciliation and strategic organization; this has greatly enhanced the transformational impact of the neighborhood churches, giving them the united strength to affect issues of housing, food, employment, education, economic growth, and spiritual development.

As a partner with Vision Chicago, Willow Creek's role is to provide money and volunteers to help carry out the plans and projects developed by the church coalitions. We are also directly involved with several church-based employment initiatives, a building materials distribution center, and CityLINC, a volunteer placement service.

One of CityLINC's placements led our fifteen-year-old son, Todd, and a group of his friends from our high school youth ministry to a rubbish-filled three-flat in Chicago's Pilsen neighborhood. After six Saturdays of cleaning, painting, laying tile, arranging furniture, and making beds, the kids celebrated the building's transformation into a church-based shelter for foster children, senior citizens, and mentally impaired adults. I hope the building will be a place where God's love can touch human lives. I know that the experience of working on the building touched my son. He was touched by the competence, compassion, and commitment of the owner of the building, who is a single black mother and a professional woman with a heart that breaks for the neglected in her community. He was touched by the gray barrenness of the city streets and by the dark emptiness of the eyes that watched him and his friends climb into a church van and head back to the suburbs. He was touched by the grace of God that had blessed him in so many ways and by the call of God to join the ranks of those who become brokers of those blessings.

Our vision is to have much of this "brokering" happen through our small-group ministry as individual groups from various subministries "adopt" projects, support them financially, and ultimately offer their time and talents as well.

"JUDEA" AND "SAMARIA"

The second area of focus in International Ministries is the neighboring nation of the Dominican Republic. We chose this country as our first major international outreach because of its tremendous need and because its close proximity to the U.S. permits extensive personal involvement by Willow Creek attendees.

In the future as the concept of the worldwide church becomes more entrenched in the cultural mind-set of the Willow Creek body we will be able to connect with neighbors more distant.

In the meantime the Dominican Republic presents more than enough needs for us to address. As a member of Willow Creek's International Ministries assessment board, I was overwhelmed as I walked through the dusty barrios of Santo Domingo, where scraps of tin and discarded plywood define a structure loosely called "home." It appeared at first glance to be a place devoid of hope. But that first impression proved false. Members of a church-based community group, mostly mothers determined to provide adequate housing, clothing, food, and education for their children, described to us their plan for acquiring loans with which they would start microbusinesses such as sewing, selling vegetables, repairing bikes, or making food, candles, and blankets. A short way from where the mothers' group met, a brick-making factory and a bakery, both subsidized by ministry loans similar to those sought by the women, each provided employment for ten to twelve workers who would otherwise be unemployed and whose families would be destitute. In rural villages, where death rates among children have been alarmingly high, health care workers shared with us their commitment to providing potable water and sanitary latrines as a first line of defense against disease. At a farm school, local farmers whose overused land has become nearly barren were learning the principles of sustainable agriculture that have produced abundance on the school's terraced, green fields; the farmers and their children are also learning the principles of God's Word. Back in town, pastors spoke with us in earnest tones, eager to learn how to move their congregations out of isolation and into community involvement so they can provide a holistic answer to people's needs and earn a hearing for the Gospel.

These and similar scenes of hope are being generated by organizations such as World Vision, our primary partner in the Dominican Republic, and by our secondary partners: Habitat for Humanity, Opportunity International, and others. Again, our goal is to involve not only the finances but also the talents and time of Willow Creek attendees, through construction projects, medical assistance, job skill training programs, marriage and family classes, Christian education workshops, and ongoing relationships with church leaders.

Just weeks ago a group of Willow Creek women returned from a weeklong stay in the Dominican Republic to lay the groundwork for an ongoing involvement of our women's ministries. They returned having discovered a mutually beneficial sisterhood with the hardworking, gifted, dynamic women of the Dominican Republic. "It was wonderful to get to know them," said one Willow Creek woman. "As our team held hands and wept and prayed with the Dominican women, we knew this was just the beginning. We need to learn Spanish and go back!"

"THE UTTERMOST PART OF THE EARTH"

The third area of focus in International Ministries is international church development. On the southern coast of Spain, an energetic seeker-oriented church ministers and thrives, grateful for a recent influx of educated, talented, and spiritually hungry Spaniards. The first evangelical church officially recognized by the federal government of Spain, this church was offered an unprecedented land grant by the city government as an official affirmation of the church's positive contribution to the life of the community. For several years Willow Creek teachers and lay leaders have offered leadership training, spiritual mentoring, and encouragement to this Spanish church. Now our financial contribution allows the church to complete construction of a permanent facility designed to enhance community outreach and spiritual growth.

For years the brighter future promised by the inevitable collapse of communism kept hope alive in Poland. But the series of broken promises following communism's demise have replaced hope with a deep depression that seems to pervade the country. Sky-high interest rates, vicious crime, increasing pornography, and wrenching poverty have thrown people into a state of despair, rendering them emotionally and spiritually vulnerable. Cults of every form are thriving.

But what I saw and heard in a mountain village along Poland's southern border was clearly a manifestation of the true God at work. Vibrant Christian Poles are leading dynamic, growing, nationwide ministries to children, young people, women, married couples, prisoners, and university students. Gifted musicians and actors are effectively using the arts to communicate to seekers. In a medical clinic and counseling center, broken bodies and wounded minds are being drawn into the embrace of divine love. At a Christian women's conference attended by hundreds of representatives from countries throughout Central and Eastern Europe, dramatic scenes of reconciliation culminated in a prayer for peace offered jointly by the women from Serbia and Bosnia.

These ministries and others are all part of a nationally led evangelical organization that started in Poland not long after Willow Creek started in the U.S. The vastly different cultural contexts surrounding Willow Creek and the Polish endeavor distinguish our respective ministries in significant ways. Still, I am struck more by our similarities than by our differences. In terms of overall philosophy and strategy, the Holy Spirit seems to have bridged continents in leading our distinct ministries along parallel paths. As the innovative approach espoused by the Polish ministry forces it out from under its previous denominational umbrella we at Willow Creek feel blessed to be able to offer what the ministry needs most: encouragement, assistance in leadership training, and financial support. Our recent funding effort will subsidize a Christian conference for over one thousand Europeans, a quarterly Christian magazine, additional staff, a ministry van, and necessary building renovations.

For many of us who have been at Willow Creek since the beginning, this opportunity to join hands with emerging Christian ministries and churches throughout the world is truly like a dream coming true. We look forward to enjoying many additional partnerships such as these in years to come.

WILLOW CREEK ASSOCIATION

The recently energized thrust of International Ministries, particularly regarding church partnerships, is enhanced by the work of the Willow Creek Association. There are over one thousand member churches in the Association, and if the present growth rate continues, there will be 4,000 member churches by the year 2000. The Association sponsors church leadership conferences that have been attended by over 30,000 people from around the world. Five countries—Australia, New Zealand, England, the Netherlands, and Germany—have created affiliates of the Association in 1995 alone. The Association also produces Willow Creek resources—books, small-group curriculum, spiritual gift assessment materials, drama scripts, and music to be used by other ministries—and will eventually publish resources developed by other member churches as well. The WCA publishes a newsletter, provides a job referral publication, and answers calls from people looking for seeker-oriented ministries in various cities around the world.

"Our vision," said WCA executive director Jim Mellado, "is to see the local churches of this country better relate God's solutions to the needs of seekers and believers. . . . We're not trying to create Willow Creek clones. We just want to help churches fulfill what God intends for them and to assist them in effectively reaching their local communities with the message of Christ."

I am delighted by the impact of Willow Creek and the Willow Creek Association. Just days ago Bill and I attended a "seeker service" at a multicultural church on a tiny island in the Atlantic Ocean. After the pastor, a young white national, welcomed his congregation, a middle-aged man of African heritage performed a drama sketch written and originally performed by Sharon Sherbondy, veteran member of the Willow Creek drama team. It was fairly obvious that the congregation was moved by the drama spot, but few people were mopping up tears as we were. It is humbling and exhilarating to see ideas that have grown out of our ministry being used in settings so different from ours, to see them reinterpreted and reenergized by the Spirit. So I rejoice in the momentum apparent today in the Willow Creek movement; I believe it is inspired by God.

But I can't deny that it scares me. I fear that the vision, values, and strategies of Willow Creek will lose something crucial as they are written down, published, marketed, and applied. I fear that what has become known as the "Willow Creek model" will lack the dynamic, living, Spirit-led quality that has characterized the real thing. Published resources make it all seem so concrete and orderly and—well, finished. Here it is. The plan. The strategy. The model. Cast in stone. Complete.

That scares me. There has been, I think, a sense of constant movement at Willow Creek—not a restless addiction to change but an ongoing, rolling, vital unfolding of the Spirit's plan, complete with unexpected turns and surprise events. That has been unsettling for some people. I can understand that. I have always been the kind of person who likes to get things figured out "once and for all," who likes to chart a clear course. But I am learning in life, as well as in ministry, that the Spirit's commitment to operate "decently and in order" does not imply predictability and settledness. Where the supernatural is involved, there seems to be no room for "getting set in your ways" or feeling as if you "have a handle on it."

Last night Bill called me from California after an unplanned meeting with a Christian leader from another country, excited about a new idea for a fresh emphasis in his teaching and leadership at Willow Creek. He had thought, prior to that meeting, that he had his personal approach to ministry mapped out pretty well for the next few months at least, and now suddenly—an unexpected meeting, a fresh challenge, and a new piece to the ministry puzzle, which could only have been dropped into place by the Holy Spirit.

Time and again Bill, the elders, management team members, or other staff leaders have spun off ministries in new and unforeseen directions because of similar "leadings" from the Holy Spirit. As this book goes to print we teeter on the edge of a new challenge, responding to what we believe is the Spirit's prompting to start a new weekend service. Since our beginning in 1975, we have been known as a church for the baby boomer generation, and we have geared our outreach specifically to that group. But a new generation with distinct needs and biases seems to require a new approach. Generation X, the baby busters, are suspicious of the very ministry methods that have proven so effective in reaching their parents. Shaping an effective ministry to them—a challenge we could not have envisioned five years ago—is one of our goals for the next few years.

Another goal is to minister more intentionally to the unique needs and opportunities of our older church members, which may include offering an alternative weekend service for them. From the beginning we have been a youth-oriented church. But the forty-somethings who defined the upper age limit of our congregation when we started in the seventies are now facing retirement. How can we encourage them as they face new, and sometimes unwelcome, challenges? And how can we nurture the ministry potential their increasing free time affords them? The bell-shaped curve places an unprecedented number of our attendees in what we call the "time crunch" years of child rearing and career building, when they have limited time to devote to service within the church. As a biblically functioning community, we have a critical and growing need for the gifts, talents, and services of our senior members.

Where will these new ministries take us? What unexpected needs and additional opportunities will come our way? The challenge of church work—and the fun—is that only God knows the answers to those questions.

Willow Creek was, I believe, conceived in the mind of God. He brought together the right people with the right gifts at the right time in history, and a sort of spontaneous combustion occurred. The past twenty years of my life—my whole adult life, actually—have been lived under the shadow of that supernaturally fueled combustion. Because Willow Creek always has been, and always will be, an imperfect manifestation of God's perfect idea, to live under its shadow has been, for me personally, both an asset and a liability, the source of wonderful pleasure and excruciating pain. While I have had a privileged front-row seat from which to witness the unbelievable pageant of God's blessing, I have also been in a prime position to feel the full weight of our mistakes, our sins, and Satan's attacks. But all of that, with its good and bad, when viewed from my present vantage point, is incidental. What matters most, and what I want to state as clearly as I can, is that I know God more deeply now than I did twenty years ago. While I know that the Spirit accomplishes His work in our lives through a complexity of means that we humans could never fully discern, I earnestly believe that the ministry of Willow Creek Community Church has been one significant avenue of God's work in my life. I believe the same to be true for Bill and for our children, and I am grateful for that.

I believe God wants to use the local church to reach the lost and to draw them into intimate relationship with Himself. I believe that for all its imperfections, Willow Creek is being used by God to do just that.

NOTE

1. Bud Ipema, president, MidAmerica Leadership Foundation.

part two

chapter nine

EXPLORING WILLOW CREEK'S INFLUENCE

Having read the first part of this book, you know that we don't have all the answers to ministry. More often than not we've been making things up as we go. But as we've tried to submit ourselves to God as best we can, He has decided to create something tremendously exciting on our campus. As a result, Willow Creek has attracted a lot more interest than we had ever anticipated.

In recent years this increasing attention has prompted us to wrestle with the question of what role—if any—Willow Creek might play in assisting other churches and helping to advance God's kingdom throughout the world.

After considerable prayer and discussion, we've concluded that our best contribution is this: *to encourage church leaders to go through the agonizing but exhilarating experience of determining God's "thumbprint" for their own particular fellowship.* Let me explain.

The Bible says there's one Spirit but many ministries. Just as no two thumbprints are alike, every church is going to look different, with different leadership styles, different strategies, and a different mix of spiritual gifts. In fact, I believe that part of Willow Creek's effectiveness through the years has been due to its acute awareness of the giftedness, passion, vision, temperament, and leadership style of myself and the key players around me, including Dave Holmbo, Don Cousins, Nancy Beach, and others.

We've tried to look honestly at our strengths and weaknesses, to study what the Scripture says about building a church, to understand the unchurched people in our local community, and to stay attuned to the Holy Spirit as He guides us into a vision, mission, and strategy that uniquely fit who God has created us to be.

As the first half of this book describes, it's been an incredible ride! For me nothing has been as painstakingly difficult—nor, at the same time, as deeply rewarding—as participating in the unfolding of God's redemptive drama at Willow Creek.

Sometimes tentatively, sometimes boldly, we've grappled through the years with all sorts of "thumbprint decisions"—the buying of land, the designing of buildings, the hiring of staff, the development of leadership structures, the launching of new ministries, the producing of outreach events. In recent years we've experienced the continuing excitement of reengineering some of our ministries to accommodate future growth, including our small-group ministry, our children's program, our international ministry, and our membership system.

It's been challenging, difficult, thrilling—anything but routine! For untold hours, we've prayed and planned together, knowing that the stakes were high and that the risk of failure was always looming. And through this process, we've seen with increasing clarity—and with constant wonder—what God wants Willow Creek's thumbprint to look like.

I would never want any church leader to miss that kind of experience! That's why I urge pastors not to merely use Willow Creek as a model but to actively and prayerfully discover and explore what unique thumbprint God intends for their church.

In fact, that's the purpose behind this second part of the book—to walk through the kind of critical issues that every church should explore for itself. I'll draw on our experiences at Willow Creek as an example of how one fellowship has crystallized its mission and methodology, its vision and values. Maybe this can provide the impetus for your own church to uncover the thumbprint God has in mind for you.

But let's get real practical. Exactly how will churches around the globe discover their vision and values? Not surprisingly, God has spelled out a plan. His method depends upon the unleashing of men and women who have been given the spiritual gift of leadership.

WHAT MAKES A LEADER A LEADER?

When God wanted His people delivered from an oppressive pharaoh, He used a leader named Moses. When He needed Jerusalem's wall rebuilt, He used a leader named Nehemiah. When He wanted His people to experience a golden era, He used a leader named David. When He wanted to build a temple, He used a leader named Solomon. When He needed a statesman-prophet, He used a leader named Isaiah. And when He needed a fearless church planter, He used a leader named Paul.

Throughout history, whenever God has needed someone to initiate, organize, and carry out an important project, He has called upon leaders. And since His priority from Pentecost to today has been to build redemptive communities that would flourish in the midst of resistant cultures, it makes sense that He would turn to leaders again.

After all, who's going to cast the vision of or creatively imagine the future for a biblically functioning community? Who's going to insist that the teaching and fellowship transform lives? Who's going to uphold the value of prayer, make sure the sacraments are honored, and insist that spiritual gifts are in use throughout the church? Who's going to coordinate ministries, establish small-group structures, lift high the importance of worship, and inspire the church to reach out to spiritually lost people?

That's right—*leaders*. Romans 12:8 gives unambiguous marching orders to every man and woman who's been entrusted with the spiritual gift of leadership—*Lead, and do it with diligence!*

Unfortunately, there has been some confusion about leadership in recent Christian history. Local churches generally haven't been directed by leaders but by teachers, and these two species have distinctly different behavior patterns and areas of emphasis. As a result, a lot of churches are well taught; very few are effectively led.

Please, don't get me wrong. The church *needs* great teachers. Preaching is the core ministry of the church, and lives will not change without powerful and Spirit-inspired teaching from the Word of God. Without gifted teachers, we might as well close shop, because they're critical to fulfilling God's vision for biblically functioning communities.

And yet there are distinctions in the way teachers and leaders operate. I'm not saying one is *better* than the other, only that their approach to ministry is different. For instance, when teachers stand in front of people, their chief desire is to accurately and compellingly communicate biblical truth in the hopes of impacting lives. But when leaders have the microphone, there's another agenda. Usually they have a purpose, mission, or cause that they want people to get fired up about.

Over a period of time, teachers tend to attract learners who agree that, yes, the communication and understanding of scriptural truth are crucial for believers in order to change their lives. Teachers educate and edify, which are both very necessary. Yet leaders inspire and motivate. They tend to pull people into action and involve them in the mission that they're spearheading. Leading is active, prompting people to leap out of their chairs and declare, "That's not just a good idea, it's a compelling mission for me to commit my life to!"

Also, it's common for teachers to become so immersed in their biblical studies and message preparation that they don't pick up on subtle kinds of corrective steps that should be taken in the church. Programs may be starting to deteriorate, the financial base can be slightly eroding, or the congregation's morale could be slowly sagging, but teachers might not quickly discern the need to take prompt action.

But when a person with a leadership gift walks around the church, mental warning buzzers go off all over the place. His or her mind is racing with thoughts like *We need to pay more attention to this* and *We need to solve that* and *We need to get this back on track* and *We've got to figure out why we're still doing this when it's no longer working* and *We've got to start a new program to accomplish something else.*

What's more, some teachers don't emphasize the importance of involving people in the thrill of doing ministry. Their intention is to make sure their congregation is being biblically grounded so people aren't tossed to and fro by different winds of doctrine, and this is essential. However, leaders put a high priority on making sure people discover, develop, and deploy their spiritual gifts and that they get elbow-deep in ministry themselves.

Do you see the difference?

For the most part, teachers don't naturally gravitate toward the strategic allocation of resources. While they know this is an integral part of ministry, it generally isn't an exercise they're passionate about. On the other hand, leaders look at the church's finite pool of finances and enthusiastically envision it as kingdom capital that can make the difference between a church stalling out or taking the next hill. As a result, teachers and leaders look at the church budget from entirely different perspectives. To a teacher, the budget can be sheer drudgery; to a leader, it's laden with opportunities.

Because God has entrusted me with the spiritual gift of leadership, I tend to see everything through that lens. Sometimes I'll be walking through Willow Creek with one of our elders, whose strongest gift is encouragement. I may be mentally juggling a lot of leadership issues at the time, even down to the smallest detail of how the hallway's traffic flow is working, while her attention might lock on to someone off to the side who's emotionally hurting. She doesn't know much about strategy and resource allocation; I may not notice the person with the broken heart, if I'm not careful. In both cases, our main gift colors the way we perceive the ministry.

Of course, some people have a mixture of teaching and leadership gifts. I certainly don't want to pretend these are mutually exclusive. In my own case, my primary gift is leadership, my secondary gift is personal evangelism, and my third is teaching. But it's true that those with leadership abilities exhibit certain characteristics that are vital to advancing the church.

As I've looked through the Scriptures at those who throughout history have been unmistakably strong leaders, I've noticed certain behavior patterns and attitudes that they hold in common. Each of these eight characteristics has important implications for the local church:

1. Leaders have the ability to cast a vision.

People with the spiritual gift of leadership have a God-given capability to imagine a preferred future for whatever kingdom-related enterprise they're leading. For instance, Jesus stood before a crowd of people and said, "Someday the church is going to be like a city on a hill that cannot be hidden." One day He walked up to Peter and said, "I see a future for you. In fact, I can envision you becoming something that even you can't imagine. And so from now on I'm going to call you *Rock*."

Leaders stand up in front of congregations and say, "Do you know what we need to become? A biblically functioning community!" Then they go down the list of what constitutes a loving, serving, worshiping, praying, outreach-oriented, God-honoring fellowship of believers, and people want to come flying out of their seats to sign up!

Why is that? Because God has created human beings to respond to a worthy vision when it's passionately presented by a gifted leader.

2. Leaders have the ability to coalesce people.

People are not only dying to hear an exciting vision but they're also hungering for someone to discover the unique contribution they can make to that cause. Leaders have a talent for drawing people out of the bleachers and onto the playing field and then making sure they're in the right positions for producing the maximum difference for the kingdom.

Nehemiah is a great example. He cast a vision for rebuilding the wall around Jerusalem by essentially telling his followers, "The city of God is going to be strong and fortified again! We're not going to be the embarrassment of the world anymore. We're going to go rebuild the wall and city!" And a whole bunch of people exclaimed, "Yes! Let's do it!"

Then Nehemiah mobilized them and put them into strategic positions. His plan demonstrated leadership brilliance: he assigned families to rebuild the portion of the wall adjacent to their home. After all, people will be motivated to build a terrific wall if it's going to protect their children and themselves. So Nehemiah efficiently got everybody organized into effective units to fulfill the vision that he had cast.

Part of leadership is assessing the character, skills, life experiences, temperament, personality, and spiritual gifts of each member of the team that are available to accomplish the task at hand. Then once people are assigned to appropriate responsibilities, watch out! People flourish when they're freed up to contribute to a plan's success.

3. Leaders have the ability to inspire and motivate people.

Those with leadership gifts have a supernatural sense of when to encourage other people and cheer them on. Intuitively they know how to reignite someone's spark of enthusiasm when it begins to flicker.

For instance, when people step offstage after participating in our services, they walk very close to the area where the speakers sit. I've noticed over the years that if I'm sitting there with people who are pure teachers, they're usually so wrapped up in the sermon they are preparing to deliver to the congregation that they barely notice the vocalists or actors who leave the stage and file past them.

But when people with leadership gifts sit there, they can't help but call out, "Great job! Thanks for serving! Nobody could have done that like you!" Frankly, leaders just can't stop themselves. Why? Because they have a heart to inspire and motivate others.

4. Leaders are able to identify the need for positive change—and then bring it about.

It's not enough for leaders to have an innate sense of when corrective steps should be taken in an organization. They also need God-inspired insights about how to change course without causing a mutiny by the crew—or killing the helmsman!

For instance, many times pastors will attend a Willow Creek conference and become enthused about bringing some new ideas back to their church. That's fine, except in cases when they return home and try to instigate massive modifications without first casting an appropriate vision, laying a foundation of new values, and thinking through how to manage the transition. The end result can be a disaster for both the pastor *and* the church.

Gifted leaders have the spiritual savvy that's necessary to introduce reasonable change at a pace that a church can assimilate.

5. Leaders establish core values.

Leaders are constantly defining and honing the unique set of values that undergird their organization and keep everybody on track. The apostle Paul defined such values when he said to the other leaders of his day, "If you want to hang out in Jerusalem and build churches for the already convinced—yea, God! But I want to go out and build churches where Christ is not yet known."

Paul didn't eliminate any biblical imperatives, but he recognized that a distinct value for his ministry was to develop a church among the spiritually lost. Today leaders need to determine what values are especially needed to find that thumbprint God has for their own ministry.

In fact, establishing these core principles is so important that I'll be devoting an entire chapter to the values that Willow Creek's leaders have identified as central to accomplishing our mission.

6. Leaders allocate resources effectively.

Once a vision is described, a gifted leader begins to strategically assess what resources are available to achieve that God-given, preferred future. Leaders look at such resources as money, equipment, square footage, staff, volunteers—even time—and they begin to plan how all of them can be put to maximum use. Few things upset a leader as much as resources being frittered away when they could have been leveraged for kingdom gain.

Much of the time spent by Willow Creek's management team is devoted to ongoing discussions about how to make better use of the resources we have. Those sessions, instead of being draining, actually energize these leaders. They emerge with confidence that they've done their best to squeeze the most ministry out of whatever they have to work with.

7. Leaders have the ability to identify entropy.

In other words, leaders have a sixth sense that allows them to spot something that's beginning to fall apart, before others even realize it. The subtle deterioration of a ministry, or a fraying of morale that would be imperceptible to most people, virtually shouts out for attention to the gifted leader.

For example, in the early 1990s many people would have said that Willow Creek had a world-class small-group ministry. But those of us with leadership gifts had a God-given ability to peer behind the facade. We concluded that even though our ministry was working effectively according to most standards, it was not functioning as optimally as it could be. Certain needs were going unmet. Too many leaders were burning out. The system was stifling growth.

As we moved to address those issues some people exclaimed, "Hey, if it's not broken, don't fix it!" We had to respond, "You're right, the wheels haven't fallen off yet. But they're starting to wobble, and we want to repair them *before* the crash."

Through the planning and hard work of some very talented leaders, we retooled that ministry. As a result, today we have a stronger, healthier, larger, and more efficient small-group ministry. In fact, by the beginning of 1995 we had nearly eleven hundred groups actively operating, and five times as many group leaders as we used to. Soon we will have ten thousand people active in small groups.

The reason can be traced back to leaders who looked beneath the attractive veneer and concluded that the system wasn't as effective as people assumed it was.

8. Leaders love to create a leadership culture.

Unfortunately, many churches these days are crippled by insecure pastors who want to be the hub around which the whole church revolves. They need to be involved with every decision. When capable and spiritual people step forward and offer to take over certain responsibilities, they get pushed away. Sometimes they're even given that ultimate insult, "You're just a lay person."

Consequently, churches end up with a lot of very gifted people sitting in the pews each Sunday with their hands dutifully folded in their laps. Meanwhile the pastor complains that he's exhausted and overworked. Clearly that's *not* the biblical paradigm!

Actually, the scriptural approach is for pastors to help people discover their spiritual gifts, to equip people, mobilize them, encourage them, and unleash them so they can advance the ministry. One of the best contributions that pastors can make to their church is to create a leadership culture in which others can lead, cast a vision, and organize volunteers around different parts of the ministry. Then the role of the senior leader is to work with the other leaders to make sure everyone is contributing to the vision.

Often when my secretary sends me a fax while I'm traveling, she adds this note at the bottom: "Things are running smoothly at the church." That doesn't threaten me; it fulfills me! I love to release leadership to the appropriate people, both staff and volunteers. I celebrate when they find their niche and flourish. It encourages me to see them own a chunk of the church with enthusiasm and creativity.

I enjoy it so much that sometimes I secretly think it must be illegal. But it's *not* illegal; it's *biblical*! (See Ephesians 4:11–13.)

THE LEADERSHIP CHALLENGE

God gives leaders these eight qualities for a reason: so they can prayerfully, diligently, and humbly steward His treasure, the church. But I suspect that some of you have been reading this chapter with a lump in your throat. *Uh-oh,* you're saying to yourself. *Here I am in a leadership position, but if I'm honest, these dis-*

tinctions aren't really true for me. I don't think I have any leadership gifts. Now *what do I do?*

First of all, don't panic. First Corinthians 12:7 says you have at least one spiritual gift. It could be teaching, mercy, evangelism, encouragement, administration, or one of the other gifts. Whatever it is—celebrate the way God wired you up! Thank Him for it, because each gift has incredible value in His economy. And second, do your utmost to put your gift into play for the benefit of the kingdom. You'll be more fulfilled when you're contributing in an area that fits who you are, and your church will be better served when a spiritually gifted leader is at the helm.

But if you *are* a leader, then lead—and do it with diligence! Cast an inspiring, God-centered vision, create a succinct and compelling mission statement, carve out an effective strategy, help craft a set of biblical core values, and do your best to measure the results to make sure you're staying on track. In fact, I'll help you by devoting the next few chapters to going through these critical leadership functions, one at a time.

Don't squander the abilities God has assigned to you! You owe it to the kingdom—and to yourself—to put your leadership gift into action.

I remember going for a long, wet stroll in a park with one of the Willow Creek Association's board members during a break in a leadership conference in Cardiff, Wales. At the time, the association was in the midst of navigating some high-stakes challenges, and it seemed as if the more we talked about the issues, the faster we walked.

Finally I said, "These problems are *huge*, aren't they?"

"They sure are," he replied. And then he added something very revealing. "But don't you just love seeking God's wisdom and figuring out how to solve them?"

I had to smile. That's no teacher. That's no gifted mercy giver. That's no shepherd. *That's* a leader! I went back to my hotel room thanking God that we have spiritually gifted leaders charting the future of the Willow Creek Association.

And all around the world, churches desperately need people like him to be freed up to follow the directive of Romans 12:8—*Lead, and do it with diligence!*

chapter ten

THE VISION OF A BIBLICALLY FUNCTIONING COMMUNITY

They devoted themselves to the apostles' teaching and to the fellowship,
to the breaking of bread and to prayer. Everyone was filled with awe,
and many wonders and miraculous signs were done by the apostles. All
the believers were together and had everything in common. Selling
their possessions and goods, they gave to anyone as he had need. Every
day they continued to meet together in the temple courts. They broke
bread in their homes and ate together with glad and sincere hearts,
praising God and enjoying the favor of all the people. And the Lord
added to their number daily those who were being saved.

ACTS 2:42–47

Dr. Gilbert Bilezikian, clutching a Bible, pacing back and forth, speaking with intensity and passion, was doing what he does better than anyone I know: casting the vision for a biblically functioning community.

The setting was a church leadership conference at Willow Creek. I was sitting in the front row, riveted once again to his description of what God wants His people to experience together. "This is God's ultimate achievement—a community, a center of warm, pulsating, effervescent, outreaching Christian love, a place with all of its components united in order to become a force in this world instead of a farce," he was saying.

That wasn't a description of the kind of church that most of the leaders at the conference had grown up attending. For the most part their childhood experience was that church was boring, monotonous, and predictable. They hadn't seen life-change on a regular basis. Instead they had merely gutted out the services, yawning, rolling their eyes, and furtively glancing at their watches to see how many minutes were left until they were free and safe for another week. In the years that most of them spent in traditional churches, they never got a lump in their throat, were seldom seized by the glory of God, and rarely saw spiritually lost people find Christ.

So as Dr. Bilezikian unfolded the Bible's irresistible description of how God wants communities of believers to live I could see the pastors inching toward the edge of their chairs, both struck and saddened by the contrast between that inspiring scriptural portrayal and their own childhood experience. In many ways, I could relate to what they were feeling.

TEACHING THAT'S LIFE CHANGING

In a biblically functioning community, Dr. Bilezikian told us, the teaching is transformational. When God-gifted preachers open up the Bible and present its truth under the power of the Holy Spirit and cross paths with a congregation that's full of receptive hearts, then amazing life-change takes place at that awesome intersection.

But that's not the norm. Many people grew up listening to sermons and wondering to themselves, *Why is he yelling? Why is he so distant? Why can't I follow what he's saying? Why is this so irrelevant? Why is he so holier-than-thou?*

A few years ago I was staying at a hotel in Florida during a conference, and as I walked across the lobby to go up to my room I heard some music and laughter coming from the lounge. So I poked my head in and saw a karaoke party going on, in which amateurs from the audience took turns singing to a soundtrack.

I watched as a blonde woman sauntered up to the front, grabbed the microphone, and began crooning a country-western song with incredible gusto. She swayed her hips and belted out the words at the top of her lungs—but the whole time she was singing about a quarter-pitch flat. She finished with a big flourish and strutted back to her table as if to say, *Wynona Judd—watch out!* In the meantime everybody else was cringing and thinking, *Somebody's got to tell her the truth! She thinks she's good!*

And let's face it—there are some pastors who whip together a sermon and climb into the pulpit and pound and wave and sweat and then walk away saying to themselves, *Chuck Swindoll—get out of the way!*

But that's not what the congregation is thinking. People are wondering when somebody is going to tell him the truth. He's probably good at *something*, but it's not preaching. And as a result, lives remain stagnant.

In a biblically functioning community, the leaders make sure that the preaching is done only by those who have the appropriate spiritual gifts, who have yielded themselves to the spiritual disciplines, and who have been anointed by the Holy Spirit to teach. When that happens, life starts pulsating through the place. You show me a church that's led by leaders and well served by someone with the spiritual gift of preaching, and I'll show you a vibrant and growing community of believers.

FELLOWSHIP THAT'S WELL BELOW THE SURFACE

Then, Dr. Bilezikian said, there's life-changing fellowship in a biblically functioning community. That was a far cry from the childhood experience of a lot of his audience! The only kind of fellowship that many of his listeners had witnessed had revolved around the fifteen or twenty minutes after the service when the men would stand around the church patio and ask each other superficial questions.

"So how's it going at work, Jake?" one of them would ask.

"Fine, Phil. Say, you driving a new pickup?"

"Used," Phil would reply. "What do you have going on this week?"

"Not much."

"Well, great fellowshipping with you, Jake."

"Same here."

That was about it. They'd call the women out of the kitchen, where they were having similar conversations, and go home until next week.

But the Bible says true fellowship has the power to revolutionize lives. Masks come off, conversations get deep, hearts get vulnerable, lives are shared, accountability is invited, and tenderness flows. People really do become like brothers and sisters. They shoulder each other's burdens—and unfortunately, that's something that few of the people in that audience had experienced while growing up in church.

In many churches, it just didn't seem legal to tell anyone you were having a problem. Families that had sat in the same pew for years would suddenly disappear, because the husband and wife were in turmoil over marriage problems. Instead of coming to the church for help and prayer and support, they fled the other way, because they didn't feel the freedom to say, "We love Jesus, but we're not doing very well. Our lives feel like they're unraveling. We need some help!"

The implicit understanding was that you shouldn't have a problem, and if you did, you'd better not talk about it around the church.

I learned that lesson well. When I got old enough to stand on the church patio after services, someone would say, "So, Bill, how are things going in high school?"

And I'd give the response that I thought was expected. "Fine, Ben," I'd say. "They're just great."

I didn't feel I could tell him that my heart was being ripped to shreds because my girlfriend and I had broken up. Or that I was flat-lined spiritually. Or that I had an older brother who was drinking too much and driving too fast, and I was scared about where his life was heading.

I didn't say anything, because I felt that a good Christian just didn't admit to having those kinds of real-life difficulties. And in many churches, that's called fellowship.

It shouldn't be.

SEEKING AND SAVING THE LOST

Then Dr. Bilezikian talked about how a biblically functioning community reaches out to spiritually confused people and helps them understand and respond to Jesus Christ. That resonated deep inside the church leaders in that audience. Many of them had attended church as a youngster and wondered, *If there really is a heaven and hell, then why doesn't anyone do something for that neighborhood we can see right from the church's windows?*

They couldn't understand why the church tolerated such an obvious disconnection. Despite large numbers of lost people in their vicinity, churches were only geared up to serve the already convinced. Everything that happened—the teaching, the budgets, the services, the programs—was designed for those who were safely inside the family of God. As a result, nobody from the neighborhood across the street ever ventured into the church.

As Lynne described in Chapter 1, when I did invite a high school buddy whose personal problems had opened him up to God, his interest in Christianity was quickly extinguished by one exposure to the church. He felt like the odd man out. He couldn't relate to the music, he didn't know when to sit or stand, he couldn't recite the Apostles' Creed with everyone else, and he had to suffer through a sermon that left him convinced God is irrelevant and impossible to understand.

It was the first time I had sat through a traditional worship service with a hellbound but seeking friend on my arm, and it was the longest sixty minutes of my life. That's the day I stumbled upon the dreaded "cringe factor," that awful internal flinching that a Christian experiences when he or she begins to see the service through a seeker's eyes.

But according to Dr. Bilezikian, a biblical community of believers not only has a heart for irreligious people but it also develops a strategy for reaching them. As did the disciple Matthew, who was so concerned about his former tax-gathering friends that he invited them to a party with Jesus and the other disciples in the hope that they would rub shoulders and talk about spiritual matters. Sure, it was a far-out idea, but what alternative did Matthew have? He knew that inviting them to the synagogue would only confuse them. Maybe—*just maybe*—this kind of informal setting would spark some conversations of eternal significance.

Predictably, the Pharisees ended up crashing the party to bitterly accuse Jesus of the unthinkable: fraternizing with sinners. To their cold hearts, those buddies of Matthew were merely profane, immoral, faithless, wicked people who deserved to be written off and consigned to hell.

But Jesus said, in effect, "You just don't get it, do you? With all your learning, with all your scrolls, with all your experience, you still don't understand how much lost people matter to my Father. So maybe a metaphor will help. Imagine that everyone in this room has a terminal illness. And just pretend that I'm the great physician and I've got the cure. Doesn't it make sense that the one with the cure needs to get up close to the person who's sick?"

After that party ended and all the guests had gone home, I can picture Matthew and Jesus sitting down, exhausted, and having a heart-to-heart talk. "Thank you for coming to talk with my friends," I can hear Matthew saying. "When the Pharisees came in and started pointing their bony fingers at You, I wanted to crawl in a hole and die. I hate to see You embarrassed in public. But thanks for being here. Thanks for helping some of the people I care about."

And I can imagine Jesus saying, "Matthew, I want to tell you two things that I hope you'll never forget. First, I love your heart. You didn't abandon your friends when you came to faith. You didn't need an evangelism class; no pastor had to hype you up. You just have a soft heart for the spiritually lost. And second, I love your courage. You had the guts to innovate. Who's ever heard of a party with a purpose? I love to encourage My followers when they try to do *something* to advance the kingdom."

Biblical communities remain sensitive and loving toward people outside the faith—but they don't stop there. They get intentional by creating opportunities for spiritual seekers to come to a safe place to hear the dangerous, life-changing, and eternity-altering message of Christ. The bonus is that these communities get to see the miraculous ways that God revolutionizes human hearts, one person at a time.

SHARING THE WEALTH

Once Dr. Bilezikian got on a roll, there wasn't much that could stop his enthusiasm for the Acts 2 church. In a community that's responsive to God, the wealthy share with the poor, he said. It's right there in the text. Those with resources were outrageously generous in helping those who were in need.

Generally speaking, those in the audience hadn't seen much generosity in their churches as they were growing up. What they saw was a Mercedes-driving family sitting down next to a single mom who owned a beat-up Ford Pinto. During the service, they'd share the same hymnbook, worship the same God, and recite the same creed. But afterward the affluent family would go over to the country club and spend a small fortune on dinner while the single mom packed her belongings into a cardboard box because she was getting evicted from her apartment that week. Where was the sharing? Where was the evidence of love?

That's why we've started all sorts of ministries at Willow Creek in an effort to sensitize the affluent to the plight of the needy, both inside and outside the church. There's a food pantry and help for the homeless; there's a Benevolent Board to distribute financial assistance; there are volunteers building homes for the poor and working on projects in Chicago's inner city. And there's a ministry of auto mechanics who decided on their own to get together twice a week and repair the cars of single moms for free.

In fact, many people at Willow Creek don't trade in their old car when they buy a new one. Instead they donate it to the church, and the mechanics fix it up and give it to a family that's desperate for transportation. In a recent two-year period, the church distributed nearly seventy cars.

Once when I was coming out of our maintenance area, I noticed a gleaming Honda Accord sitting there. "Whose car is that?" I asked my brother Dan, who oversees the part of the church which includes that ministry.

Dan told me the name of a businessman from the church, a middle-management type who has a mortgage and some kids to put through college. In other words, he's not rolling in money. But when it came time to get another car, he gave his Honda to the church.

"You ought to see the family that's going to get this car," Dan said. "It's going to blow their minds."

He was right. A short time later the church got this thank-you note:

> When I became my son's sole supporter, we had nothing—only our clothes, no car, no house, no child support. I was fortunate to find a job a mile and a half away from the apartment so I could walk to work. People seemed to rally around and help me from time to time by lending me their cars so I could hold down a second part-time job that paid the bills the primary job couldn't.
>
> I learned to live day by day, grateful for each car I drove, grateful to Willow Creek for introducing me to Christ, grateful to the youth ministries for being a "father" to my son, grateful for the church's Rebuilders Ministry, which taught me that God would be my husband and so much more.
>
> Our lives have changed in miraculous ways because of this church—because people reach out and touch others in ways that feel to us like being touched by God.

I wanted you to know how hard it is to be a single mom. We don't know how to fix things when they break, and often there is no money to have them fixed by someone, so we limp along, praying for the car we're driving to get us safely where we need to go "just one more time." I've lived with the "just one more time" prayer longer than I can remember and am amazed that God honored that prayer for so long.

I can hardly take it all in that I should be the recipient of this car you have provided. I want to cry every time I get in it. It feels to me like another "loaner" car—but this time it's a loaner from Jesus. I'm driving His car. I feel blessed again and am a witness of how He gives "good things" to His children.

LOVE OF ANOTHER KIND

You tell me: what is nobler, what is loftier, what is a higher purpose in life, than devoting yourself to establishing and developing a community of believers that strives to fulfill the Acts 2 description of the bride of Christ? To creating a supportive and encouraging place where Spirit-led preaching brings a new, God-focused direction to people's lives; where believers gather in small groups to share their hearts on the deepest of levels; where people compassionately walk with each other through life's problems and pain; where everyone feels empowered to make a difference through their spiritual gifts; where prayer, worship, and the sacraments are lifted up; where the rich share their God-given resources with the poor; and where people ache so much for their irreligious friends that the church gets strategic and takes risks to reach out to them with the Gospel?

Believe me, I don't want to paint Willow Creek as being better than it is. In this book, we've tried to be honest about our shortcomings. Yes, a few of our programs have blown up in our faces, and we've made some mistakes that have inadvertently hurt people. But anyone who hangs around Willow Creek long enough will know that the signs and marks of a biblically functioning community are manifesting themselves in greater and greater ways as each year goes by.

That's what fires me up. It's not Willow Creek's size or campus or creativity that inspires me to keep going. It's the fundamental realization that people are trying their best, under the power of the Holy Spirit, to build a community that operates according to the plan that God has described in Scripture. I *need* to be part of that.

And you can bring about the same kind of environment in your own church if you catch the vision for it. You don't have to change the name on the sign or toss out the organ or make your church more contemporary. That isn't what renewal is about. Renewal happens when the internal force at the core of your church is simply this—*love of another kind*. It's the giving and receiving of the sort of outrageous love that Jesus called us to express to each other.

Let's face it. Jesus was scandalously generous in distributing love. In Luke 7, when He was dining at the invitation of the Pharisees, the neighborhood prostitute barged in and fell down before Him, her tears bathing His feet. It was the social embarrassment of the month! But Jesus didn't whack her for her wicked life. He didn't throw her out to demonstrate that He hadn't had any prior acquaintance with her. He didn't sermonize on morality.

Instead He looked into her eyes and discerned that her tears of repentance were genuine. Then He assured her that her moral debt had been canceled by love of another kind.

Do you know the shocking message that we've got to communicate to your neighborhood and mine? *That love of another kind is still available.* We've got to tell people who are right in the midst of fouled-up lives that there's a gift of redemption that Christ has purchased with His death on the cross and which He is freely offering to anyone who'll receive it in repentance and faith.

We need to be reckless purveyors of saving grace. In the end, it's only this love of Christ that can change our attitudes, reshape the way we relate to others, and make us more forgiving, more generous, and more loving. Ultimately, it is this love that can turn our churches into authentic biblical communities.

THE SOURCE OF HOPE

The scene was the San Juan airport. Lynne and I were on our way back from a vacation in Puerto Rico. I was reading as we waited in the gate area.

From the other side of my newspaper, I heard a tussle starting. I glanced over the paper and saw two little boys, probably six or seven years old, who were pushing each other around. *Well, the parents will come and break them up soon,* I mused. *No problem.* I went back to reading my paper.

But then all of a sudden I heard a loud *slap*. One of the boys had just walloped the other kid so hard that his face instantly glowed red. *Where are those parents now?* I thought. *This is getting serious.*

That's when the other kid rolled up his fist and smacked the first boy with such force that he was knocked to the floor. Blood erupted from his nose. One thing was clear: both these kids knew violence. They weren't playfully wrestling around like my brother Dan and I did when we were little. They had probably been beaten themselves, because they clearly knew how to dish it out.

My insides started churning, and I was thinking, *Where are those parents? This is awful! They've got to stop this.*

Then the second youngster took the bloodied one by the hair and started pounding his skull on the quarry tile floor. *Pounding it!* I couldn't stand it anymore. I threw down my paper, ran over to the fight, and picked up the kids to get them away from each other. They were swinging and fighting and biting and screaming, but finally I spun them off in opposite directions, just as the loudspeaker announced the last call for my flight.

I grabbed my carry-on bag, walked to the plane, and slumped down into my seat. I can't tell you how much I wanted to just put on the earphones and flip through a sailing magazine. I hate violence and wanted to get my mind off it.

But God had other plans. It was as if the Holy Spirit impressed upon me, *Don't put your head in the sand, Bill. Think about what just happened. Think about those two boys.*

And I did. As we were approaching cruising altitude, I said to myself, *Well, let's see. With boiling cauldrons of hatred inside them, these kids probably aren't destined to become honor students in junior high school. And they probably aren't going to get inducted into the National Honor Society in high school, either. Are they going to date cheerleaders? Are they going to go to the right college, get good-paying jobs, marry their sweethearts, buy homes in suburbia, and become deacons in a church? No, probably not. The course of their lives isn't soaring northbound; it's plummeting southbound. If they're hitting each other with closed fists at age six or seven, then they'll be using sticks in junior high, knives in senior high, and then who knows what? Sooner or later somebody's going to get killed.*

So what in the world can change the trajectory of their lives? Is the government going to start a program that will save them? Can Congress pass a law that will redirect them? Is some businessman going to sell a product that will alter the condition of their hearts? Will the media improve their value system? Is a college professor going to utter some brilliant words that will reshape their character?

Of course not. It's going to take a fully devoted follower of Jesus Christ from your church or mine who gets alongside them at some point in their lives and says, "Listen—it's pretty obvious that you didn't get much love in the home you grew up in. But I'm here to tell you that there's a love in heaven with your name on it. And if you'll open yourself up to the grace of Christ, over time He will revolutionize who you are. Love of another kind can gradually transform the composition of your heart. You can be pardoned through Christ for your wrongdoing, and you can join a biblically functioning community in which the teaching is transformational. You'll grow and mature through relationships that are rich and real. You'll be loved and surrounded by people who will really be on your side. Your soul will be replenished through prayer and worship. You'll discover your spiritual gifts and find a new purpose for your life. And sooner or later you'll end up pass-ing on the trajectory-changing message of Jesus Christ to someone who is just like you used to be."

On that airplane between Puerto Rico and Miami, this realization struck me anew—*church leaders really do hold the hope of the world in their hands*. They have more power than politicians, more influence than business leaders, more answers for the world's calamities and heartbreaks than any university scholar or media pundit.

The answer is love of another kind, expressed through the cross and through the bride of Christ—communities of His people who are committed to fulfilling His vision for the church.

What greater mission—what more critical enterprise—can you possibly invest your life in?

chapter eleven

A MISSION AND A STRATEGY

The multitiered classroom at Harvard Business School was arranged in a semi-circle around a massive green chalkboard. The students—future leaders of commerce and industry—sat behind cardboard signs on which they had written their names. After all, half their grade was based on classroom participation, and they wanted to make sure the teacher gave credit where credit was due.

The professor prowled the room, barking questions, extracting answers, eliciting opinions, dashing back and forth to the chalkboard to write down a particularly insightful observation. The discussion was animated; the atmosphere was electric.

In their quest for lessons about effective business practices, these students were accustomed to critiquing case studies of multinational corporations. But for the first time in the school's history, they were examining a local church, mining Willow Creek for clues about how a nonprofit organization should serve its constituents.

Suddenly the professor stopped in front of a student who had been quiet until then. He got up close to her, looking her straight in the eyes. "What do you think of the one-sentence mission statement of Willow Creek Community Church?" he demanded.

"Well," she said, gathering her composure, "they say they're trying to turn irreligious people into fully devoted followers of Christ."

The professor shook his head. "No, no, no—I didn't ask you what the mission statement *was*. I want to know what you *think* about it! What's your visceral reaction? How do you *feel* about it?"

She was clearly flustered. "Uh, I don't come from a religious background," she started. "But when they say they're trying to turn irreligious people into fully devoted followers of Christ, it sounds to me like they're ... well ... *they're trying to turn atheists into missionaries.* And frankly, I see that as being one hell of a challenge!"

The class burst into laughter, but her comment was more than just a slightly coarse remark to me. It triggered something deep inside. The way she said it—turning atheists into missionaries—gave me new clarity. *No wonder it's so hard to do what we're trying to do!*

We're not just wanting to keep Christians happy and growing. We aren't attempting to lure believers from other churches by having glitzier services and better programs. We're starting with hard-core skeptics and trying to transform them into zealously committed disciples of Jesus.

And that's *really* hard!

THE SHEEPISH TRUTH

To be truthful, most churches aren't actively engaged in that process. In fact, let's get real honest about what happens in a lot of them. Not your church or mine, of course, but with too many pastors in traditional churches on the corner of Elm and Vine.

After they get out of seminary, these pastors are assigned a little flock of sheep and given a pen to keep them in. They see their job primarily as keeping the existing sheep safely within that corral. So they feed them a little, they give them something to drink, they pat them on the head, and if the sheep get too close to the fence, they warn, "Get back! Get back!" From time to time, they even shear the sheep—but not too closely. And they encourage them to give birth to little lambs, because that's the way the church grows.

If they perform well, then in a few years they receive a bigger flock and a larger pen. And if they do that three or four times without fouling up, they're moved to headquarters, where they don't even have to mess with sheep anymore!

Is that cynical? OK, maybe it is. But there's also some truth in there.

Those of us who started Willow Creek decided early on that we didn't want to spend our lives just trying to keep sheep in a pen. Instead we wanted to do what Jesus told us in the Great Commission: "Therefore go and make disciples of all nations, baptizing them in the name of the Father and of the Son and of the Holy Spirit, and teaching them to obey everything I have commanded you" (Matthew 28:19–20).

In other words, reach them and teach them. Find lambs who aren't part of the flock and enfold them through what Christ has done. Then don't just pat them on the head. Turn those grass-munchers into spiritual champions—fully devoted followers of Christ who unapologetically orient their entire lives around Him.

That means we needed to pay attention to both parts of the Great Commission. Yes, we wanted to be a worshiping church, but that doesn't fulfill the evangelistic imperative of Christ's command. Sure, we wanted to reach seekers with the Gospel, but that wouldn't achieve the second directive: to grow up believers in their faith. We needed to do both—and to do it according to the unique thumbprint that the Holy Spirit had in mind for us.

So we developed a clear vision statement: *We want to become a biblically functioning community.* Then we summarized our mission in one sentence: *We want to turn irreligious people into fully devoted followers of Christ.* Anything less than that would not do justice to Jesus' marching orders in the Great Commission. But what's next? We needed an effective, God-honoring plan to accomplish that mission.

The strategy we pursued intuitively for many years took shape when I wrote it down one day on a napkin in California. Every believer at Willow Creek sees it as their blueprint to accomplish our mission. We call it our seven-step strategy, and it's part of our "thumbprint" as a church.

STEP 1: BUILD AN AUTHENTIC RELATIONSHIP WITH A NONBELIEVER

Once some religious leaders wanted to sting Jesus with the most devastating insult they could conjure up. What's the ugliest slur they could sling at Him? What's the most embarrassing and deflating affront imaginable? After wracking their brains, they finally sputtered, "You ... You ... *You friend of sinners!"*

But Jesus wore their words like a badge of honor. He pleaded guilty to attending raucous weddings, hanging around with crooked tax-gatherers, talking with women of ill repute, and mingling with riffraff from the wrong side of town. His motivation was simple: Jesus befriended sinners because they mattered to His Father!

As Christians, we're supposed to model our lives after Christ's. Yet somewhere along the way, some pastors began beating the "come apart and be ye separate" drum. They twisted a verse that calls on us to lead a distinctly Christian lifestyle into one that justifies our ignoring spiritually lost people. The result was the development of an "us versus them" mentality that makes nonbelievers the enemy instead of the object of our prayers and love.

I wonder how many church leaders and their congregations can worship God so sincerely, study and pray so fervently, raise their children in the faith so determinedly, and pursue many aspects of church life so fully but care so little about hell-bound people within a nine-iron shot of their own home.

I understand that it's a lot more comfortable to pal around with brothers and sisters in Christ. They speak the same language, say the same prayers, read the same

Bible, laugh at the same kind of jokes. It's clean, it's easy, it's safe. And I admit that the minute you step outside that circle, everything's up for grabs. The language is ugly, the values are different, the morals are loose, the jokes are off-color.

But I'll say flat out: *In our current culture, the cause of world redemption is going to be won or lost depending on whether Christian leaders build relationships with unchurched people and then—by teaching and example—encourage those in their church to do the same.*

Today's skeptic isn't likely to pull over and repent at the sight of a Christian bumper sticker. If he's handed a tract, he's probably going to pitch it into the first wastebasket he sees. If he's approached by a stranger, he's going to raise his defenses. But there's credibility in relationships. There's trust. There's a track record of caring and love. And so the typically irreligious individual needs someone who will build an authentic friendship with him, who will answer his questions and sincerely discuss his problems, who will live out his faith before him in a humble and honest way, and who will—over time—earn the right to delve into the sensitive topic of faith.

At Willow Creek we've put all our eggs into the basket of relational evangelism. We barely do any advertising, we aren't on television and radio, and we don't use direct mail or visit strangers door-to-door. Other churches may find those approaches helpful, but that's not the thumbprint the Holy Spirit has impressed upon our church.

Through our *Becoming a Contagious Christian* training course, as well as through other teaching and modeling, we instruct and encourage our believers to proactively build relationships with irreligious people for the ultimate purpose of leading them to Christ.

That's how God's kingdom advances—one life at a time.

STEP 2: SHARE A VERBAL WITNESS

A few years ago Lynne and I were enjoying an idyllic second honeymoon aboard a sailboat that a friend had loaned us. We dropped anchor in a picturesque Caribbean harbor and went ashore to enjoy the beach for a while.

While we were there we met another sailor who had chartered a seventy-foot boat. "Why don't you come over for cocktails tonight?" he asked us. When I mentioned that we weren't really drinkers, he said, "Aw, that's OK. Come on over anyway. We'll have a good time."

So at the appointed hour, Lynne and I motored our dinghy to his boat and climbed aboard. We were greeted by six couples from the East Coast, and they were definitely in a party mood. The piña coladas were flowing, the conversation was lively—and then after we had spent some time getting to know one another, somebody asked, "So, Bill, what do you do for a living?"

I thought my response might sink the boat. "Well," I said, "I'm a minister." But as it turned out, we had gotten to know each other well enough that it didn't seem to be a barrier. We continued to talk and joke around until it was time for Lynne and me to head back to our boat, which was anchored nearby.

Lynne climbed down the ladder and got into the dinghy. But as I was about to climb in—I had one foot on the sailboat's ladder and the other in our skiff—the woman who had asked me what I did for a living called out, "Say, Bill! Before you leave, can you answer a question? I've always wanted to ask a Christian what it means to become one. Can you tell all of us?"

I looked up at the slightly inebriated group of twelve, most of them clutching drinks with little umbrellas in them, and I did a quick mental computation. I figured I had forty-five seconds to a minute at most to summarize the only message in the universe that was capable of changing their eternities.

Hit the pause button.

It's not enough to merely enter into the world of nonbelievers, build relationships with them, and live out our faith in front of them. At some point, if we're praying for them, the Holy Spirit is going to open up a window of evangelistic opportunity, and we've got to know how to respond. As the apostle Peter cautioned, "Always be prepared to give an answer to everyone who asks you to give the reason for the hope that you have" (1 Peter 3:15).

So let me ask: are *you* prepared?

Not only should the ten percent of Christians who are gifted evangelists be poised to share their faith, but *every* Christian needs to be ready, because opportunities are surely going to arise if we are actively involved with spiritual seekers. We teach the people of Willow Creek to practice verbalizing their testimony about how Christ changed their life. Then we show them how to master several techniques of communicating their faith in a graphic and concise way. I used one of these illustrations with the people on the boat.

Now hit play.

"Here's a brief way I can explain it to you," I told them. "I spell religion D-O. It's what people *do*. It's the good things they do to try to offset God's anger at the bad things they've done. Religious people are always on that religious treadmill, trying to do more, give more, serve more, attend more church services—to try to reach some mysterious quota at which point they think they can say, 'Phew! I think I finally paid off my bad deeds.' Religion frustrated me incredibly for years, and I've bailed out of the D-O plan."

171

They nodded as if to say, *Us too! We don't want any part of that plan, either!*

"But Christianity is different," I said. "It's spelled D-O-N-E. It's what Jesus Christ, the Son of God, has *done*. When He died on the cross and took the punishment for my sins and foul-ups, He paid the penalty in order that forgiveness could be granted to me as a gift. So I got off that performance treadmill and just trusted in what Christ had done on the cross. It changed my heart, it changed my life, and it has changed my eternity.

"That's the best way I can summarize it right now," I added. "If any of you has questions or wants to talk any further, we're on the boat right over there, and we'd love to discuss it some more."

These people had neither the time nor the tolerance for a theological lecture; they merely needed to hear the fundamentals of the Gospel explained in a way that connected with them. I don't know if I'll see any of them in heaven, but I do know I did my best under the circumstances to crisply point out to them what Christianity is about.

By themselves, these first two steps—building relationships with seekers and being equipped to share your faith—are enough to revitalize a church that has been following the "keep the sheep in the pen" approach. If people would prayerfully enter into the redemptive drama, their own lives would change, and all of a sudden some new Christians would be walking around. And that inevitably softens everybody's heart toward seekers.

But Christians do require help in the evangelistic process. They need a partner.

STEP 3: BRING THE SEEKER TO A SERVICE DESIGNED ESPECIALLY FOR THEM

Linda and Leslie were best friends. Linda was a Christian and part of a solid Bible church. Leslie, having grown up with virtually no church experience, was in spiritual neutral, not knowing whether God was fact or fantasy.

In the course of their relationship, when credibility and trust had been firmly established, Linda told Leslie the story of how Christ had changed her life, and she spelled out the Gospel with as much clarity as she could muster. Leslie was genuinely interested, especially since she could see consistency between Linda's beliefs and her day-to-day behavior. But Leslie always stopped short of taking a step of faith herself.

Linda felt stuck. She had done everything she had learned in various evangelism courses, and now she didn't know what to do next. Even so, she knew intuitively what *not* to do—bring Leslie to her church. After all, the church only offered a worship service. How could Leslie praise a God she wasn't sure existed?

She would be required to sing lyrics she didn't believe; she would be embarrassed when the pastor told everybody to look up a Bible passage and she didn't know how; she wouldn't understand the Christianese or the rituals; she wouldn't know when to sit or stand; the offering would seem coercive to her; and the sermon would be irrelevant to someone who was on the outside of the faith looking in.

Then Linda read about a newfangled church called Willow Creek, which was holding weekly "seeker services" in a nearby theater. Linda and her husband, Jerry, checked out a service and knew immediately it was perfect to help Leslie take the next step in her spiritual journey.

They invited Leslie and, because she trusted Linda, she accepted. Sure enough, she was blown away by the service. She loved the contemporary music with Christian lyrics; she was moved to tears and laughter by the drama; her mind was stretched by the multimedia presentation; and most of all, she was impacted by the message. "It was like the pastor had a window into my heart," she told Linda.

Soon a pattern developed. Leslie would attend the seeker service with Linda each Sunday, and afterward they'd discuss it in detail. Specifically they'd focus on how the message applied personally to her. She would ask questions and seek elaboration—until one day when all the puzzle pieces fell into place. She prayed to receive Christ as the forgiver of her sins and leader of her life, and the spiritual transformation of her entire family began.

That's what we call "team evangelism."

Here's the deal we've struck with the Christians at Willow Creek: you build meaningful relationships with irreligious individuals, pray for them and care for them, describe to them how Christ has changed your life, and explain the Gospel as the Holy Spirit opens up opportunities. And then, as a tool you can use in your personal evangelistic efforts, those in the church who are gifted as musicians and actors, producers and teachers, dancers and vocalists, will knock themselves out to present the basic truths of Christianity in a creative, compelling, and Spirit-anointed way. And together—*as a team*—we'll reach our community for Christ; one friend, one neighbor, one colleague, one family member, at a time.

A CLOSER LOOK AT TEAM EVANGELISM IN ACTION

We call our part of the bargain "seeker services." Everything from the music to the printed program is designed specifically for unchurched people. We have services on the weekend, because if nonbelievers finally decide to attend church, that's when they expect to go. We do them fifty-two weekends a year so that there is always one when it's needed. We minimize the "cringe factor" by maintaining excellence. We preserve the anonymity that seekers so desperately want to protect.

Nothing we have done has been more effective in bringing people to Christ or more widely misunderstood by the Christian community than our seeker services. That's surprised us, because our approach isn't very different from what Billy Graham has done with nearly universal blessing for the last several decades.

Before a typical Graham crusade, his team goes out in advance and trains Christians how to build relationships and share their faith with unchurched people, as well as how to invite them to a rally where they can learn more about Christianity. The event is held in a neutral setting, usually a stadium or civic center. The music, stage design, terminology—everything that happens in the service—is planned with the nonbelieving person in mind. The program culminates with Graham giving a concise scriptural message that nonbelievers can understand. He then challenges them to receive Christ right then or, if they're not ready, to continue to investigate Christianity further.

Our approach is similar. What may have caused some misunderstanding, though, is our contemporary approach. Because we began in the mid-seventies, while Graham started in an earlier era, and because we were trying to reach a different generation, we've used cutting-edge communication methods: contemporary Christian music, drama, multimedia, video, and dance. But we have merely harnessed those art forms in the same way that Graham has used soloists, choirs, and testimonies. Our approaches may differ somewhat, but our driving values are identical.

Even so, our use of the arts has prompted some misinformed people to assume that we're only trying to entertain people. They suspect we're preaching a superficial message, because so many seekers show up on weekends.

But our seeker services aren't fluff. Anyone who has attended them for a period of time knows that. Our music has God-honoring lyrics with biblical integrity. The drama, video, and media touch people on an emotional level to help thaw the deep pools of spiritual longing that often lay frozen beneath the surface.

And while we've felt the freedom to vary the method with which the Gospel is communicated, we don't tinker with the message itself. Our sermons don't shrink back from spelling out the fullness of the Gospel, including the difficult elements of sin and repentance. Actually, most seekers these days *want* someone to be straight with them and give them the unvarnished truth of the Bible. A couple of years ago we spent twenty-six consecutive weeks going through the Sermon on the Mount at our seeker services—verse by verse, chapter by chapter—and that season we baptized several hundred new believers.

Sure, we discuss topics that are relevant to seekers—their marriages, their priorities, their emotions, their finances, their parenting, their quest for fulfillment, their sexuality. But it's always from a biblical perspective, to help them understand that Christianity isn't just true but that it also can *work* in their lives. And throughout the year, we weave in explicit evangelistic messages to help bring people across the line into God's family.

The beauty of the seeker service is that it involves the entire congregation in personal evangelism, not just people who are gifted in sharing their faith, or those with outgoing personalities. A few years ago we encouraged those who were being baptized to be accompanied by the individual who was most instrumental in bringing them to faith. During the service, I noticed that one rather shy woman was the person who had witnessed to four or five people. She certainly didn't look like an extroverted, raw-meat-eating evangelist type to me. So at a reception afterward, I mentioned her to one of the people who had been baptized. "She must really be something," I said.

"Let me tell you about her," he replied. "She works in my office, and she doesn't throw Bibles around or anything like that. She is just the most loving, truthful, and life-giving person in our department. She made me want to ask, 'What's going on that would make you like you are?' She didn't really give me an understandable answer. She just said, 'Come to church with me.'"

He looked me in the eye and added, "Then you and the others filled in the pieces."

That's team evangelism.

Should Willow Creek continue to do weekly seeker services? Absolutely, because that's part of the Holy Spirit's unmistakable thumbprint for our ministry. He has led us to develop an effective, fruit-bearing outreach tool that is a perfect fit for those of us at the core of the church.

Should *your* church do a weekly seeker service? Maybe, maybe not. It's really a question to ask God. But whatever course you take—whether it's a monthly seeker-sensitive event, a quarterly outreach breakfast, or some other approach—every church needs to figure out, under the guidance of the Holy Spirit, how to fulfill the front end of the Great Commission.

Naturally, the second component of the Great Commission needs to be fulfilled as well. So at Willow Creek, once people make the decision to receive Christ as their forgiver and leader, we encourage them to continue through the next four steps.

STEP 4: REGULARLY ATTEND A SERVICE FOR BELIEVERS

A few years ago I invited several irreligious guys to join me in racing a sailboat during the competitive season on Lake Michigan. One of them, a harddrinking party animal named Tom, ended up committing his life to Christ a while later. I've continued to mentor him in his spiritual development, although it hasn't been easy because he lives three hours away. One way I've helped is by mailing him books and other resources, and a couple of times I sent him some bootleg tapes of our entire midweek New Community service.

The next time we got together, his enthusiasm took me off guard. "Hey, whatever that Dieter guy does," he said, referring to our New Community worship leader and teacher Dieter Zander, "I *really* like that."

"Tommy," I replied, "that's just another indication of the work the Holy Spirit's doing in your life. You're learning to love worship."

That's what happens when people are freshly adopted into God's family. They're so bowled over by God's amazing grace and so thoroughly ambushed by love of another kind that their natural reaction is to want to thank and praise God. We offer them that opportunity on Wednesday and Thursday nights at our believers services.

As Lynne mentioned earlier, we weren't always a worshiping church. In the early days, we basically had song times followed by a Bible study. But then I was invited to speak at a conference at Jack Hayford's church in California. As I was waiting to appear, Jack told the congregation, "Before our speaker comes to deliver the message, let's just worship God."

No problem. I figured this wouldn't take too long.

An hour and twenty minutes later I felt as if I needed to take a shower. For the first time in my life, I had experienced worship. Freed-up worship, in which the Holy Spirit was active, the songs had a flow and purpose to them, lyrics mattered, and we were gently brought to the throne of God and invited to empty our hearts to Him.

Since then we've strived to make worship a central focus of our New Community. Sometimes it's celebratory, other times it's reflective, but we spend thirty to forty-five minutes exalting God together. It has become a refreshing oasis for those who spend most of their week working in spiritually parched territory.

New Community is also where believers are nurtured and encouraged, challenged and inspired, edified and even chastised when appropriate. We celebrate the Lord's Supper each month, handling it with profound respect as the sacrament that commemorates Christ's sacrifice for us. And we learn together, going through the Bible book by book and focusing on themes—such as "downward mobility" from Philippians 2—that become rallying cries throughout the church.

One of the advantages of having separate services for seekers and believers is that each service can be optimally focused. Every week, the New Community creates what is, in essence, a core meeting of the church, where I can exert leadership among the family. I can shore up a sagging value, talk about a new opportunity, or point out the next hill we're going to take, and we can have confidence that we're handling "family matters" without boring or confusing seekers.

However, when any church spends a large part of its resources and energy trying to reach irreligious people, sometimes there's a temptation to merely toss a few crumbs to its believers. Unfortunately, they tend to get warmed-up leftovers. And regrettably, sometimes that's what we gave them.

But we've come to realize that as New Community goes, so goes the church. The hearts of our believers need to be filled to overflowing with love of another kind if they're going to be able to live the compassionate, sacrificial, and authentic Christian lifestyle that will be salt and light to seekers.

STEP 5: JOIN A SMALL GROUP

Ray was dying of cancer, but he wasn't dying alone. His small group got together and vowed, "We're going to walk with him right until the end. We're going to love him and care for him and pray for him, because he's our brother in Christ."

And they did. They'd go over to his house and hold hands in a semicircle around his bed, singing together the New Community worship song that had become his theme: "Be bold, be strong, for the Lord your God is with you."

That's what it's like to be in a small group. It's a place of loyalty and compassion, commitment and caring, prayer and mutual sacrifice. It's a supportive little platoon in which people can share their lives with each other, expose their faults and fears, seek counsel and encouragement, hold each other accountable, grow together spiritually, and give and receive love of another kind. It's no accident that even Jesus surrounded Himself with a small, close-knit band of followers.

I've seen incredible life transformation take place across a dining room table, where people get elbow-deep in each other's lives and lovingly but firmly challenge one other to become more like Jesus. Please don't misunderstand—I believe in the power of preaching to bring change into people's lives, but we also need to acknowledge that small groups have the important added advantages of direct interaction and follow-up.

This really struck me a few years ago when Lynne and I were leading a discipleship group with four other couples. Halfway through a get-together at our house, one person asked a question. That's not unusual, except that it was the *exact* question I had just spent thirty minutes answering in my sermon that morning!

I thought he was kidding. "Hey, that's what my sermon was about," I said with a laugh.

He replied, "It was?"

Those of us who preach like to believe that all a person needs in order to grow spiritually is to pay attention when we speak. And while Spirit-empowered preaching can be transformational, sometimes the pastor's three finely honed points fade from the minds of listeners a lot more quickly than he likes to admit.

However, small groups provide the optimal environment for incubating the maturing process. Where there is trust and transparency, and where there are extended periods of time to help each other apply biblical truth to real-life situations, suddenly scriptural truths that seemed theoretical become concrete and practical. As Proverbs 27:17 says, "As iron sharpens iron, so one man sharpens another."

In fact, virtually every significant decision and step of growth I've made in the last two decades of ministry have come in the context of community, in which brothers and sisters who know me well have gotten up close to me and said, "Bill, you've got to face this thing that you don't see. You've got to root this sinful pattern out of your life. You've got to grow in this character area. We'll help you, we'll cheer you on, but it's time to change."

That's why we want Willow Creek not to be a church that *offers* small groups but to become a church *of* small groups. One of my biggest regrets is not improving our small-group structure earlier in order to accommodate growth and ensure that leaders were dealing with a reasonable span of care so they didn't burn out.

Thanks to Jim Dethmer, we began implementing a variation of the metachurch model, which uses a system of leaders, apprentice leaders, and an "open chair" in each group so that groups can increase in size and then birth into new groups. He helped implement a group-leader apprentice program with an eye toward training new leaders and dividing and multiplying groups. The result was better care and fewer leader casualties. For the first time in our church's history, leaders feel adequately trained and empowered to perform their shepherding task.

Our goal: we want every person who calls Willow Creek their home church to be connected in a little platoon of believers.

STEP 6: DISCOVER, DEVELOP, AND DEPLOY YOUR SPIRITUAL GIFT

As a young pastor, I felt obligated to visit everyone from the church who was hospitalized. And frankly, it was a very frustrating experience for me—and probably for them too. I didn't know where to sit, what to say, or what questions to ask, and so I felt awkward and uncomfortable. It seemed as if people ended up feeling worse after my visits instead of better.

Then one of our elders came into the room where I was visiting a patient. He was gracious and compassionate, saying the right things, asking the right questions, encouraging the person in just the right way, praying the right prayer, always having the right tone of voice. That *really* made me feel awful!

Later he put his arm around me and said, "Bill, it's OK. I happen to have a spiritual gift of mercy, and it's not one God gave to you. But you don't have to have all the gifts. Why don't you just concentrate on the gifts that God did give you and then surround yourself with others who can complement you?"

He was right. All Christians are supposed to be compassionate, but some have a specific spiritual gift of mercy—a divine enablement to minister cheerfully and appropriately to those who are suffering. As I've mentioned, my particular gifts are leadership, evangelism, and teaching. Others have gifts of administration, craftsmanship, encouragement, or a number of others listed in Scripture. The Bible assures us that all Christ followers have at least one gift and that God places gifted individuals just as He desires in His church.

So at Willow Creek we don't start with a volunteer position that we desperately need to fill—like teaching fourth graders or cleaning the building—and then browbeat people into reluctantly agreeing to serve. That's a formula for frustrating the individual and demotivating the church. Instead we start with the person. What spiritual gifts has God bestowed on him or her? What kind of passions, temperament, and personality does he or she have? Once that's determined, we try to match the individual with a position in one of our ninety-four ministries that fits him or her well.

The result: people serve with joy and effectiveness, with fulfillment and longevity, and everyone is left marveling at how God created His church as an interconnected, interdependent community in which each person can make a unique contribution.

As a leader, few things are as satisfying to me as watching people serve God with their gifts, whether it's stocking the food pantry, shepherding a small group, or handling administrative tasks. I can remember sitting through a New Community service and watching one of our teaching pastors, John Ortberg, use his phenomenal preaching gift.

"John," I told him afterward, "you were created by God to do what you just did tonight. By gift, by passion, by personality, by training, by life experience, by the way God wired you up, you delivered exactly what the church needed."

God lets people not only contribute to His work but also find soul satisfaction in doing it. What a kingdom coup!

STEP 7: STEWARD YOUR RESOURCES IN A GOD-HONORING WAY

Uh-oh. Here it comes. The collection plate.

During my college days, I'd often do a quick mental calculation as the offering began in church. I'd have, for example, a twenty-dollar bill, a five, and a single in my pocket, and I assure you—the twenty was safe. It was really a decision between the five and the one.

I'd quickly think about the amount of gas in my car. I'd run through my schedule for the day—was I going out to eat? Did I have a date? And depending on my gas gauge, my hunger, and my social life, I'd decide which bill to sacrifice. Usually it was the dollar, and sometimes it was neither.

That was my attitude for quite a while. That is, until one day I was reading the last book in the Old Testament, where God said to the prophet Malachi, "I'm absolutely heartbroken by something that's happening among my people." Wow—that really intrigued me! What had disappointed God so much?

I discovered that God had specifically told His people that when it comes to sacrificing a burnt offering, it should be their best lamb. The one without blemishes. The one that's worth the most in the marketplace. This sacrifice was to foreshadow God giving *His* best in the form of Jesus Christ, the lamb of the world, to take away our sins.

But over time God's people began cheating. They would search their flocks for a sick, lame, or blind lamb, and they'd hustle it to the altar before it died. And God was saying that He was hurt and angry about that. In fact, He said He'd rather have someone bolt the temple door shut than for His people to cynically offer Him their castoffs. He actually accused them of stealing from Him. Think about it. They were robbing the very God they claimed to love!

I choked back tears as I read that. *Oh, God, I'm so sorry,* I prayed. *I'm terribly ashamed for how I've wounded You by giving You blemished lambs. I'm sorry for robbing You of what You rightfully deserve for all You've done for me.*

That's when I made a promise to consistently honor God with my giving. Not as an afterthought but as an integral part of my life. And I've never regretted it. God has repeatedly proven faithful to His promise in Malachi 3:10: "Test me in this . . . and see if I will not throw open the floodgates of heaven and pour out so much blessing that you will not have room enough for it."

At Willow Creek we don't employ professional fund-raisers, put thermometers on the wall, or make arm-twisting visits to people's homes. We just teach the New Testament value that all we are and all we have belongs to God and that we should honor Him by giving at least the historical ten percent called the tithe.

This is incredibly countercultural today. Before people encounter Christ, their attitude is, *I've earned everything I've got, so it's my money. If I save it or spend it, if I squander it or waste it, it's nobody's business but my own.*

Yet when people surrender their life to Christ, they surrender everything, including their treasures. God becomes Lord over all they have, because everything ultimately belongs to Him. But although all of our possessions and riches are registered to His name in the spiritual realm, He graciously entrusts us to manage and steward them under His direction. What a responsibility!

So we've tried to tell people, "Look, you're in a relationship with a God who loves you irrationally, a God who can be trusted, a God who is very specific about how you ought to handle your money. You ought to avoid debt like the plague. You ought to live within your means. You ought to be frugal and unselfish. And you ought to believe that if you're generous with God's work, He will be generous back to you in ways that go far beyond just dollars and cents."

In the end, financial stewardship isn't a money issue. It's a heart issue. And that's why it's the last of the seven steps. A human heart needs to be transformed before a person's wallet reflects full devotion to God.

AN ACTION PLAN FOR CHANGE

That's a summary of one church's strategy to fulfill the Great Commission. We want our people to build friendships with Unchurched Harry and Mary, share their faith with them and explain what the cross of Christ is all about, and then invite them to a weekend service so we can do "team evangelism" together. Once Unchurched Harry and Mary have put their trust in Christ and become Believing Harry and Mary, we want them to learn to worship and participate in the sacrament of communion at New Community, to experience life change through deep and loving interaction in a small group, to uncover their spiritual gift and put it into play, and to honor the Lord through the way they manage their resources.

What's next? Harry and Mary build a relationship of integrity with Unchurched Larry and Sheri, and the whole process begins again. Our strategy isn't a linear progression as much as it's a cycle that repeats itself.

Other churches may take a different approach; they have a different thumbprint. And that's fine. But *every* church needs to grapple with the question of how to follow the specific instructions that Jesus gave all of us: "Therefore go and make disciples of all nations, baptizing them in the name of the Father and of the Son and of the Holy Spirit, and teaching them to obey everything I have commanded you."

It's not enough to have a succinct mission statement engraved on a plaque and hung in the hallway where it can inspire everyone. While that's a good step, it's only wishful thinking unless there's a concrete, Spirit-inspired game plan to turn it into reality.

chapter twelve

VALUES THAT DISTINGUISH
A MOVEMENT

Several years ago one of our most visible vocalists at Willow Creek slipped into a pattern of disobedience to God, an era of confusion and chaos that disintegrated into deceitfulness and ever-deepening sin.

She forfeited her position with the vocal team and as the church began to follow scriptural principles regarding discipline she lost heart and left the church. We grieved that her life, once so influential in pointing seekers toward the hope of Christ, looked as if it were ending up in a ditch.

Time passed and eventually she started coming back to the church, her once-rebellious attitude now replaced by genuine repentance. The church leaders searched the Scriptures for guidance and followed its instructions: if there's specific evidence of heartfelt repentance, then she should be carefully restored with gentleness. We felt it was appropriate that whatever scope of ministry her life had touched, those individuals ought to be enfolded into the restoration process.

So first with the elders, then with the vocal team, there was repentance and reconciliation. Next she went to the New Community, where this brave young woman stood in front of thousands of our core of believers to confess her sinful detour and describe her long path back to participation in the church.

"One step remains," she said, "that you too would offer me forgiving grace. I'm sorry for what I've done, but if you would give me forgiving grace, I would steward it carefully, and I would become a sister in this body once again. I'd give anything for you to look at me not as someone who fell but as someone whom grace has restored."

Immediately the entire New Community erupted in a warm and loving standing ovation, thanking God for His restorative powers and expressing their compassion and affirmation. It was their way of saying, *As God has forgiven us, we forgive you.*

It was a memory that all of us will take to heaven. And to me it was one more sign that we're inching closer and closer to becoming a biblically functioning community.

Ever since I was an idealistic student in college, when Dr. Bilezikian kept reading Acts 2 with such fervency, I've been convinced to the core of my soul that biblically functioning communities can and will flourish again. It's not going to happen because we're talented or special or because we have all the answers or because we're laser-age technocrats who create the right environment for it. It will come about because the Bible says it ought to happen, and the Bible is absolutely true.

As I look around at churches that are pursuing this vision for ministry I don't see a denominational common denominator. However, I do see some commonly held convictions that distinguish these ministries. In other words, in addition to all of the biblical characteristics that are supposed to mark a community of believers, there are certain tenets that are especially distinct in these churches. For purposes of clarity and focus, I've distilled them down to ten distinguishing core values:

1. We believe that anointed teaching is the primary catalyst for transformation in the lives of individuals and in the church.

"For the Word of God is living and active," says Hebrews 4:12. "Sharper than any double-edged sword, it penetrates even to dividing soul and spirit, joints and marrow; it judges the thoughts and attitudes of the heart." Acts 20:32 says, "Now I commit you to God and to the word of his grace, which can build you up and give you an inheritance among all those who are sanctified." And in our creedal passage, Acts 2:42 says Christians in the early church "devoted themselves to the apostles' teaching."

We believe that the Word of God is not only totally true but that it is the primary change agent in the lives of individuals and in the church itself. By "anointed" teaching, we mean preaching that is empowered by the Holy Spirit from preparation to presentation and which goes beyond mere scriptural accuracy to a relevant application of truth that can change sinners into saints. Danger lurks whenever we depend on anything else.

In this book, you've already read about the Train Wreck of '79, when Willow Creek was shaken to its foundation and nearly destroyed. By hindsight, we've seen clearly how we were weak and vulnerable because of imbalanced teaching.

It was my fault. In spite of the fact that every message I gave was absolutely biblical, certain themes were stressed to the near exclusion of others. In that era, I inadvertently emphasized grace but not holiness, and as a result, we adopted a kind of careless Christianity. In fact, every time the church has ventured dangerously close to a reef, we can trace it back to some minor variation in the balance—not the accuracy—of the teaching. That's a sobering truth for me, as the primary teacher. But we've learned some lessons that I believe will keep us sailing strong and steady in the future. For example:

- *Watch out for going overboard with "felt-need" or "helpful" messages.* When you're involved in a seeker ministry, it's tempting to go for long periods of time on what I call junk-food preaching diets. In other words, giving people biblical wisdom to improve their relationships, smooth their emotions, deal with their daily problems, and put some zip back in their marriage. Believe me, I'm a proponent of dealing with felt needs from time to time, because it demonstrates that biblical truth can indeed improve our day-to-day lives, which is a valuable lesson for seekers to learn. But we are responsible for teaching the whole counsel of God in a balanced, biblical, and mature fashion so that the teaching diet accurately reflects Scripture as a whole. The reality is that you'll never grow up fully devoted followers of Christ on a diet of spiritual Twinkies.

- *Watch out for overprotecting seekers and new believers.* I've learned that when something needs to be said from God's Word, it doesn't need to be couched five different ways because you're worried that seekers will recoil. These days, seekers are coming to church in a more desperate state than ever before—their lives are more battered and broken—and as a result, they just want someone to unashamedly give them the straight scoop from Scripture.

- *Watch out for the shadow side of team teaching.* I believe one of Willow Creek's most helpful contributions to the contemporary church has been team teaching, which rescues senior pastors from self-destructive schedules and allows the congregation to hear God's voice through multiple speakers. One warning might be in order: the senior leader in the church must retain the ultimate authority to draw a line in the sand and say, "We in this church, on the basis of God's Word, are going to take *that* hill." Other teachers can't give those clarion calls to action, because this is really the unique role of the senior pastor.

- *Watch out for the sizzle of programming talents, and the temptation to make everything produced and slick.* Nancy Beach would be the first to say that the use of the arts has always been intended to support and lead up to that moment in the seeker service when the Bible is opened and taught from. Preaching should always be the central focus, because ultimately it's the Word of God that's capable of changing lives.

I remember attending a graduation ceremony and having to endure four or five speeches in which, one by one, speakers spooned out nuggets of pure, unadulterated pabulum: "Go for it!" "You can be anything you want to be!" "Remember to have fun!" It was a sobering reminder to me that there is an increased desperation for truth in our culture and that only the Bible—taught under the power of God and in a relevant, uncompromising, and application-oriented fashion—is "sharper than any double-edged sword."

2. We believe that lost people matter to God and therefore ought to matter to the church.

A couple of years ago I was meeting in California with leaders of seeker-style churches, and because of some difficulties in my life I was probably the least motivated and most pessimistic person to walk into the room.

But then I asked these pastors to stand up, one after the other, and describe the most exciting thing God was doing in their life. I expected a lot of talk about programs and services, buildings and bottom lines. And yet half of these leaders said something like, "The most exciting thing to me is the relationship I'm building with a guy down the street" or "I've been getting to know a person at the health club for the last six months, and he's finally opening up to me" or "The most exciting development is that I've been able to have a breakfast and Bible study every Friday with my brother-in-law."

I was nearly overcome with emotion! If seeker-oriented churches around the world are being led by pastors actively engaged in leading lost people to Christ, then we can all be optimistic about the future of the church!

You see, that's a major distinction of the seeker movement—its leaders don't just give lip service to evangelism; they are deeply immersed in personal evangelism in their daily lives. Inevitably, this affects everything they do—the way they pray, the way they allocate resources, the way they hire staff, the way they preach. The entire orientation toward ministry is different when pastors have a couple of hell-bound individuals they are working on.

I remember hanging out after a sailing regatta on Lake Michigan a while ago. I was standing in a light rain near a competitor whom I'd seen around for a couple of years but had never met. As the rain let up a bright rainbow arched across the sky.

"I know who you are and I know you're a Christian," the man said to me. "One year ago tonight my sister was killed in a car accident, and there was a rainbow that night. This is the first rainbow I've seen since then." His eyes started to mist. "I don't know why it had to happen," he added softly. "I don't understand God. I don't understand eternity. If someone would just tell me . . ." The tender conversation that followed will remain in my memory for a very long time.

Every time I have an experience like that, I think of the privilege, the adventure, the high stakes, of sharing God's truth with people who are spiritually confused. They matter to God; may they forever matter to His church.

3. We believe that the church should be culturally relevant, while remaining doctrinally pure.

Jesus was one of the most effective, relevant communicators of all time. Whatever was hot in first-century society, whatever had captured the people's attention, whatever was woven into the fabric of their everyday experiences, Jesus would draw from it. He would say, "Look at the fig tree" or "Consider the mustard seed," and everybody knew what He was talking about. When He told an anecdote about a man whose son had asked for his inheritance early, the whole crowd knew what He meant. Once, He picked up a Roman coin and asked, "Whose face is on this?" Another time, He referred to eighteen people who had been killed by a collapsed tower. He was fresh and current. I doubt if it ever crossed His mind to time-warp His teaching five hundred years into the past.

Seeker services merely apply Jesus' methods to our generation. While He told parables, we use drama. While He built upon the common knowledge of His day, we tap into our current events. While He addressed crowds from a mountainside or boat, we enhance our communication through twentieth-century technology.

The potential pitfall is to concentrate so much on being timely and topical that we lose our biblical distinctiveness. If we do that, we become just a Christian *Oprah Winfrey Show*, mirroring the culture but not bringing scriptural truths to bear on it. I've learned over the years that if I get an A for cultural relevance and a C for doctrinal purity, I've failed.

And both seekers and the church lose.

4. We believe that Christ followers should manifest authenticity and yearn for continuous growth.

Then Jesus went with his disciples to a place called Gethsemane, and he said to them, "Sit here while I go over there and pray." He took Peter and the two sons of Zebedee along with him, and he began to be sorrowful and troubled.

187

Then he said to them, "My soul is overwhelmed with sorrow to the point of death. Stay here and keep watch with me." Going a little farther, he fell with his face to the ground and prayed, "My Father, if it is possible, may this cup be taken from me. Yet not as I will, but as you will" (Matthew 26:36–39).

I remember reading that text a long time ago and being floored by the vulnerability of Jesus. It's one thing to swallow a little pride by saying you're not hitting home runs or triples, or that you're not on top of your game right now. But here's the sinless Son of God telling His closest companions that He's in such bad shape that He's grieved to the point of death. In other words, He's so overcome with anguish that He feels as if He's going to die!

Jesus set the standard for appropriate authenticity. He basically said that when Christians are in community, there shouldn't be any pretense or hiding. They should just be real with each other. And one important legacy of the seeker movement is that it has spawned churches in which people don't have to pretend that they're more important than they are or that they're smarter than they are or that they've got their whole life in perfect working order.

Sometimes I'm asked why it's so easy for me to be open with the congregation, and I respond that I don't have the energy to cover up the obvious. It takes a lot more effort and scheming to watch what you say and make sure your tracks are covered. Frankly, it's a lot less work to say, "Here's where I think I'm doing OK, and here's where I'm not doing too well, and I'm open for feedback either way."

From the beginning, there was no question that Willow Creek Community Church was going to be pastored by a sinner. The only issue was whether he was going to be an honest one or add deceitfulness and cover-up to his list of sins.

Archibald Hart once said that pathological pastors don't deal with their distortions, wounds, and sins, and the result is that they make their whole church sick. But it's also true that those who value authenticity and continue to grow spiritually, relationally, academically, recreationally, and psychologically are much more apt to bring a healthy perspective to their congregation.

5. We believe that the church should operate as a unified community of servants stewarding their spiritual gifts.

"It's different at Willow Creek," pastors kept telling me. "People buy in more." "The commitment is deeper." "The ownership is higher." "People are willing to pay a greater price."

I wasn't convinced their observations were accurate, but enough church leaders had made these comments over the years that I began to analyze why the value of servanthood is so deeply ingrained at Willow Creek. And I concluded that it goes back to the earliest days of the church, when Dr. Bilezikian would teach over and over on the topic of radical servanthood. In fact, one of the greatest challenges that Jesus faced, Dr. Bilezikian would tell us, was to reorient the disciples' me-first mind-set into a servant mind-set.

Consider these verses: "If anyone would come after me, he must deny himself and take up his cross and follow me" (Mark 8:34). "If anyone wants to be first, he must be the very last, and the servant of all" (Mark 9:35). "Whoever wants to become great among you must be your servant, and whoever wants to be first must be slave of all. For even the Son of Man did not come to be served, but to serve, and to give his life as a ransom for many" (Mark 10:43–45). "When he had finished washing their feet, he put on his clothes and returned to his place. 'Do you understand what I have done for you?' he asked them. 'You call me "Teacher" and "Lord," and rightly so, for that is what I am. Now that I, your Lord and Teacher, have washed your feet, you also should wash one another's feet. I have set you an example that you should do as I have done for you'" (John 13:12–15).

In an achievement-oriented world where success means more recognition, more power, more limelight, and more perks, Jesus thoroughly redefined for us what greatness is in God's eyes. It's humility, availability, downward mobility, servanthood. And through Dr. Bilezikian's teachings, we got a steady dose of this until we began to identify a little with Paul's description of himself as a bond servant of Christ.

Yes, God gives His people spiritual gifts. Yes, it can be fulfilling, exciting, and satisfying to serve consistently with those God-given abilities. But fundamentally, we're supposed to be Christ's bond servants who will do whatever we can to advance His kingdom, who will invest our resources and time in His church, who will get under the heavy end of the log and help lift it. Not to the point of self-abuse and unhealthiness but as humble and committed servants of Christ.

When there are Christians who are deploying their spiritual gifts and who are sacrificing out of a servant mind-set, and when there are no restrictions by gender or race, that's when there's a cohesive unity of purpose within the church. That's when an audience turns into a powerful, organized army!

6. We believe that loving relationships should permeate every aspect of church life.

The apostle Paul was breaking the news to the leaders of the Ephesus church: after three years of ministering to them, he felt compelled by the Holy Spirit to leave for Jerusalem. The announcement knocked the wind out of them. They cried, they hugged him, they kissed him repeatedly. It was obvious that he had been more than a spiritual mentor or professional clergyman to them. Their hearts had become knit together because of their close and loving relationships.

Ministry ought to be like that. And yet when you open yourself up to that sort of emotional entanglement, the stakes go way up. You're exposing yourself to the risk of reaching the highest highs you can imagine—and the lowest depths you'll ever experience.

Some pastors refuse to take the gamble. They maintain rigidly narrow boundaries, refusing to become more than just a professional shepherd, because they fear that their heart will get ripped out by the congregation. Their staff interactions are guarded. And ministry usually becomes more of a lonely drudgery than an exhilarating adventure.

In recent years I've decided that being in loving relationships is the best revenge I can have against the exceedingly difficult aspects of church life that will inevitably take big chunks out of my hide. In other words, if I have to work through five agonizingly difficult discipline cases with the elders, then sweet revenge to me is to have warm, supportive, and loving relationships with them while we sort it all out. If I'm going to lead the management team through an agenda that's filled with policy land mines, then I can retaliate by spending the first hour of our meeting talking openly and lovingly about our lives.

The truth is that we ought to be as concerned with the *process* of doing tasks in the church as we are with the tasks themselves. For instance, we used to have volunteers who would mow the church's lawn once a week. Getting that job done is important, but so is the way it's done. So nowadays before a person mows the grass, he sits down with a few other volunteers, and they spend time together in community, praying for each other, encouraging each other, and sharing each other's lives. Pretty soon they're deep friends. The mowing becomes secondary— which is the way it ought to be.

The first time I stayed after class to ask Dr. Bilezikian if I could meet with him in his office, it was a moment of truth for me. Would he brush me off? Would he coldly say he was too busy? Would he be condescending toward this unknown student? Instead he said, "Sure, Bill, let's get together."

And the moment I walked into his office, the professor-student dynamic fell by the wayside. I didn't even know it was legal for a student to have a friendship with a Ph.D.! At the conclusion of our meeting, he said, "Why don't you come back sometime, and we can talk further?" I said, "Sure, I'd like that." After we met a few more times, he said, "I've got a garden in my backyard. I'd love to fix you a salad, if you'll come down to my house." And I started realizing, *This really is a friendship. There's love here.*

190

That's what Willow Creek was built on. Not dreams of bigness but a commitment to being in loving relationships. First and foremost, before we can minister to people through the church, we need to be the church to each other.

Key question - 'What would the loving thing be to say/do in this situation?'

7. We believe that life change happens best in small groups.

Talk about a rapidly growing church—Acts 2 describes how *three thousand* people gave their lives to Christ on Pentecost. The verses that follow outline the characteristics of this first-century megachurch, saying the Christians "broke bread in their homes and ate together with glad and sincere hearts" (Acts 2:46). In other words, they gathered in small groups. In fact, home-based get-togethers were an integral part of the early church. Paul went "from house to house" with his teaching (Acts 20:20). Priscilla and Aquila hosted a house church (Romans 16:3–5), and so did Philemon (vv. 1–2).

While large-group events are well suited for certain aspects of Christian growth, such as preaching, there appears to be a Holy Spirit-prompted migration in which Christians gravitate toward smaller gatherings so they can experience the life change that occurs most optimally in community.

So I believe our task as leaders isn't to merely create a small-group program that's just one more activity in the church and then try to crowbar people into participating. It's to develop a structure that effectively facilitates this supernatural migratory desire that Christians will feel as the value of community is lifted up and they develop an increasing thirst for close relationships.

I've already discussed in the previous chapter why life change is synonymous with small groups. That's why we've developed a variety of small-group options for people, ranging from couples and singles groups to groups specifically geared toward handling issues unique to men or women.

Even spiritual seekers have found that small groups provide a safe and supportive place to freely express opinions and to check out what it means to follow Christ. In fact, Garry Poole—our evangelism director, who pioneered these groups—has a motto he likes to tell seekers: "Just try one meeting." That's usually all it takes for them to see how stimulating it is to investigate spiritual matters in the context of relationships.

It's in these seeker groups that the most revolutionary sort of life change takes place: people give their lives to Christ.

8. We believe that excellence honors God and inspires people.

While I was doing some Scripture memory exercises with Tom, my sailing buddy who has become a Christian, I taught him Colossians 3:23: "Whatever you do, do it heartily as unto the Lord." As you're deepening your spiritual roots, I told him, take it seriously. As you're trying to improve your relationships, be conscientious and honor God with them.

Shortly after that, Tom was steering the sailboat in a regatta, and we were coming up to a buoy around which we had to make a sharp turn. Suddenly as we were sailing along at about six knots he turned aggressively to tuck inside another boat. But the other boat went broadside and—*crash!* We rammed the other boat, knocking all of us to the deck, ripping our spinnaker, and prompting the other crew to heap well-deserved abuse on us. We had to do two 360-degree circles because of our infraction, and while we were doing that the whole fleet passed us, which put us out of contention for first place.

As we were cruising back to the harbor afterward, I sat down next to Tom. "I really didn't like that move," I told him. "I think you were trying for something that just wasn't there."

Tom looked at me with a twinkle in his eye. "Hey, Bill," he said, "I was just steering heartily as unto the Lord!"

I had to laugh. "This must be a new record!" I exclaimed. "You've been a Christian for six months, and you're already wrenching verses out of context!"

That verse is referring to excellence. First Corinthians 10:31 says, "Whatever you do, do it all for the glory of God." As you read Scripture you get the idea that when Solomon was overseeing construction of the first temple, when Nehemiah was erecting the wall around Jerusalem, and when Ezra was rebuilding the temple, their desire to give God the best possible gift fueled a spirit of excellence.

"Good enough" is just not good enough when it comes to honoring God through the church. In response to His holiness and greatness, in gratitude for His monumental sacrifice for us, our attitude ought to be to pay tribute to Him with the best we can offer. I'm not talking about obsessive perfectionism but rather an attitude of excellence that permeates all we do in the church and in our personal lives. After all, what we do as Christians reflects on the Christ we serve.

Inevitably, there's something about doing a task in a quality fashion that lifts our spirits and makes our souls feel noble. Beyond that, others are inspired. When the bar of performance is raised, everybody is motivated to do their best.

And seekers are attracted, because they are accustomed to striving for high standards in the marketplace. When they see a church that has a strong sense of belief, purpose, and dedication as reflected in the high quality of its campus and services, it invariably draws their attention and arouses their curiosity.

9. We believe that churches should be led by those with leadership gifts.

In his book *Today's Pastors*, Christian researcher George Barna offers a statistic that should scare anyone who yearns to see churches thrive: only six percent of senior pastors claim they have the spiritual gift of leadership.

Consistently preaching good sermons can create a big Bible study, but the building of a biblically functioning community requires more than that. Leaders are needed to cast a vision, summarize a mission, develop a strategy, undergird values, measure results, and coalesce people to advance the kingdom together. And to do it all with humility as servant-leaders who diminish self but lift up Christ.

That doesn't mean that senior pastors who are primarily teachers should step down. Instead they need to surround themselves with Spirit-enabled leaders who are elders, deacons, or in other positions of influence in the church. These people should be freed up to exercise their leadership gift while the pastor concentrates on transformational preaching.

Much is hanging in the balance. It's my conviction that the crisis of mediocrity and stagnation in today's churches is fundamentally a crisis of leadership.

10. We believe that full devotion to Christ and His cause is normal for every believer.

King Solomon, the wisest man in history, had blown it. He ignored God's dire warning that his heart would be corrupted if he married women from pagan tribes. And sure enough, Solomon ended up reducing himself to worshiping their false gods, and as a result, his entire kingdom was eventually torn apart.

What was at the root of Solomon's demise? The answer is in 1 Kings 11:4: "His heart was not fully devoted to the Lord his God, as the heart of David his father had been."

Those words stung me as I read them during my devotional time several years ago. Opening my journal, I wrote, *"Ninety-five percent devotion to God is five percent short."*

In the previous point, I stressed the importance of godly leadership. But a critical prerequisite is godly followership: to yield ourselves totally to Jesus Christ. Our goals, our ambitions, our pathological pushes, our talents, our desires—all abandoned, as best we can, in favor of divine plans. With the help of the Holy Spirit, we should want to become "just say the word" followers of Jesus, ready to jettison our agenda in order to pursue His intentions.

This isn't a onetime commitment; it's a daily surrender. Time after time I've promised to open my life fully to God's leadership—only to shrink back and fail once more. But I've always sunk to my knees again and reiterated that it's the

193

sincere desire of my heart to obey Christ unconditionally and become His fully devoted follower.

That's not heroic. In fact, it ought to be the norm in churches. Leaders should challenge congregations to become "just say the word" disciples who submit themselves unreservedly to the authority of Christ in every area of their life. As Jesus reassured Peter in Mark 10, anyone who chooses to become His unconditional follower will receive a hundredfold blessing in this life and in the age to come.

Total yieldedness—that should sum up the objective of Christ followers. That isn't the same as merely saying we should do more, give more, volunteer more, sacrifice more, serve more. Sometimes when you open yourself up to Christ's leadership, His marching orders will be for you to relax, to slow down, to chill out. The point is, it's His call. We merely cooperate. Our trust in Him ought to be great enough that we're willing to subordinate ourselves to Him and follow His lead wherever He takes us.

That goal—never totally achieved this side of heaven but always worthy of enthusiastic pursuit—was captured colorfully in this anonymous composition:

> I am part of the "Fellowship of the Unashamed." I have Holy Spirit power. The die has been cast. I've stepped over the line. The decision has been made. I am a disciple of His. I won't look back, let up, slow down, back away, or be still. My past is redeemed, my present makes sense, and my future is secure. I am finished and done with low living, sight walking, small planning, smooth knees, colorless dreams, tame visions, mundane talking, chintzy giving, and dwarfed goals!
>
> I no longer need preeminence, prosperity, position, promotions, plaudits, or popularity. I don't have to be right, first, tops, recognized, praised, regarded, or rewarded. I now live by presence, learn by faith, love by patience, live by prayer, and labor by power.
>
> My face is set, my gait is fast, my goal is heaven, my road is narrow, my way is rough, my companions few, my guide reliable, my mission clear. I cannot be bought, compromised, detoured, lured away, turned back, diluted, or delayed. I will not flinch in the face of sacrifice, hesitate in the presence of adversity, negotiate at the table of the enemy, ponder at the pool of popularity, or meander in the maze of mediocrity.
>
> I won't give up, shut up, let go, or slow up until I've preached up, prayed up, paid up, stored up, and stayed up for the cause of Christ.
>
> I am a disciple of Jesus. I must go till He comes, give till I drop, preach till all know, and work till He stops.
>
> And when He comes to get His own, He'll have no problems recognizing me . . . my colors will be clear.

chapter thirteen

GROWING FULLY DEVOTED FOLLOWERS

Most people saw Jim as a successful midlevel business executive with a suburban company. But actually, he was a liar and a cheat. He had lost a job for stealing. What's more, he was openly hostile to spiritual matters. When his wife suggested that they take their two children to church, he said, "There's no way I'm going to let anyone pollute their minds with that God junk."

One day he announced to his wife that he didn't love her anymore, and he walked out on his family. The truth is, he had found another woman. They moved in together, and everything was going well until she said that she just *had* to go to church every Sunday. It didn't matter what she was doing beforehand or afterward; she just needed to spend an hour each week inside a church building. That's the way she had been raised.

So reluctantly Jim accompanied her to church, where the minister spent his sermon trying to convince everyone that members of their denomination had a leg up on everyone else. As they left, Jim told her that the message was, in so many words, baloney. "If God existed," Jim said, "he certainly wouldn't judge people on the basis of their denomination."

"Fine," his girlfriend replied. "*You* pick the church next week."

That posed a problem. The only church Jim vaguely knew about was the one his secretary had described several times over the years. She had respectfully tried to explain to him what Jesus meant to her life, but he had always stopped her cold. Now he was trying to remember the church's name. *Willow something,* he thought. *Willow Creek. That's it.*

As they pulled onto the campus the following Sunday the well-maintained property caught his attention. So did the theater-style auditorium. *Is this really a church?* he asked himself.

When the music started, he found himself actually liking it, because it was the style he usually listened to, although the content was certainly different. As for the short drama put on before the minister spoke, Jim was impressed by the quality of the acting, and the relevance it had to his daily life. And when the person giving the announcements invited visitors *not* to contribute to the offering, the church *really* had his attention.

But it was the message that succeeded in chipping away at the corrosion of Jim's heart. That morning I talked about patience, using myself as a prime example of someone who desperately needed God's help in that area. As it turned out, my willingness to admit my shortcomings prompted Jim to begin examining his own life—and he didn't like what he found.

"I thought that if people really knew me, they would run in the opposite direction," he explained years later. "I figured that God was the same. If He existed, I knew that based on my lifestyle, I was in big trouble. But then I heard at Willow Creek that I mattered to God. No matter what. No matter where I was in life. A glimmer of hope slipped into my mind: *Could this possibly be true?*"

LIKE COMING HOME

Jim's girlfriend didn't connect with Willow Creek, but he was intrigued. *What was that experience all about?* he wondered. *Was it a fluke? If there is a God, could I possibly matter to Him?* Those questions caused Jim, for the first time in his life, to attend church by himself the following weekend. He walked out feeling challenged and encouraged, and so he returned on the third weekend. This time my message was on different kinds of faithfulness—marital, relational, and spiritual. It didn't take much soul-searching for Jim to realize that none of those qualities were true in his life.

Something prompted Jim to call his estranged wife the following week. "Would you go to church with me on Sunday?" he asked. She was shocked and skeptical—but she accepted.

They hardly talked in the car on the way to Willow Creek, and they didn't converse during the service. As they were driving away Jim asked cautiously, "Well, what do you think?"

She reflected on the service. The message didn't particularly make an impression on her, but those vocalists—they really seemed to believe what they were singing. All the people appeared to be . . . well . . . sincere. Authentic. They weren't just playing church. She felt strangely attracted to the atmosphere of community that she had sensed. "I really loved it," she replied. "It was like . . . *coming home.*"

During the next several weeks, Jim wrestled with the sometimes confusing spiritual thoughts that kept pestering him late into the night. Finally he asked his wife if he could move back home. After some thought she agreed, and they began marriage counseling. Then during a weekend service at Willow Creek, they submitted a card asking for someone to specifically spell out what Christianity was all about. Two Willow Creek volunteers met with them and presented Christ's plan of salvation, and while neither Jim nor his wife was ready to receive the gift of Christ's grace that day, they both agreed they should thoroughly investigate the faith.

So they did. After six months a weekend message encouraged them to decide, once and for all, whether Jesus was who He claimed to be. Jim made his choice. With tears glistening on his face, he asked Christ to forgive his ugly past and to lead his life from that moment onward. "I felt as if a two-ton weight had been removed from my shoulders," he said.

A few months later his wife made her own decision to follow Jesus. Now that God was starting to reshape their attitudes, their marriage slowly healed and grew stronger.

They started attending New Community services, in which they learned about small groups. "Once we got in a group," Jim said, "we learned more about who it was we'd come to believe in." They also were prompted to explore and develop their spiritual gifts, and that brought some real surprises. "This is how I discovered that God has a sense of humor," explained Jim. "He took this very irreligious tightwad and gave him the gifts of evangelism and giving!"

Jim and his wife enthusiastically put their gifts into action, initially as part of our Seeds Tape ministry and later as small-group leaders. More recently Jim started a new ministry at Willow Creek. Its purpose: to give tours to newcomers.

But these guided visits are tours with a difference. When Jim points to the auditorium, he tells visitors, "You may be impressed by the number of seats in here. But look at *this* seat. This represents one person who matters to God." Then he gives his first-person account of sitting in that very seat as a cynical, hardhearted adulterer and how God miraculously touched his life—and eventually the lives of his entire family.

THE MARKS OF A CHRIST FOLLOWER

We have an expression that's caught on around Willow Creek: "*Yea, God!*" That's what we say when we encounter stories like Jim's, stories about world-toughened men and women who are dragged to the church kicking and leaving heel marks on the sidewalk but who ultimately emerge as tenderhearted followers of Jesus. What else but the life-transforming power of God can account for such an amazing metamorphosis? And what other mission in life could be more important than building a church that's wholeheartedly committed to that eternity-changing process?

When I look at Jim's life, I see the unmistakable marks of a Christian who is walking down the path toward full devotion to Christ. And that's important for church leaders to track. In other words, if Willow Creek's goal is to turn irreligious people into fully devoted followers of Christ, then how do we know when we're fulfilling that objective? What external behavior do we look for to tell us that something is happening inside a person's heart? How can we measure the changing characteristics of a person like Jim who's being transformed by Christ?

We've wrestled with that in recent years at Willow Creek, especially as we tried to create a new membership system that would be congruent with the New Testament's vision of the church. Under our previous system, there were some people whose names were on the rolls but who were no longer participating in the life of Willow Creek, and others who were greatly involved in the church but had never bothered to become official members. So we needed to work through the question of what a real "member" of a church should look like.

While the Bible never explicitly uses the term "church member," it's clear that the concept of membership is biblical. As we studied the Scriptures we observed that two kinds of members were described. The first are those who have received grace through Christ and have been adopted into God's family. At the moment of their conversion, they become permanent "positional members" of the church universal.

Then the Bible invariably depicts Christians as continuing to grow by becoming "participating members" of a specific local body of believers. These participating members share certain characteristics. So instead of seeing membership as a hoop for people to jump through, we strived to develop a membership system that describes those qualities of a person who is becoming fully formed in Christ.

We call this description of participating membership the Five Gs—five specific qualities that describe a Christian like Jim who's progressing toward full devotion to Jesus. The Five Gs aren't a finish line or a rigid checklist to be achieved through legalistic efforts. They're more like a baseline of maturity that indicates a person has appropriated God's grace and is cooperating as the Holy Spirit conforms him or her, over time, into the image of Christ. We use this standard of commitment to determine who's really a participating member of the church. In effect, Willow Creek succeeds only when God uses the church to produce Christians whose lives reflect the Five Gs.

As I go through each one of the Five Gs think about your own spiritual situation. Can you honestly say that these qualities describe your life? If not, what specific steps can you take to ensure continued growth in your relationship with Christ?

1. Grace

Christ followers have abandoned their attempts to earn God's favor through their own accomplishments and have individually received Christ's free gift of eternal life—by His grace alone—through repentance and faith. Like Jim, they've come face-to-face with their own sinfulness and have humbly accepted Christ's payment on the cross on their behalf. Then, in obedience to Christ's command, they have been baptized as a way of identifying with His burial and resurrection and also to proclaim to the community their intention to be His disciple.

2. Growth

Growth is our ongoing response to God's grace over a lifetime. Growth is encouraging the Holy Spirit to reshape us from the inside out, and it's also owning our responsibility for deepening our faith through the spiritual disciplines as well as by resisting those things that would retard our growth.

Christ followers have an ever-increasing desire to nurture their spiritual development through authentic prayer, sincere worship, and application-oriented Bible study. They want to be wholly obedient to the teachings of the Bible, which they regard as the final authority in all areas in which it teaches. When they slip into sin—as we all do—they confront it and seek to turn away from it under the power of the Holy Spirit. In addition, Christ followers are so grateful for God's grace that they want to share it with others through personal evangelistic endeavors.

3. Group

Relationships aren't optional in church; relationships *are* the church. Christ followers enter into the community of believers so that they can grow in Christlikeness, express and receive love, and carry out the ministry of the church. This means not only participating in corporate gatherings of the church for the purposes of worship, teaching, and communion but also being related to a small group of believers in which they can be encouraged, supported, challenged, and lovingly held accountable.

In fact, Christ followers are committed to honoring God in all of their interactions with others. They want to abandon impure relationships, reconcile broken friendships, and immediately take steps to resolve conflict whenever it arises. They abide by the teaching in Romans 12:18, which says, "If it is possible, as far as it depends on you, live at peace with everyone."

4. Gifts

The church isn't an organization as much as it's an organism, an interdependent community of believers who selflessly offer their unique, God-granted talents for the purpose of furthering the ministry of the church. In a way, the church's strength comes through its diversity, which is clearly seen as different people express different spiritual gifts where God has specifically placed them in the body. A strong sense of unity and common purpose is achieved when these gifts of the Spirit are combined with the fruit of the Spirit as described in Galatians 5:22: "love, joy, peace, patience, kindness, goodness, faithfulness, gentleness and self-control."

5. Good Stewardship

In Jesus Christ, Christians have a daunting example of giving: He gave up all He had so that the world could be reconciled with God. His followers, realizing that their eternities have been purchased with His blood, consider everything they have as belonging to Him. So they strive to be responsible caretakers of what He has entrusted to them, giving generously as they increasingly submit their resources to His authority. Their money management demonstrates a clear departure from the world's values of status-seeking and selfishness.

In reality good stewardship is the result of a heart that is responsive and thankful to God and that trusts in His promise to reward those who honor Him with their giving.

THE POTENTIAL OF A FIVE-G CHURCH

A Five-G Christian *is* a participating member of the church. But that's not the approach most churchgoers are used to. Sometimes when I'm greeting people after a service, a person will pump my hand and say with great eagerness, "This is my first time here, and I really love this place. Point me to the right booth so I can go sign up to become a member." I have to gently explain that in our view, membership isn't about a onetime signing on the dotted line as much as it's a description of a person's growing devotion to Christ and of that person's engagement with this particular body of believers.

There is, of course, a procedure we encourage people to follow to be formally recognized as members. At their own pace, they first complete a personal

Bible study that walks them through the Five Gs. The second step is an affirmation process, in which they evaluate for themselves whether the marks of a participating member are present in their own life. Third, they are interviewed by a trained volunteer—preferably their own small-group leader, who already knows them well—who confirms that the Five-G characteristics are present. Any difficult issues are referred to a staff member or elder. And finally, new participating members—sitting together with their small group—are presented at the New Community so that everyone can rejoice together at another example of God's handiwork.

This new approach has been enthusiastically received as a defining moment for the participants and as a fulfilling experience for the small-group leaders who are involved in the interviews. From the church's perspective, it helps us identify who's committed to this body and who's still in the tire-kicking stage. And it has been an inspiring testimony to God's grace that so many people have been affirmed as being thriving Five-G disciples of Jesus. They're on their way to becoming the end result that the Great Commission envisioned.

Often when journalists ask me about the future of Willow Creek, it's the faces of these participating members that I bring to mind. It's newcomers like Jim, who spent their Sundays slamming down beers a few years ago but who are now sold-out, prayed-up, unabashed zealots for Christ. It's veterans like Nancy Beach, Rory Noland, Laurie Pederson, and others, who have emerged from Willow Creek's first twenty years more in love with the church than ever before. It's the leaders, who sacrifice daily for the cause of Christ; the humble difference-makers, who practice quiet servanthood; and the godly staff, who would rather do what they do with each other than with anyone else in the world.

Then I tell the reporters that I don't know what God has in store for the next two decades. I honestly don't. But I do know that regardless of how the future unfolds, doing ministry with this core of believers is bound to be a ride that none of us would want to miss!

And for that we all say, *"Yea, God!"*

EPILOGUE

Washington, D.C., is a center of incredible power. When I've visited there over the years, I've ended up sitting across the table from a number of people who have wielded enormous authority and influence. And it has never ceased to be an eye-opening experience for me.

But it hasn't been an eye-opener because of the allure of political clout. I am taken aback by the power that the people in Washington *don't* have.

Politicians can rearrange stuff on the surface of life. They can spend money and enact legislation and draw attention to a cause. But they can't bring fundamental transformation into the life of one individual. They can't rewrite the eternal address of a single person. They can't order genuine reconciliation between two estranged human beings. They can't instill character into anybody. They can't turn a selfish heart into a servant heart, or a granite heart into a giving heart.

And *this* is what our country desperately needs the most.

Sometimes when I'm driving away after meeting with a person who has heavyweight responsibilities in government or business, I think to myself, *My job is a lot weightier than his or hers.* So are the ministries of people around the world who are investing their energy into turning irreligious people into fully devoted followers of Jesus Christ.

The reason is simple: the product of our efforts is destined to endure in heaven forever.

I'm in awe of what God, in His sovereignty, has chosen to accomplish through Willow Creek during its first twenty years despite our often-inept efforts. And I'll say it straight out—my experience with this church has convinced me to the core of my soul that nothing on this planet is more important, more strategic, and more urgently needed than the local church.

I'm not talking about stale churches that do business as usual. I'm referring to authentic biblical communities that are the conduits through which Jesus Christ can rescue a world gone awry.

So let's commit ourselves to praying that God would energize His people and breathe renewing life into His church. And let's go out—*all of us*—to surprise a lost and bewildered world with the most unexpected, outlandish, irrational, and ultimately life-changing message of all: *You matter to God.*

COMMONLY ASKED QUESTIONS
ABOUT WILLOW CREEK COMMUNITY CHURCH

In starting Willow Creek, volunteers went through the neighborhoods to ask people why they didn't go to church and then made adjustments in order to attract them. Isn't that tantamount to telling people only what they want to hear?

It's amazing how the lore about our community survey has grown up through the years and distorted our real intentions behind it. Actually, from the beginning we had a clear vision of what we wanted to establish—a biblically functioning community. The scriptural elements of what constitutes a viable and biblical church were nonnegotiable. The Bible—not a door-to-door canvass—should determine how a community of believers operates.

The purpose of the survey was merely to determine what particular sensitivities existed in that community and to gather information that would help us meet the particular spiritual needs of that area. For instance, were there a lot of young couples with children in the vicinity? If so, that would influence the kind of ministries we offered. Were there a lot of atheists and hard-core unbelievers, or were most people Christians who had decided to stop attending church for certain reasons? That information would be helpful in fine-tuning the approach we would take in our services. Were people especially turned off by appeals for money? Then maybe we should downplay the request for funds.

Nobody should create a church based only on what people want. The blueprint should come from the Bible, but it's legitimate to have some flexibility in the methodology in order to reflect the particular needs of each community.

Theologian Alister McGrath of Oxford University commented in his book *Evangelicalism and the Future of Christianity* that "Willow Creek is an excellent example of a church that has pioneered an approach that breaks down incidental barriers [that keep seekers away from church]. . . . Yet the Gospel is proclaimed effectively." He added that "there is no doubt that this church and an increasing number of imitators throughout the Western world are getting a hearing for the Gospel among those who would regard a traditional church setting as a no-go zone."

In trying to attract unchurched individuals, aren't you tempted to avoid the tougher truths of Christianity, such as sin, hell, and judgment?

It's a misconception that seekers only want to hear the soft side of the Gospel. In fact, they insist on hearing the *whole* truth before taking such a drastic step as committing themselves to Christ.

In Acts 20:27 the apostle Paul told the church at Ephesus that he had "not hesitated to proclaim to you the whole will of God." Likewise, we strive to provide a balanced and complete account of the Gospel to those who attend Willow Creek. And that certainly includes the "tougher truths" of Christianity. Where we've noticed an imbalance at certain times in our history, we've taken corrective steps.

We encourage anyone to go through our Seeds Tape catalog to see that we have addressed all major doctrinal subjects through the years.

Willow Creek is known as being a "safe place" for people to visit. But isn't the Gospel by its very nature threatening to the "safety" or comfort level of seekers?

We describe Willow Creek as being a safe place where seekers can hear the very dangerous, life-changing message of Jesus Christ. It's safe because we have tried to eliminate the artificial barriers that discourage people from focusing on the central message of the Gospel. We want only one thing to be offensive at Willow Creek: the Cross of Christ.

If seekers leave Willow Creek because they're unwilling to face the truth about their sinfulness and rebellion against a holy God, then that's their choice. They've heard the Gospel and made an informed decision that they'll have to live with for eternity. But if they leave because they're bored or frustrated or because we've inadvertently offended them by being insensitive, then we've failed as a church.

As an example, we've found that many seekers prefer to be anonymous during their early walk down the road toward Christ. We feel comfortable with allowing them that anonymity as long as they're continuing to make progress toward a decision about putting their trust in Him. We won't water down the Gospel to keep them happy, but we will create an environment in which they can grow in their understanding of Christ at their own pace, free from the worry that they will be put in the spotlight or pressured into something prematurely.

In a seeker-oriented church, isn't there a risk that new believers won't be adequately discipled, because so many of the resources are devoted to outreach?

Yes, that risk exists. We need to be conscientious in fulfilling *both* parts of the Great Commission—to reach seekers with the Gospel and then disciple them into fully devoted followers of Jesus.

In the early days of Willow Creek, we didn't have many Christians, and so we weighted our resources toward the front end of that command. When we began to see some converts, we gradually shifted some resources to balance things out. Today a greater proportion of our resources is devoted to the discipleship of believers than to reaching seekers, because there are so many Christians who desperately need nurture and training.

Adjustments are constantly being made in this area. When we've gotten out of alignment at Willow Creek, we've tried to move expeditiously to rectify the situation. At any church, leaders must continually make evaluations to determine whether efforts and finances are being appropriately allocated for both the evangelism and discipleship components of the Great Commission.

Isn't it inevitable that using modern art forms and language to communicate the Gospel will subtly change its content?

We don't believe this is inevitable, but we are acutely aware of the potential for this taking place. That's why we regularly bring together our best minds to make sure we're not accidentally distorting the Gospel. Every service we conduct is promptly evaluated by our elders, as a safeguard against inadvertently straying from a responsible proclamation of the historical Christian message.

It's also important to keep in mind that art isn't used to teach at Willow Creek. Its purpose is to pique curiosity, to evoke ideas, and to till the soil of the soul so that the seed of God's Word can be planted there. Music, drama, video, multimedia, and dance are only used as a prelude to a thirty- to forty-minute message that then brings strong biblical clarity to the topic of the day. It's this preaching of God's Word that ultimately has the power to change lives. Art plays a secondary—though important—support role.

In terms of using contemporary language, a distinction from theologian William Hordern might be helpful. He stresses the difference between *transforming* and *translating* the Gospel. Those who transform the Gospel are watering it down into something it isn't, in order to make it more palatable to seekers. That's totally unacceptable, and that's not what we're doing at Willow Creek.

We're committed to keeping the Gospel intact while merely translating it into words and images that our modern audience can understand. This has to be done carefully so that the original meaning of the Scriptures is captured, but we are convinced that it's essential to use contemporary communication in order to help today's seekers grab ahold of biblical truths.

The ironic downside of not translating the Gospel has been described by evangelist Alan Walker: "An idolatry of words has grown up in evangelism. There are people who, if they fail to hear the repetition of phrases and words with which they are familiar, make the sometimes absurd claim that the Gospel is not being preached."

Willow Creek has said that one reason why unchurched people don't attend church is because it makes them feel guilty. But the Gospel declares that they are guilty. Isn't it the role of the church to point that out?

Surprisingly, most seekers don't object to being told about their depravity. For many of them, it's hardly news! What they find offensive, however, is when the church focuses on their guilt but fails to clearly spell out a solution to their situation in language that they can understand and act upon.

John 16:8 tells us that part of the Holy Spirit's ministry is to convict people of their sin. But His ultimate purpose isn't to make them feel permanently ashamed and dirty; it's to lead them to the Cross of Christ, where they can find redemption and cleansing from their guilt. Romans 8:1 says, "Therefore, there is now no condemnation for those who are in Christ Jesus."

That's why we are committed not only to helping seekers realize that they've rebelled against God but also to helping them understand that Jesus Christ is offering forgiveness and grace so that they can be rescued, once and for all, from the ultimate consequences of their sin.

How big do you expect Willow Creek to grow? Why doesn't the church spin off some satellite congregations instead of just continuing to expand?

From the beginning, we haven't discerned the Holy Spirit leading us to directly plant other churches. Instead our ministry has been to work through the Willow Creek Association to encourage church leaders around the world who have been led by God to start new churches and overhaul stagnant ones. We've seen numerous churches planted and rejuvenated as a result of our church leadership conferences, and we've provided resources and other assistance to many of them.

Besides, we have seen some tremendous benefits to having a large church. Because of our size, we're able to provide a wide-ranging inventory of ministries to help seekers and believers alike, as well as to make an impact for Christ in our local community.

How large will Willow Creek grow? We don't know the answer to that. There are 1.5 million people living within a twenty-minute drive of our campus, and yet we're only reaching one percent of them in a typical weekend service. So there's certainly potential for growth!

Willow Creek has more than fifteen thousand in attendance on a weekend. Don't some of your people—even your most involved and committed people—get lost in that large crowd? What keeps Willow Creek from becoming an impersonal, corporate entity, where folks feel as if they're only a part of a machine or an elaborate program?

We believe that our new system of small groups will continue to make the church small and personal to those who choose to get involved. With so many opportunities to experience life change in the context of these groups, there's no reason for anyone to get the feeling that Willow Creek is an impersonal place.

In addition, people are given the opportunity to be difference-makers in the church by discovering their spiritual gifts and putting them into action in one of our nearly one hundred different ministries. A by-product of this is an increased sense of ownership of the church; people feel needed and appreciated for the contribution they make.

Also, the large weekend gatherings aren't the only place where teaching happens at Willow Creek. We provide a variety of smaller settings where interactive biblical teaching is offered on a wide range of life issues.

Willow Creek obviously has a large front door through which thousands come to church. But doesn't it also have a big back door through which many people leave?

Because we want to grant seekers the anonymity they desire in the early stages of their spiritual pilgrimage, we resist the temptation to track them, and so it's difficult to precisely measure how many of them come for a while and then leave. Certainly, some of them do come and then go—although many of those will end up returning to the church at a future time when their once-smooth life has hit unexpected turbulence.

It's also true that there have been various times in our history when people were not getting assimilated into the life of the church as readily as they should have been. That's why we've retooled our small-groups ministry and instituted other improvements. Our goal: make sure that nobody slips through the cracks.

Who is providing the financial help to make Willow Creek happen? Surely a church the size of yours can't be supported merely on the giving of its congregation.

Although occasionally a person from another place will contribute to a special project at the church, that is certainly the exception. The overwhelming majority of our giving is willingly and cheerfully offered by everyday individuals who have been taught biblical principles of stewardship and who earnestly want to honor God with the way they handle their finances.

We have no pledge plan, no envelope system, no elders knocking on doors, no outside fund-raisers, no thermometers on the wall, no coercion or emotional appeals.

We've found that when Christians understand that all they have belongs to God, and when they sense that the church is authentically committed to helping them grow in their faith, their natural response is to demonstrate amazing generosity.

Willow Creek is obviously built on Bill Hybels' personality and charisma. Won't the church disintegrate if he was to leave?

We're aware that the departure of a founding pastor can create a considerable amount of trauma at any church, but we've already taken steps to ensure that the impact of my absence would not be debilitating at Willow Creek.

One safeguard has been team leadership. I'm one of eight elders, one of seventeen board members, and one of ten management team representatives. So the entire leadership core of the church would remain intact if I was to leave. Similarly, I'm one of four senior teachers, which means that the congregation is already receptive to teaching from a variety of individuals.

There's no question that the church would have to make adjustments in the event I was to depart. However, conversations are being held periodically to try to figure out how to best position Willow Creek so that it will continue to flourish in my eventual absence.

Since Willow Creek was built on reaching baby boomers, what happens as that generation ages?

Interestingly, a study conducted in the early 1990s shows that the median age of Willow Creek attenders exactly matches the median age of the baby boom generation. But as any waistline-expanding, hair-receding forty-something will tell you, that generation is getting up in years. In fact, the leading edge of the boomers will hit the age of fifty in 1996.

As a result, in recent years Willow Creek began taking steps to continue ministering to boomers while stepping up its efforts to reach the preceding and following generations. In 1995 plans were being implemented to begin a weekly service aimed at reaching the so-called baby busters, the generation following the boomers. This group, also known as Generation X, has its own culture, its own language, its own issues—and its own desperate need for the Gospel. At the same time, plans were afoot to create a new ministry to address the unique needs of older members of our congregation.

We're still trying to determine how these new ministries will play out. But even if both baby busters and seniors end up with their own services each week, the entire church will continue to get together at New Community for vision-casting, expository preaching, communion, and just *being* the church together. We believe it's biblical for all generations to gather on a weekly basis as the body of Christ.

Isn't Willow Creek's emphasis on excellence really just a product of unhealthy perfectionism?

We've found that in all areas of life, whatever you care deeply about, whatever you hold most dear, whatever you believe in most passionately, you're going to do with excellence. And that holds true for ministry.

We sincerely love the church, because we see it as the bride of Christ. And so it's only natural for us to want to offer our best. In 1 Corinthians 10:31 it says, "Whatever you do, do it all for the glory of God." We strive to honor Him with the sacrifice of our service.

Willow Creek defines excellence as "doing the best we can with what we've got." It's pursued in an atmosphere of grace and acceptance. When we see it being taken to unhealthy extremes, we step in and discuss the matter in order to neutralize those tendencies.

But we are convinced that excellence is important in the church. Franky Schaeffer provided an interesting perspective in his book *Addicted to Mediocrity,* in which he observed: "The idea that 'the Spirit can work somehow,' that God can bring something out of it if we just sort of throw it out there, is unjustifiable from those who aim to know the living God and can see His integrity and dedication to quality in His Word and the world around us."

Is Willow Creek's stance concerning women a product of biblical research, or is it intended to appease seekers, who tend to believe strongly in equal rights for women?

In all attempts to understand and put into practice appropriate relationships between genders in the body of Christ, our sole authority is the will of God as expressed in Scripture. Although a few isolated texts are debated, we believe that when the Bible is interpreted correctly and in its entirety, it teaches the full equality of men and women in status, giftedness, and opportunities for ministry. This is the basis of our position concerning women at Willow Creek, not any pressure to be "politically correct" in the eyes of society.

We believe that the Bible teaches that men and women were created by God and equally bear His image (Genesis 1:27). God's intention was for them to share oneness and community (Genesis 2:23), even as God Himself experiences oneness within the Trinity. However, human oneness has been severed by the Fall. The struggle for power, and the desire to "rule over" another gender, are part of the curse that resulted from human sin (Genesis 3:16) and were not in God's original plan for human beings.

However, God has acted in Christ to redeem the human race and to offer to all people the opportunity to be part of the new community of His church. It is God's intention for His children to experience the oneness that exists between the Father and the Son (John 17:22). This means that old divisions and hierarchies between genders are not to be tolerated in the church, where all are "one in Christ Jesus" (Galatians 3:28).

In the formation of the church at Pentecost, the Holy Spirit was poured out on women and men alike, as in fact had been predicted long before the coming of Christ (Joel 2:28; Acts 2:18). The Spirit sovereignly bestows gifts on all members of the church, without giving anyone preferential treatment based on gender (Acts 2:1–21; 1 Corinthians 12:7, 11). Every believer is to offer his or her gift for the benefit of the body of Christ (Romans 12:4–8; 1 Peter 4:10–11), and so we believe that preventing anyone from properly exercising his or her spiritual gift would be a form of quenching the Spirit.

What is Willow Creek's attitude toward major social and political issues, such as abortion?

Our approach has been to teach unapologetically on social topics that the Bible addresses, including racism, poverty, injustice, abortion, homosexuality, pornography, the environment, and so on. Then we encourage our attenders to be sensitive to the individual promptings of the Holy Spirit regarding their own social and political involvement in these causes through appropriate organizations.

As a church, we've been scrupulous about staying out of partisan politics, because there can be legitimate differences of opinion among Christians about how certain biblical values can best be translated into political policies in a pluralistic society.

On a person-to-person level, Willow Creek has been heavily involved in social issues. For instance, we have ministries designed to help women choose adoption rather than abortion and have helped finance agencies that place unwanted babies in Christian homes, and we've fought hunger and homelessness through our Food Pantry and Community Care ministries.

As a corporate body, however, we're committed to maintaining a tight focus on what we feel we have been primarily called to do—reach lost people with the Gospel and help them mature in their faith. We're convinced that, ultimately, a person's perspective on social issues won't fundamentally change until his or her heart is transformed by Jesus Christ.

As Chuck Colson writes in *Against the Night*, "In the absence of a deeper conversion of perspective . . . minds are rarely changed on single policy matters, no matter how persuasive our arguments."

That "deeper conversion of perspective" comes when Jesus Christ works in a person's life. That's why we believe that our greatest contribution to society is through helping to bring irreligious people into an authentic relationship with Him.

*Learn more about applying the strategy found in **Rediscovering Church** in these titles:*

Becoming a Contagious Christian

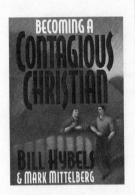

Bill Hybels and Mark Mittelberg

Becoming a Contagious Christian is a proven action plan for impacting the spiritual lives of those around you. Based on their own experiences, the authors' powerful stories will help you get rid of your misconceptions about evangelism and develop your own "contagious" Christian character.

Hardcover   0-310-48500-2
Audio Pages   0-310-48508-8

Fit to Be Tied
Making Marriage Last a Lifetime

Bill and Lynne Hybels
Writing openly about their own marriage, Bill and Lynne Hybels give a biblical perspective to the realities of married life. From understanding your spouse's temperament to ways of courting creatively, this book gives honest, helpful insight into developing a healthy, loving Christian marriage.

Softcover   0-310-53371-6
with discussion guide
Audio Pages   0-310-53378-3

Available at your local Christian bookstore.

Honest to God?
Becoming an Authentic Christian

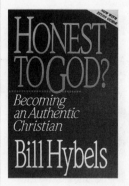

Bill Hybels

Go beyond just talking about faith, and learn the deep joy and fulfillment that comes from truly living what you believe. Hybels gives concrete examples and down-to-earth counsel for living an authentic Christian life.

Softcover   0-310-52181-5
with discussion guide
Audio Pages   0-310-52188-2

Descending into Greatness

Bill Hybels and Rob Wilkins

Do you find yourself placing your desires before God's? Through powerful teaching and touching, real-life stories, the authors show how "downward mobility"—putting God's Kingdom first—can lead to a life of spiritual fulfillment and satisfaction.

Softcover   0-310-54471-8
Audio Pages   0-310-54478-5

Available at your local Christian bookstore.

WILLOW CREEK RESOURCES

This resource was created to serve you.

It is just one of many ministry tools that are part of the Willow Creek Resources® line, published by the Willow Creek Association together with Zondervan Publishing House. The Willow Creek Association was created in 1992 to serve a rapidly growing number of churches from all across the denominational spectrum that are committed to helping unchurched people become devoted followers of Christ.

The vision of the Willow Creek Association is to help churches better relate God's solutions to the needs of seekers and believers. Here are some of the ways it does that:

- **Church Leadership Conferences**—4-day events, generally held at Willow Creek Community Church in South Barrington, IL, that are being used by God to help church leaders find new and innovative ways to fulfill and expand their ministries.
- **The Leadership Summit**—a once-a-year event designed to increase the leadership effectiveness of pastors, ministry staff, and volunteer church leaders.
- **Willow Creek Resources®**—to provide churches with a trusted channel of ministry resources in areas of leadership, evangelism, spiritual gifts, small groups, drama, contemporary music, and more. For more information, call Willow Creek Resources® at 800/876-7335. Outside the U.S. call 616/698-3231.
- **WCA Monthly Newsletter**—to inform you of the latest trends, events, news, and resources.
- **The Exchange**—to assist churches in recruiting key staff for ministry positions.
- **The Church Associates Directory**—to keep you in touch with over 1000 other WCA member churches.

For conference and membership information please write or call:

Willow Creek Association
P.O. Box 3188
Barrington, IL 60011-3188
(708) 765-0070

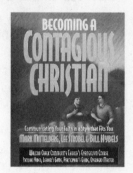